Lumber Widths and Thicknesses

Lumber is ordered by thickness, width, and length. When you order in U.S. or imperial measurements (2 inches x 4 inches x 8 feet, for example), the thickness and width figures (in this instance 2x4) refer to nominal size—the dimensions of the piece as it left the saw. But what you get is the smaller, actual size remaining when the piece has been planed smooth; in actual fact, a piece 1½ inches x 3½ inches x 8 feet. (Length is not reduced by the processing.)

Metric measurements, on the other hand, always describe the actual dimensions of the processed piece.

Nominal size in inches	Actual size in inches	Actual size in millimeters
1x3	(¾ x 2½)	16 x 64
2x2	(1½ x 1½)	38 x 38
2x4	(1½ x 3½)	38 x 89
2x6	(1½ x 5½)	38 x 140
2x8	(1½ x 7¼)	38 x 184
2x10	(1½ x 9¼)	38 x 235
4x4	(3½ x 3½)	89 x 89
4x6	(3½ x 5½)	89 x 140

Metric Plywood Panels

Plywood panels come in two standard metric sizes: 1,200 millimeters x 2,400 millimeters and 1,220 millimeters x 2,400 millimeters (the equivalent of a 4 foot x 8 foot panel). Other sizes are available on special order. With sheathing and select sheathing grades, metric and inch thicknesses are generally identical. The metric sanded grades, however, come in a new range of thicknesses.

Metric thicknesses

Sheathing and Select Grades		Sanded Grades	
7.5 mm	(5/16 in.)	6 mm	(4/17 in.)
9.5 mm	(⅜ in.)	8 mm	(5/16 in.)
12.5 mm	(½ in.)	11 mm	(7/16 in.)
15.5 mm	(⅝ in.)	14 mm	(9/16 in.)
18.5 mm	(¾ in.)	17 mm	(⅔ in.)
20.5 mm	(⅘ in.)	19 mm	(¾ in.)
22.5 mm	(⅞ in.)	21 mm	(13/16 in.)
25.5 mm	(1 in.)	24 mm	(15/16 in.)

THE FAMILY Handyman®

Woodworking
Room-by-Room

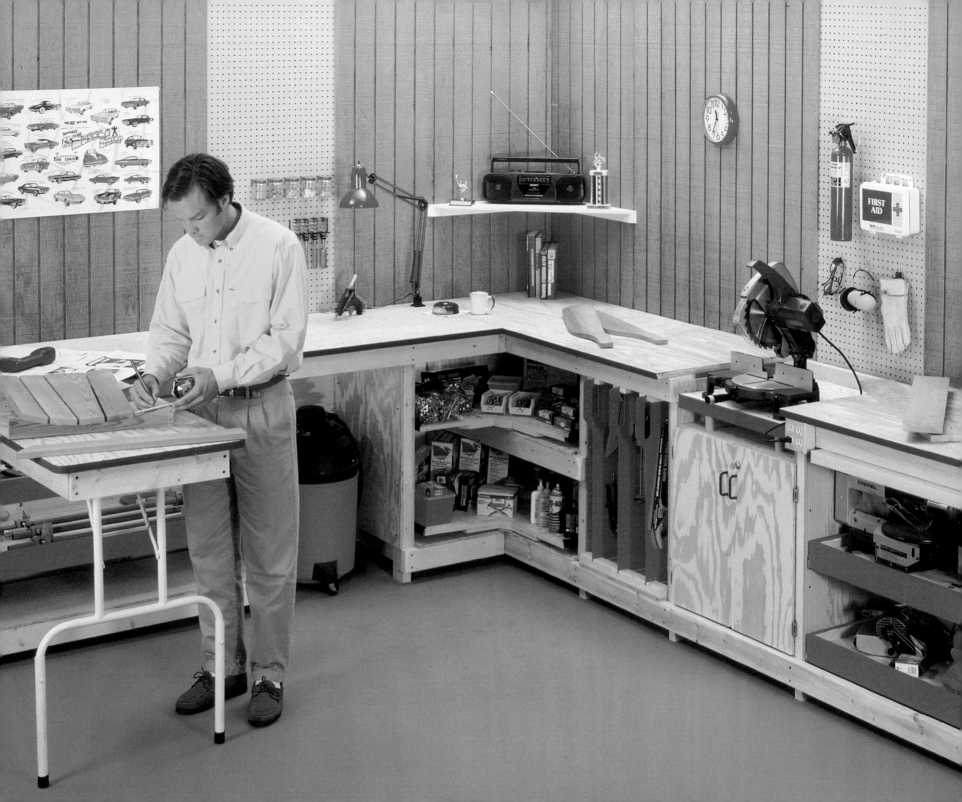

THE FAMILY Handyman®

Woodworking Room-by-Room

Furniture, Cabinetry, Built-Ins & Other Decorative Projects

THE READER'S DIGEST ASSOCIATION, INC.
Pleasantville, New York/Montreal

A READER'S DIGEST BOOK

Produced by Roundtable Press, Inc.
Directors: Susan E. Meyer, Marsha Melnick
Executive Editor: Amy T. Jonak
Project Editor: William Broecker
Editor: Thomas Neven
Assistant Editor: Megan Keiler
Design: Sisco & Evans, New York
Production: Phil Fabian, Steven Rosen

For The Family Handyman
Editor: Gary Havens
Senior Editor: Ken Collier
Associate Editor: Spike Carlsen

For Reader's Digest
Executive Editor: James Wagenvoord
Editorial Director: John Sullivan
Design Director: Michele Italiano-Perla
Managing Editors: Diane Shanley, Christine Moltzen
Editorial Associate: Daniela Marchetti

Library of Congress Cataloging in Publication Data
The Family handyman woodworking—room by room : furniture, cabinetry,
    built-ins, and other decorative projects for the home.
        p.   cm.
    Includes index.
    ISBN 0-89577-686-3
    1. Furniture making—Amateur's manuals.   I. Reader's Digest
Association.   II. Family handyman.   III. Title: Woodworking—room by
room.
TT195.F36   1995
684.1'04—dc20   94-45302

A Note from the Editor

Ask professional carpenters or woodworkers about their favorite work, and nine out of ten will describe the kind of projects that fill this book— ornamental woodwork and straightforward furniture. This is the dress-up stuff—the finishing touches, the little details, the finely milled wood. It's furniture, moldings, and clever joints.

These are projects you can quit working on when you tire and resume when you're ready. They are projects people can see and touch when you're done. This is the work that brings compliments. I know, because I'm a carpenter by trade. I've done all this stuff, many times over. And it's still fun, just as it was at the beginning.

I am not a great natural-born craftsman. I had to learn from masters. I learned by watching; then I tried to imitate as best I could. The kind of teaching that helped me is here, just for you. Each project comes from the pages of *The Family Handyman* magazine. Each was built by an experienced carpenter, cabinetmaker, or furniture builder. They designed the projects. They wrote the text as well as the captions and labels on the photos and diagrams. All I did was ask them questions along the way.

I'm hoping I asked the right ones. Did I keep them from using technical words that are hard to understand? Did I remind them to tell about the hard stuff that you wouldn't know about? Did I make them describe how to use the special tools that will make some projects easier?
You tell me.

Gary Havens, Editor
The Family Handyman

FAMILY HANDYMAN

Woodworking Room-by-Room

Introduction

Wood is a material with a soul. Its grain reminds us of the tree from which it was cut; its texture, warmth, and color enhance any room. Wood is strong and durable, yet easy to cut and shape. Much of the pleasure of woodworking is in the process; the final result, whether a piece of furniture or an architectural improvement, provides additional pleasure long after the work is done.

The projects in this book provide both craft pleasure and "pride of achievement" pleasure. There are designs for both advanced and novice woodworkers, and a great variety of techniques—cutting a drop-leaf joint, applying iron-on veneer, creating detailed curves and molding, and many others that you will use again and again.

Each special technique, like each overall project, is explained in detail, from tools and materials to procedures to helpful tips from experienced professionals. Just follow the step-by-step instructions carefully and you can't go wrong.

An important part of any project is working safely. Always wear eye and ear protection when cutting, sanding, drilling, or routing. Keep chisels, planes, and other cutting tools sharp. Keep all tools clean, and make sure power cords and plugs are not frayed or broken. Follow the manufacturer's directions when operating power tools and when using chemicals and solvents. Some photographs in this book show power tools with the blade or safety guards removed. Keep in mind that this was done only for clarity; when you work, always use the safety guards on all your tools.

Setting Up Shop

This is the best all-around workbench you'll ever own. It's easy to build —

only the most basic tools are required. And because it uses common materials,

mostly 2x4's and 1/2-inch plywood, it's inexpensive.

Build the Ultimate Workbench

No two workshops or garages are exactly alike, so the instructions here first show you

how to build a basic workbench module that you can expand with additional

full- or partial-size modules to fit your workspace.

The instructions then show you how to add a number of special features.

When you're finished, you'll have a workbench customized for your shop and the kind

of woodworking projects you want to do.

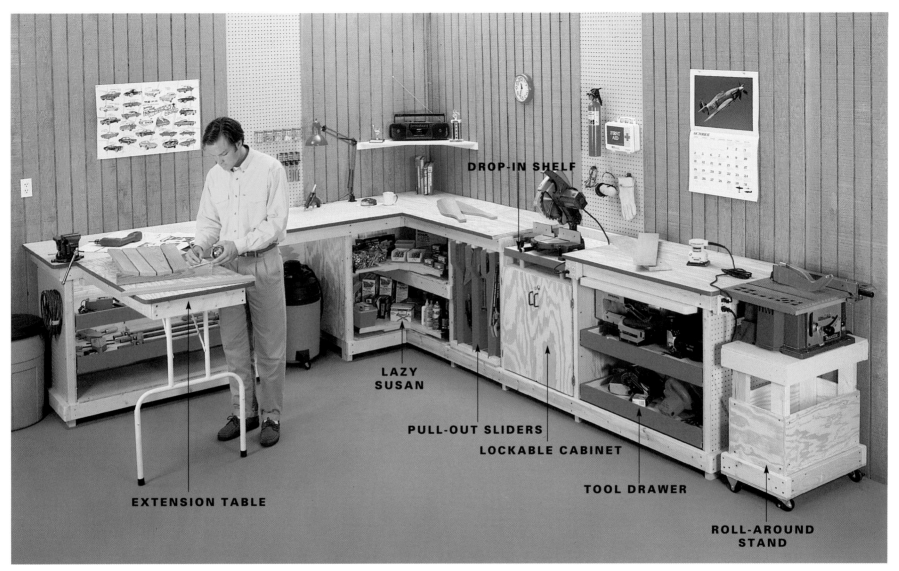

DROP-IN SHELF

LAZY SUSAN

PULL-OUT SLIDERS

LOCKABLE CABINET

TOOL DRAWER

EXTENSION TABLE

ROLL-AROUND STAND

This versatile and extensive workbench is constructed from easy-to-build basic modules. Special features include a fold-up extension table that stores in the space near the floor; an open section for a roll-around vacuum; lazy susans for maximum corner storage; pull-out sliders for hanging small tools; an adjustable drop-in shelf for bench-top tools; a lockable cabinet for safe storage; drawers for large portable tools; and a roll-around stand for a table saw. You can include any or all of these features in making your own custom-designed workbench.

Planning Your Workbench

Tool sliders offer hanging storage on both sides. A lazy susan makes best use of corner storage space.

Because you are going to customize a workbench to your particular needs with a selection of special features, you must plan the project carefully. Read through this entire chapter before deciding on the size and configuration of your bench. Then develop a detailed plan based on the construction plans and data given here, the measurements of your specific work area, and your preference in the height of a work surface. Note that features such as the lazy susan and drop-in shelf require special calculations or additional space to accommodate them. In your planning, consider the following.

Give yourself plenty of room

Build your workbench as large as possible so you have room for lots of features and have plenty of bench-top workspace. The maximum length of the basic workbench is 8 feet. If you need more, build additional modules anywhere from 4 to 8 feet long, according to the same plan. Bolt them together—in line or around a corner—for a sturdy and stable workbench that exactly fits your space.

Plan for additional storage space

Build readily accessible storage inside the workbench and add features that let you get at tools and supplies quickly and easily.

A big lazy susan will make maximum use of the corner of an L-shaped workbench. It can hold fasteners and other hardware, small tools, and similar items.

Sliding panels of 1/4-inch perforated hardboard (perf board) will hold a variety of small and medium-sized tools on hooks. They can virtually double storage space because you can hang tools on both sides.

Heavy-duty drawers can house large portable power tools when they are not in use. Lockable cabinet doors across a section of drawers will make dangerous tools and chemicals inaccessible to children and pets, but easy to get at when you need them.

Provide storage room for bulky extra equipment. For example, leave open space under the bench for a shop vacuum, or an air compressor, or both. If you decide to build a fold-up extension table, be sure to include storage space for it.

Position power tools where you need them

Provide a drop-in shelf to hold bench-top tools such as a power miter saw at the best working height. The shelf is located under a lift-out section of the workbench top. Its working height is adjusted by changing support pegs beneath it.

Build a roll-around stand for a table saw so you can move it away from the bench easily, or put it at any position to use the bench top as a support for the material being cut. For safe cutting, make the cabinet tall enough to put the saw table just a little higher than the level of the bench top.

Have safe power where you need it

You can install electrical power almost anywhere on this workbench. Mount electrical power strips on the workbench and plug them into nearby wall outlets. Or, for a permanent installation, run plastic-sheathed cable from a wall outlet or power panel to various spots on the workbench, protecting it with metal conduit, and install surface-mount electrical boxes and receptacles on the edge of the workbench under the overhanging bench top. A special section (page 31) explains how to wire receptacles.

Large drawers on heavy-duty glides can hold a great variety of portable tools or packaged supplies.

A drop-in shelf adjusts the working height of interchangeable bench-top tools.

A roll-around stand can put a table saw, drill press, or other tool wherever it's needed.

Draw a plan

Once you have decided on the size of your bench and what shape would work best for you, draw up detailed plans on graph paper. Show where special features such as drawers, a lazy susan, or a drop-in will be located, calculate the spaces required, and mark the measurements on the plan. For example, if you want to store a 20-inch diameter shop vacuum under the bench, you'll need to plan for a space at least 24 inches wide in order to get it in and out easily.

Use this information to calculate positions for the legs, which can go anywhere within the frames at any spacing up to 54 inches apart. Remember to allow for the thickness of the structural elements. For example, the legs are constructed of 2x4's sandwiched between two pieces of 1/2-inch thick plywood, for a total thickness of 2-1/2 inches.

When planning, give yourself at least a 2-inch toe space beneath the workbench. The bottom framing pieces of the bench are mounted to the legs above that point.

Use materials efficiently

The more time you spend planning things on paper, the better your workbench will be. Take maximum advantage of standard-size pieces of lumber, so as to have as little waste as possible. For example, make the leg assemblies 24 inches from front to back, so you can cut 4x8 sheets of plywood in half lengthwise to get the leg panels. Similarly, make the leg panels 32 inches long so you can get three of them out of each half-sheet of plywood (3 x 32 = 96 inches, or 8 feet).

Calculate the lengths of the 2x4 framing elements to use standard 8- and 12-foot lengths of lumber with minimal waste. Also consider both economy and practicality in choosing wood for the workbench. You can use construction grade lumber and plywood for the bench framing, shelves, and leg panels. But for the top, buy A/C or B/C grade plywood (in Canada, G1S or Select grade) and put the higher grade, sanded side facing up. This will give you a smooth work surface.

Construction Plan: Basic Workbench

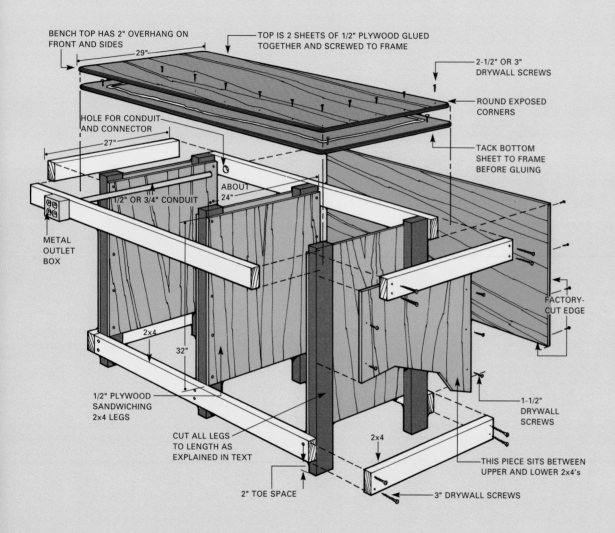

BENCH TOP HAS 2" OVERHANG ON FRONT AND SIDES

TOP IS 2 SHEETS OF 1/2" PLYWOOD GLUED TOGETHER AND SCREWED TO FRAME

29"

2-1/2" OR 3" DRYWALL SCREWS

ROUND EXPOSED CORNERS

HOLE FOR CONDUIT AND CONNECTOR

27"

TACK BOTTOM SHEET TO FRAME BEFORE GLUING

1/2" OR 3/4" CONDUIT

ABOUT 24"

METAL OUTLET BOX

FACTORY-CUT EDGE

2x4

32"

1/2" PLYWOOD SANDWICHING 2x4 LEGS

1-1/2" DRYWALL SCREWS

CUT ALL LEGS TO LENGTH AS EXPLAINED IN TEXT

2x4

2" TOE SPACE

THIS PIECE SITS BETWEEN UPPER AND LOWER 2x4's

3" DRYWALL SCREWS

WORKBENCH

Materials for Basic Workbench

Quantity	Size and Description

BENCH TOP

Quantity	Size and Description
2 sheets	4' x 8' x 1/2" plywood, cut 29" wide
20	3" drywall screws
6	1" nails
1 bottle	Wood glue

EACH LEG

Quantity	Size and Description
2	2x4 cut to accommodate your height
2 pieces	1/2" plywood
20	1-1/2" drywall screws

FRAME

Quantity	Size and Description
4	2x4 x 89"
4	2x4 x 27"
40	3" drywall screws

BACK

Quantity	Size and Description
1 piece	1/2" plywood (left over from top)
8	1-1/2" drywall screws

COMPARTMENT SHELVES; BASES

Quantity	Size and Description
3+ sheets	4' x 8' x 1/2" plywood
As needed	2x4's for front, rear, and end supports

EACH ELECTRICAL OUTLET ASSEMBLY

Quantity	Size and Description
1	UL-listed power strips or 4" x 4" x 2-1/8" surface-mount electrical box with raised metal outlet cover plates
2	Standard or GFCI receptacles per electrical box
1	10 x 32 green ground screw
Approx. 30"	3/4" metal conduit per electrical box, two conduit connectors, and one conduit strap
As needed	Two- or three-conductor grounded NM-B cable (in Canada, NMD cable); No. 14 wire for 15 amp circuit; No. 12 wire for 20 amp circuit

Build the Basic Workbench

The first thing to build is the basic workbench module. Everything else will be oriented around this. The most efficient approach is to prefabricate various parts of the bench, then combine them to form the finished bench. For example, cut and construct the top and bottom frames and set them aside, then build the leg assemblies. Once you have the basic bench together, you can concentrate on the special features.

Tools You Need

Circular saw

Table saw (optional)

Framing square

Pencil

Pipe clamps

Jigsaw or saber saw

Electric drill with twist bits, 1-1/4" spade bit, and Phillips bit

7/8" hole saw

Hand saw

Hammer

Cable ripper

Wire stripper

Needle nose pliers

Adjustable wrench

Sander

Build the frame

The top and bottom frames are made from 2x4 stringers joined at the ends by 2x4's. Cut the stringers to the length of the bench minus 3 inches, the combined thickness of the two 2x4 end pieces. Cut the end 2x4's to the front-to-back depth of the bench plus 3 inches for the combined thickness of the two 2x4 stringers.

Use the longest, straightest 2x4's possible. Cut the front and back frame members to length, then clamp them together.

Refer to your plan and use a framing square and pencil to transfer the leg positions across all the front and back pieces. Write on the lumber which features go where (Photo 1).

Cut 2x4's for the frame ends and screw them to the ends of the long 2x4's with 3-inch drywall screws (Photo 2). If you have spaces of different widths between any two sets of legs, make sure your pencil marks match on the front and back frame members.

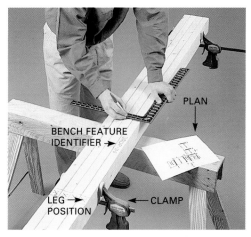

Photo 1. Mark the leg positions on all of the frame pieces at one time, using a framing square. Clamp the frame pieces together before marking. Follow the measurements on your plan.

Photo 2. Build all the frames and set aside. Drive screws through the sides of the short end pieces into the ends of the long front and back pieces.

Build the leg assemblies

The leg assemblies are vertical 2x4's sandwiched between panels of 1/2-inch plywood. To determine the length of the 2x4 legs, stand straight and have a helper measure from the floor to the middle of your hip. The final finished height of the workbench will be this measurement plus 1 inch, which is the thickness of the bench top.

Your plan tells you how many leg assemblies to build; you need two 2x4's for each assembly. Mark and cut the 2x4's all to the same length from straight pieces of lumber. Be accurate and consistent in making measurements and cutting the pieces.

You can use lower-grade, cheaper plywood for the panels of the leg assemblies, since knots and patches won't matter here. When cutting the plywood, make sure the panel is well supported close to both sides of the cutting line; this will prevent the panel from sagging and binding the blade in the kerf. Use a plywood cutting blade in your circular saw or table saw for a good, clean edge.

Cut a 4x8 sheet exactly in half lengthwise to get two pieces just slightly under 24 inches wide. Cut each of those pieces into three 24 x 32-inch panels. If the legs are less than 32 inches tall, cut the plywood panels at least 2 inches shorter than the legs. Note that the two outside pieces of plywood are cut even shorter, to fit between the upper and lower 2x4's at the ends of the frame (see plan).

To assemble a leg, position a plywood panel on two 2x4 legs, one at each edge (Photo 3). Align the bottom of the panel with a line marked 5-1/2 inches from the bottom of each leg. This allows for the 2-inch toe space plus the width of the bottom 2x4 stringer. Fasten the panel with five 1-1/2 inch drywall screws evenly spaced along each 2x4 leg. Turn everything over and fasten a panel on the other side of the legs in the same way. You may want to substitute perf board at the outside ends of the workbench to create additional storage hangers.

Assemble the workbench base

The leg assemblies fit inside the frame stringers. Lay the frames back side down, slide the legs into their marked positions, and use 3-inch drywall screws to join the pieces (Photo 4). Screw all the legs to one side, then turn the base over and fasten the frame on the other side.

The plywood back adds rigidity. It also helps square the workbench if you use the factory-cut edges as a reference. You can use a piece left over from cutting the bench top from a full sheet of plywood. But you must make sure the back piece has two intact factory-cut edges that form a 90-degree corner. If you cannot use scrap, cut a full piece to fit the opening in the back.

Place one factory-cut side of the back piece on the ledge of the bottom stringer. Pull the top of the frame sideways until it's aligned with the other factory edge running up along the side of the bench. This ensures that the bench frame is square. Maintain that alignment and screw the plywood back to the legs (Photo 5). The workbench frame is now square, straight, and true, but don't assume it will stand level, since your shop floor may not be. Level the bench with shims once you have put it in place.

Add the top

If you are not going to install any special features—lazy susan, tool sliders, drawers, electrical outlets—in the workbench, you can put on the top now. However, if you are going to build in additional features do not build the top at this time. It would only get in the way and make the job much harder. Instead, complete the other features at this time, then return to the instructions here to complete the top.

The top is constructed of two pieces of plywood cut 29 inches wide to provide a 2-inch overhang at the front, and long enough for 2-inch overhangs at the ends. If you are covering two or more modules joined together, screw a 2x4 filler block between the legs where two pieces of bench top join.

Photo 3. Build the leg assemblies by cutting all of the 2x4's and all of the 1/2-in. plywood panels first. Mark the panel positions on the 2x4's, and then screw the parts together.

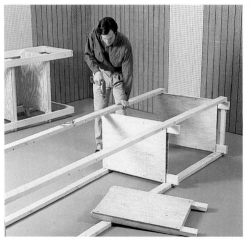

Photo 4. To assemble the base, set the frames on the floor, place the legs in the marked positions, and secure them with drywall screws through the frames. Turn the base over and fasten the other side.

Photo 5. Square the base assembly when attaching the back. Align the bottom frame and an end leg with the factory-cut edges of a sheet of plywood, then drive screws through the back into all the legs.

Use grade A/C or B/C (in Canada, G1S or Select) grade plywood for the top layer, a lesser grade for the bottom layer. Position the bottom piece on the frame and adjust it for front and end overhangs; there is no overhang at the rear. Tack the bottom piece in place with a few nails, then spread wood glue evenly across it with a piece of scrap wood or a sponge.

Place the top piece on top of the bottom piece and drive 3-inch drywall screws through both pieces into the frame. Lay some weights on the center while the glue dries.

If you plan to build the drop-in shelf, screw the top to the frame on only one side of the drop-in area now. Complete fastening the top after building the drop-in (see page 24).

ELECTRICAL OUTLETS

Extending electrical power to various points on the workbench lets you plug in power tools without having cords draped everywhere. You can use outlet strips or you can install duplex (dual-outlet) receptacles in electrical boxes mounted on the workbench.

Outlet strips

Ready-made electrical outlet strips mounted on the workbench and plugged into nearby wall outlets will provide power quickly and easily. Use strips that have built-in ground fault circuit interrupt (GFCI) protection, or replace the receptacles you plug into with GFCI receptacles. The added safety is well worth the extra cost.

Receptacles in bench-mounted boxes

A permanent method for bringing power to your bench involves running cable from a wall outlet or electrical panel to receptacles in metal outlet boxes on the workbench

(Photo 6). If you connect the cable to an existing GFCI receptacle circuit breaker, the workbench outlets will be protected. Otherwise, install one GFCI receptacle and one standard receptacle in each box on the bench to provide GFCI protection for both.

Boxes

Use 4 x 4-inch metal outlet boxes 2-1/8 inches deep so you can install two duplex receptacles side by side. Put the boxes close to legs of the bench; drilling holes in the center would weaken the frame. A box will fit under the 2-inch bench-top overhang with the face exposed just enough for easy access.

Mount the box with screws. You'll also need a raised metal outlet cover plate for each box.

Cable

Use NM-B plastic-sheathed cable (NMD cable in Canada), such as Romex, that has No. 12 circuit wires and a ground wire. Two-conductor cable designated 12-2G has black- and white-insulated circuit wires, and a bare or green-insulated ground wire. Use it to connect two receptacles to a single circuit.

Three-conductor or 12-3G cable has black-, red-, and white-insulated circuit wires, and a ground wire. Use this cable to connect two receptacles to separate circuits, or use two 12-2G cables for the same purpose.

Conduit

By electrical code, you must use metal conduit with NM-B or NMD cable; you cannot run cable through the legs of the bench or leave it exposed. A 3/4-inch conduit can hold two cables, giving you more options in wiring the receptacles.

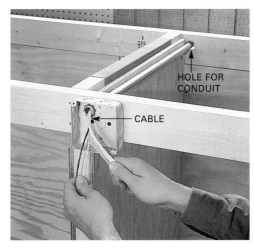

Photo 6. Install electrical outlets wherever useful on the workbench. Use square metal boxes that hold two duplex receptacles. Wire the receptacles with NM-B cable run through metal conduit.

To install the conduit, drill holes through the workbench frame large enough to accommodate the conduit connector. If you're not running the cable directly into a stud wall cavity behind the workbench, you must run it in conduit along the back of the workbench. The cable cannot be exposed. Secure the conduit to the bench frame with metal conduit straps. Be careful not to puncture the conduit with screws when fastening down the workbench top.

Wiring

Connect the cable to the receptacles in the workbench boxes before connecting it to a power source. See Wiring Workbench Receptacles (page 31) for instructions on making the connections in the boxes.

Hire a licensed, certified professional electrician to make the final connections at the main electric service panel.

Construction Plans: Lazy Susan and Tool Sliders

Materials List

Quantity	Size and Description

LAZY SUSAN

Quantity	Size and Description
1 sheet	4' x 8' x 3/4" plywood
1	12" diameter ball-bearing lazy susan base
1	10-1/2' plastic landscape edging

TOOL SLIDERS

Quantity	Size and Description
1 or more	4' x 8' x 1/4" perforated hardboard
1	2 x 2 x compartment length per set (bottom front stop)
1	1 x 4 x compartment depth per slider (top cleat)
4	1 x 2 x compartment depth per slider (guides)

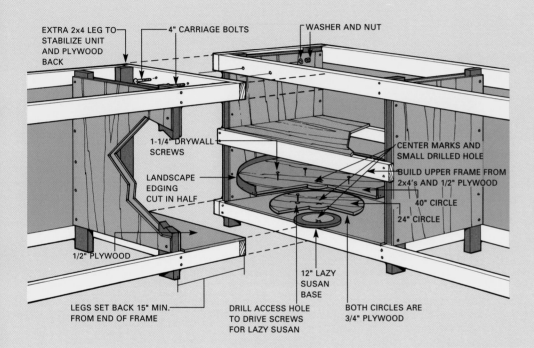

EXTRA 2x4 LEG TO STABILIZE UNIT AND PLYWOOD BACK

4" CARRIAGE BOLTS

WASHER AND NUT

1-1/4" DRYWALL SCREWS

LANDSCAPE EDGING CUT IN HALF

1/2" PLYWOOD

CENTER MARKS AND SMALL DRILLED HOLE

BUILD UPPER FRAME FROM 2x4's AND 1/2" PLYWOOD

40" CIRCLE

24" CIRCLE

12" LAZY SUSAN BASE

LEGS SET BACK 15" MIN. FROM END OF FRAME

DRILL ACCESS HOLE TO DRIVE SCREWS FOR LAZY SUSAN

BOTH CIRCLES ARE 3/4" PLYWOOD

LAZY SUSAN

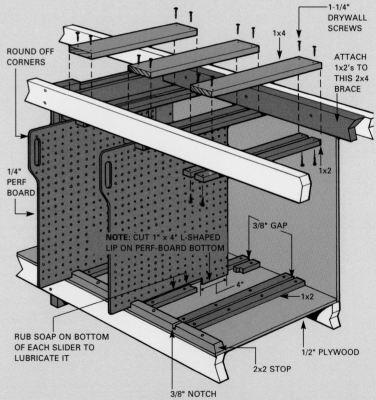

ROUND OFF CORNERS

1-1/4" DRYWALL SCREWS

1x4

ATTACH 1x2's TO THIS 2x4 BRACE

1x2

1/4" PERF BOARD

3/8" GAP

NOTE: CUT 1" x 4" L-SHAPED LIP ON PERF-BOARD BOTTOM

4"

1x2

RUB SOAP ON BOTTOM OF EACH SLIDER TO LUBRICATE IT

1/2" PLYWOOD

2x2 STOP

3/8" NOTCH

TOOL SLIDERS

Build Additional Features

LAZY SUSAN

The lazy susan (Photo 7) is a circular shelf at the L-shaped corner where two workbench units join at right angles. It consists of a double layer of plywood mounted on a rotating metal base, available at home centers and specialty woodworking stores. A 24-inch diameter circle of plywood mounted on top of the metal base serves as a support for a 40-inch diameter circle of plywood which is the actual storage shelf.

Provide room for a lazy susan

To ensure adequate space for the rotating shelf, you must set back the legs at the end of one workbench frame at least 15 inches. Then add a 2x4 as an extra stabilizing leg at the rear where the two workbench frames meet. Build a lower shelf of 1/2-inch plywood in the bench frame, using 2x4 cleats screwed to the leg assemblies as support. While building the workbench, clamp the two frames together where they meet. Once the bench is complete and in place, drill holes and bolt the frames together.

Cut the circles

To get perfect circles for two lazy susans, use a scrap piece of perf board 22 to 24 inches long as a trammel—a kind of bar compass. With one end of the trammel anchored with a screw at the center of the intended circle,

the other end can rotate around that pivot point. A pencil inserted through the end will mark a circle as the trammel rotates.

You can cut material for two lazy susans out of one 4x8 sheet of 3/4-inch plywood. Draw two circles each 40 inches in diameter (pencil 20 inches from the pivot screw in the trammel) at diagonally opposite corners of the plywood (Photo 8). Between them draw two circles 24 inches in diameter (pencil set 12 inches from the trammel pivot). The circles will slightly overlap. Use a saber saw to cut out the 24-inch pieces as full circles. Each large circle will have a small section cut out at the edge; this won't matter because you will notch them to fit the corner.

Notch the circles

The plywood circles must have a 90-degree section cut out of them where they overhang the L-shaped corner of the workbench. Drill a small hole completely through the center of one 24-inch circle (where the trammel pivoted). Drill another hole centered in the bottom shelf of the workbench where the lazy susan will be mounted.

Position the 24-inch circle exactly in the corner of the workbench with its bottom side facing upward, and insert a nail through its center hole and the hole in the workbench shelf. Mark the section of the plywood circle that has to be cut out to conform to the "L" at

Photo 7. A lazy susan revolves on a ball-bearing base secured to the workbench shelf. The plywood shelf has a raised edge to retain small items. Build one or two lazy susans as you require.

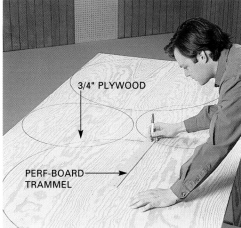

3/4" PLYWOOD

PERF-BOARD TRAMMEL

Photo 8. Make a trammel out of perf-board scrap. Insert a pivot screw in one end, a pencil in the other. You need one 24-in. and one 40-in. circle for each lazy susan. Cut the circles with a saber saw.

the corner where the bench frames come together (Photo 9). Remove the plywood circle and center the metal lazy susan base on it. Mark the curve of the outer edge of the base where it crosses the notch to be cut out — now use a saber saw to cut the notch out of the plywood circle: straight in from each edge, and around the curve in the center.

Drill a small hole in the center of a 40-inch circle of plywood, place the notched smaller circle over it, and drop a nail in the center holes to align the circles. Mark the notch on the large piece and extend it all the way to the edges; then cut it out. If you are making two lazy susans, use these notched circles to mark the other two for cutting.

Mount the lazy susan

The ball-bearing lazy susan base has two revolving flanges with holes for mounting screws. Each flange also has a larger diameter access hole. Center the base on the bottom face of the smaller notched plywood circle. Align the access holes in the flanges, mark that point, and remove the base. Drill a 3/4-inch diameter hole all the way through the plywood. This will give you access later to screw the base to the workbench shelf.

Center the metal base on the bottom of the small circle once again and rotate the access hole on the bottom flange so you can drive screws through the mounting holes of the upper flange into the plywood (Photo 10). Then turn the plywood face up and center it and the attached base on the workbench shelf. Drop a nail through the center holes to align them, as before. Rotate the plywood so the access hole you drilled in it exposes the

mounting holes in the bottom flange of the lazy susan base one at time (Photo 11). Drive a screw through each hole to fasten the base to the bottom shelf of the workbench.

Before mounting the large plywood circle, give it a retaining lip. Take a length of vinyl landscape edging 10-1/2 feet long and cut it in half along its length. Screw it along the edge of the plywood, flush with the bottom face and extending up above the top face. Then center the large circle over the small one mounted on the workbench and fasten it to the support with screws.

If your plans call for two lazy susans, complete the one on the bottom shelf of the workbench first. Then build a frame of 2x4 stringers into the corner opening for an upper shelf of 1/2-inch plywood. Assemble and install the second lazy susan there as you did the first.

Photo 9. Mark the 24-in. circle, centered face down in the corner, for a notch. Then center the metal base on the plywood circle and mark its edge curve in the notch. Make the cut with a saber saw.

Photo 10. Mark the notched circle where the access holes in the metal base line up and drill a 3/4-in. hole. Screw the base to the circle, working through the access hole in the bottom flange.

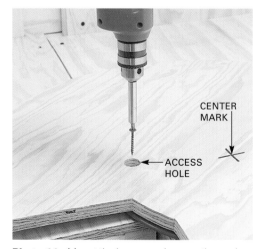

Photo 11. Mount the lazy susan base on the workbench shelf by rotating the plywood circle and driving screws through the access hole. Then center the large plywood circle and attach it with screws.

Photo 12. Tool sliders are vertical pull-out panels. Hooks on either or both sides hold small tools and other items. The number and spacing of sliders depends on the size of items to be hung on them.

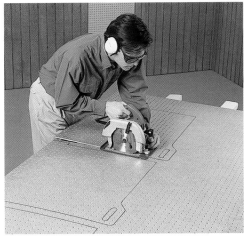

Photo 13. Lay out the tool sliders on a sheet of 1/4-in. thick perf board. Make all the straight cuts with a circular saw. Support the panel well to prevent binding; wear eye and hearing protection.

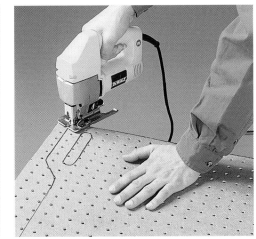

Photo 14. Cut the handle curves and the notched section in each slider base with a saber saw. To cut out the opening in the handle, drill a starter hole and insert the saw blade through it.

TOOL SLIDERS

The tool sliders (Photo 12) are cut from a 4x8 sheet of 1/4-inch perf board (1/8-inch board is too flimsy) with the front edge cut away to make a pull-out handle. The distance from the front of the slider handle to the back edge of each slider should not be longer than 24 inches — half the width of a sheet of perf board. The bottom is cut away to leave a 1x4-inch lip at the rear of the slider. This prevents accidentally pulling the slider all the way out of the bench.

Cut the perf board

Mark the shape of each slider on a sheet of perf board and use a circular saw to cut along the straight lines (Photo 13). Use a sharp plywood blade to get a good, clean edge. Cut out the handle openings and all curves and notches with a saber saw (Photo 14). Drill a starter hole to cut the openings.

Paint the sliders if you wish. Hardboard is porous, so prime it first. Use a roller to apply both coats of paint.

Install the sliders

Each slider rests on the bottom shelf of the workbench and moves in 3/8-inch wide channels built out of four 1x2's. The bottom 1x2's are 1-1/2 inch shorter than those at the top because they fit behind a 2x2 front stop that is notched for each slider.

You can divide the workbench section for as many sliders as you wish, but you'll probably want to space them at least 4 inches apart. This will provide room for the long hooks needed to hang larger tools. If some tools require more clearance so adjoining sliders can move in and out without interference, take that into account. For thin, flat tools, 3 or perhaps even 2 inches of clearance between sliders may be adequate. Cover the exposed tops of the 1x2's with 1x4's to keep the sliders from riding up in their channels. Before installing the 2x2 front stop at the bottom, mark the channel spacing on it. Use a circular saw and a chisel to cut notches 3/8 inch wide by 3/4 inch deep for the sliders. Rub a bar of soap to lubricate between the channel 1x2's and the bottom of each perf-board slider before putting it in its appropriate place.

Construction Plans: Drop-In Tool Support and Tool Drawers

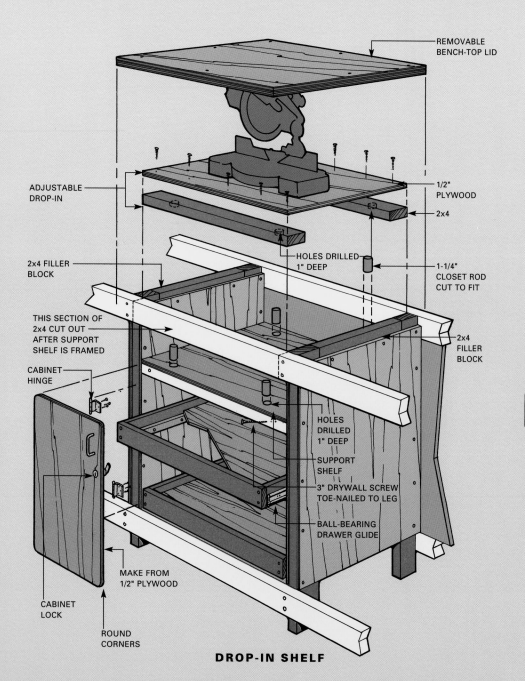

REMOVABLE
BENCH-TOP LID

ADJUSTABLE
DROP-IN

1/2"
PLYWOOD

2x4

2x4 FILLER
BLOCK

HOLES DRILLED
1" DEEP

1-1/4"
CLOSET ROD
CUT TO FIT

THIS SECTION OF
2x4 CUT OUT
AFTER SUPPORT
SHELF IS FRAMED

2x4
FILLER
BLOCK

CABINET
HINGE

HOLES
DRILLED
1" DEEP

SUPPORT
SHELF

3" DRYWALL SCREW
TOE-NAILED TO LEG

BALL-BEARING
DRAWER GLIDE

MAKE FROM
1/2" PLYWOOD

CABINET
LOCK

ROUND
CORNERS

DROP-IN SHELF

Materials List

Quantity	Size and Description
2 or more	4' x 8' x 1/2" plywood
As needed	1x2's and 2x4's (supports, fillers, cleats, frames)
	Cabinet hinges, lock, and handle
	22" ball-bearing drawer slides

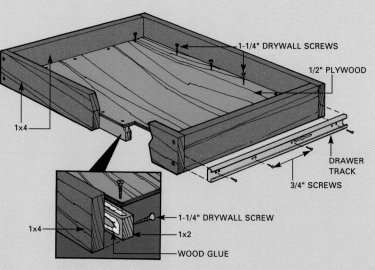

1-1/4" DRYWALL SCREWS

1/2" PLYWOOD

1x4

DRAWER
TRACK

3/4" SCREWS

1-1/4" DRYWALL SCREW

1x4

1x2

WOOD GLUE

DRAWER

DROP-IN TOOL SUPPORT

The drop-in (Photo 15) is an adjustable shelf located below a lift-out section of the bench top. Complete the drop-in before installing the top permanently.

Build a support shelf

Provide a shelf to support the drop-in by toe-screwing two 2x4's to the frame, about 6 inches down, depending on the dimensions of the tools that will fit inside (Photo 16). Screw a 1/2-inch plywood shelf to these 2x4's. Then use a handsaw to cut away the top frame stringer (Photo 17). Brace the adjacent leg sections by installing 2x4 filler blocks inside the plywood panels at the tops of the leg assemblies.

Build the drop-in

Make the drop-in itself by cutting 2x4's and plywood as for the support shelf. Screw the plywood to the 2x4's. This adjustable shelf rests on pegs of various heights that fit into socket holes in its underside and into matching holes in the support shelf.

To create the sockets, make a drilling template out of a 2x4 cut to the width of the opening in the workbench. Mark one side "top" and drill two 1-3/8 inch diameter holes all the way through it, about 2 inches from each end. Place a tape flag on your drill bit 2-1/2 inches up the shaft (the thickness of the 2x4 template plus 1 inch). The tape is a depth gauge; when it hits the top of the template, you've drilled a hole 1 inch deep.

Clamp or screw the template in place at the rear of the support shelf with the side marked "top" facing up and drill two holes 1 inch deep (Photo 18).

Photo 15. A drop-in shelf sits on pegs of various lengths to adjust the working height of bench-top tools. When not in use, its space is covered with a lid to provide more bench-top working surface.

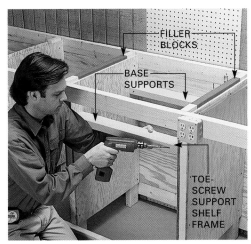

Photo 16. Build a support shelf for the drop-in. Toe-screw two 2x4's laid flat to the legs at the front and rear. Install 2x4 filler blocks in the top of the legs next on each side of the drop-in opening.

Photo 17. Use a handsaw to cut away the upper frame stringer across the drop-in opening. You can install the 1/2-in. plywood for the support shelf before or after cutting away the stringer.

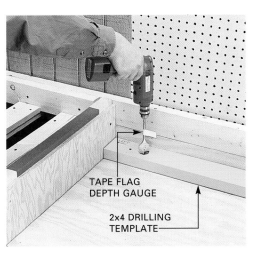

Photo 18. Use a 2x4 template to drill matching holes for the drop-in pegs in the support shelf and the drop-in shelf. Mark the drill bit with masking tape for a hole 1 inch deep below the template.

Move the template to the front of the shelf and drill two holes there. Now turn the drop-in shelf face down and clamp the drilling template to one of its 2x4's. Be sure the side of the template marked "top" is now down, facing the 2x4; that's because you're drilling into the underside of the shelf. Drill two 1-inch deep socket holes. Move the template to the other 2x4 and drill two more sockets. The goal is to end up with four holes in the support shelf and four holes in the drop-in that are exactly aligned with each other.

Cut support pegs

Support pegs will raise the adjustable drop-in to support a tool at whatever working height you prefer. To cut pegs to the proper length, put the drop-in into the workbench space, directly on the support shelf. Put a tool on the drop-in and measure up from its worktable to the working height at which you want to use it. If you want it flush with the finished bench top, remember to add 1 inch for the thickness of the top; if you want it to be above the bench top, measure up to the appropriate height.

Whatever height you get, add 2 inches to account for the 1-inch socket depth in the support shelf and the drop-in. Cut four pieces of 1-1/4 inch closet rod to that length to be support pegs when you use that tool. Do the same for your other tools. Although you may have several tools, you'll probably find that only a few different peg lengths are required to accommodate them all. Sand or file a mild taper on each peg end so they fit easily into the holes (Photo 19). Color-code each set of pegs with paint if you wish. You may want to mark the positions of various tools on the drop-in and drill mounting holes. Use bolts and wing nuts to make tool changes simple.

Cut the drop-in cover

When the drop-in is not in use, the opening is covered by a lift-out portion of the bench top. When you install the top (see page 18), cut the lift-out portion as follows.

Fasten the top to the frame at just one side of the drop-in section. Mark a cutting line on each side of the section that is centered over the thickness of the leg assembly under it.

Set your circular saw blade to just barely cut through the 1-inch thick top, and cut along the line on the side that is fastened to the frame (Photo 20). Slide the cut-off piece in tight, closing up the saw kerf, and cut through the line on the other side of the drop-in opening. Without shifting the top further, fasten the loose half to the frame, leaving the lift-off portion free. The removable portion is supported by the filler pieces in the tops of the leg assemblies and is snug fitting, but has a clearance one saw kerf wide so it will lift out easily.

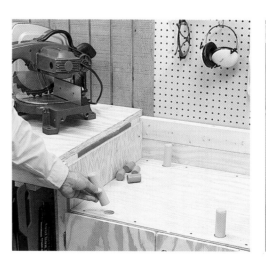

Photo 19. Cut pegs of different lengths, based on trial measurements from tools placed on the drop-in shelf. Color-code the various sets of pegs, so you can find the pegs of each set easily.

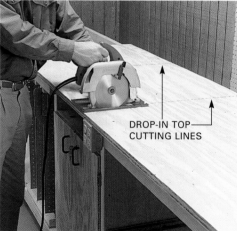

Photo 20. Make a lid for the drop-in section by cutting through the workbench top above the leg assembly on each side. Follow the text instructions to get a close-fitting lid that is easy to remove.

DRAWERS AND A LOCKABLE CABINET

Sturdy pull-out drawers (Photo 21) can hold tools, supplies, and materials. Adding doors across a workbench section creates a convenient but secure cabinet.

Build the drawers

Make the drawers 1 inch narrower than the width of the opening to provide 1/2 inch on each side for the drawer slides. Build the drawer frames with 1x4 boards and the bottoms with 1/2-inch plywood. Butt the drawer sides to the fronts and backs and use wood glue in addition to 1-1/4 inch and 2-inch drywall screws to assemble them. Use 1x2 boards as support cleats for the drawer bottoms (Photo 22).

The drawers ride on full-extension ball-bearing slides, and each drawer can support 100 pounds (Photo 23). When purchasing the 22-inch slides, check their weight rating, and be sure to buy ball-bearing versions. You can also buy 150-pound versions, but they cost more. Install the guides according to the directions supplied with them. Be sure to mount the slides for the bottom drawer with the required clearance above the workbench frame, so the drawer will not scrape or bind.

Build a lockable cabinet

To create a cabinet you can add doors to a drawer section (Photo 24), or to another section fitted with adjustable steel shelving brackets. Cut cabinet doors from scrap pieces of 1/2-inch plywood and add hinges and cabinet pulls. To make the cabinet secure, install a cabinet lock in a hole drilled through one door, or add a hasp and padlock to the face of the doors. You may want to install magnetic catches inside to hold the doors shut when unlocked.

Photo 21. Large drawers are a great asset in a workbench. You can choose heavy-duty glides that support loads of 100 or 150 pounds per pair. Drawers are assembled with both glue and screws.

Photo 22. Build drawer frames from 1x4's. Use 1/2-in. plywood for the bottoms, supported on 1x2 cleats. Make the drawers 1 in. narrower than the opening to provide space for the slides.

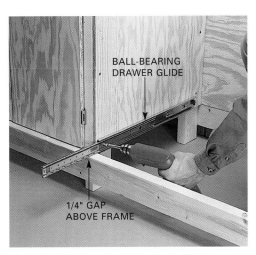

Photo 23. Attach the drawer slides with drywall screws driven through the access holes. Position the bottom drawer slides to provide a 1/4-in. gap between the bench frame and the slide.

Photo 24. Add plywood doors to a workbench section to create a storage cabinet. Put a lock on the doors if you plan to keep dangerous materials in the cabinet, to keep them away from children and pets.

Construction Plans: Extension Table and Roll-Around Saw Stand

Materials List

Quantity	Size and Description
2 or more	4' x 8' x 1/2" plywood
Approx. 40'	2x4 lumber for frames
4	Caster wheels, 2 locking, 2 nonlocking
	Metal folding table legs
	Metal strapping or washers
	1" metal conduit
	1-1/4" closet rod

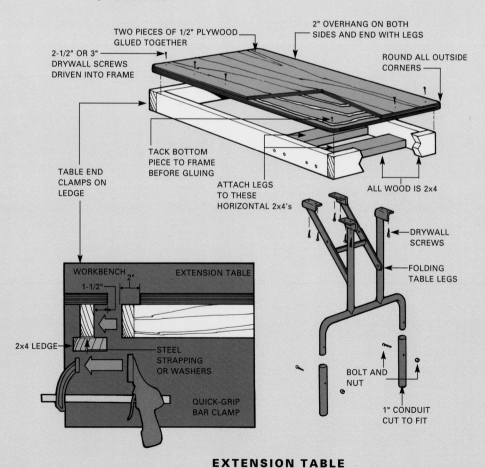

TWO PIECES OF 1/2" PLYWOOD
GLUED TOGETHER

2" OVERHANG ON BOTH
SIDES AND END WITH LEGS

2-1/2" OR 3"
DRYWALL SCREWS
DRIVEN INTO FRAME

ROUND ALL OUTSIDE
CORNERS

TACK BOTTOM
PIECE TO FRAME
BEFORE GLUING

TABLE END
CLAMPS ON
LEDGE

ATTACH LEGS
TO THESE
HORIZONTAL 2x4's

ALL WOOD IS 2x4

DRYWALL
SCREWS

FOLDING
TABLE LEGS

WORKBENCH   2"   EXTENSION TABLE

1-1/2"

2x4 LEDGE

STEEL
STRAPPING
OR WASHERS

QUICK-GRIP
BAR CLAMP

BOLT AND
NUT

1" CONDUIT
CUT TO FIT

EXTENSION TABLE

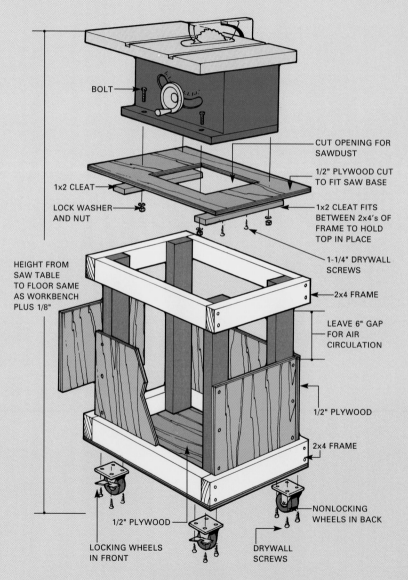

BOLT

CUT OPENING FOR
SAWDUST

1x2 CLEAT

1/2" PLYWOOD CUT
TO FIT SAW BASE

LOCK WASHER
AND NUT

1x2 CLEAT FITS
BETWEEN 2x4's OF
FRAME TO HOLD
TOP IN PLACE

1-1/4" DRYWALL
SCREWS

HEIGHT FROM
SAW TABLE
TO FLOOR SAME
AS WORKBENCH
PLUS 1/8"

2x4 FRAME

LEAVE 6" GAP
FOR AIR
CIRCULATION

1/2" PLYWOOD

2x4 FRAME

1/2" PLYWOOD

LOCKING WHEELS
IN FRONT

DRYWALL
SCREWS

NONLOCKING
WHEELS IN BACK

ROLL-AROUND STAND

EXTENSION TABLE

The extension table (Photo 25) is supported on one end by a pair of metal legs. The other end rests on a ledge on the workbench frame, to give you access to three sides of a workpiece. When not in use, the legs fold into the top and the table stores on a shelf in the workbench base.

Build the frame top

Build the table frame from 2x4's, with 2x4 cross braces for attaching the legs. You can buy a pair of steel folding table legs at many home centers. Use drywall screws to fasten them into the 2x4 braces beneath the table. To raise the legs to the height of the workbench, cut 1-inch metal conduit to length and bolt it in place.

Build the tabletop as you did the bench top, with two sheets of 1/2-inch plywood glued and screwed together. The table shown is 4 feet long (the width of a plywood sheet) and 2 feet wide (so it will store under the workbench). Make a 2-inch overhang on both sides and the end farthest away from the workbench. But do not cover the 2x4 at the end that rests on the bench ledge. The overhang of the workbench top will fill that space when the table is put in position.

Build a bench ledge

Attach a 2x4 ledge to the top workbench frame piece where the extension table will be used. You may want to attach a ledge in

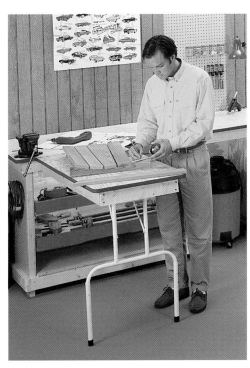

Photo 25. An extension table increases the available working area when needed, and lets you move all around a workpiece. One end is supported by a ledge added to the workbench frame.

Photo 26. Store the extension table under the workbench, in a space just 5 or 6 in. tall. The metal legs fold up into the wood frame and lie against the double-layer plywood top.

more than one location on the workbench frame, so you can use the extension table in various positions.

Secure the ledge to the bottom of the frame piece with drywall screws. Insert washers, steel strapping, or some other thin material between the 2x4 ledge and the bench frame (detail, Extension Table plan) before fastening it in place. The shim provides the small bit of extra space to allow the 2x4 edge of the extension table frame to slip easily into place, resting on the ledge, under the overhang of the bench top. Note the details in the plan carefully because they are critical for an easy-fitting extension table.

To use the extension table, just open the legs, set its end on the 2x4 ledge on the workbench, and clamp the table and workbench frames together for security.

Build a storage shelf for the extension table under pull-out drawers (Photo 26) or other shelves. The storage space should be about 5 inches high and long enough for the extension table; the maximum length of the table shown, when folded, is 48 inches.

ROLL-AROUND SAW STAND

The roll-around stand (Photo 27) lets you position a table saw, band saw, or other tool wherever you need to work. For example, you can place it so the workbench serves as a support for long or wide stock. The roll-around has four caster wheels; use locking casters for the front two wheels, and lock them in position whenever you use the tool mounted on the stand.

Build a 2x4 frame as shown in the plan, modifying it as necessary for the dimensions of your saw. Make it tall enough to place the saw table 1/8 inch higher than the work-

bench top. Be sure it isn't lower; this is potentially hazardous because wood can catch against the edge of the bench and bind against the saw blade (Photo 28).

Cut an opening in the plywood top and then attach the saw to it with bolts. You can make additional tops to fit other tools. The opening prevents sawdust from building up directly under the saw. Fasten 1x2 cleats to hold the top in place so it can be easily lifted off to empty the collected sawdust or replace it with another tool mounted on a duplicate top. Do not completely enclose the bottom of the roll-around, because of the risk of a sawdust explosion if there's no air circulation.

FINISH THE WORKBENCH

When your workbench is complete, put it in position and shim the legs if necessary to level it. If you built an opening for a shop vacuum, use a handsaw to remove that portion of the lower frame so you can roll the vacuum in and out.

Take a few minutes to round off all sharp corners, including those on the drawers, with a sander or file.

You can paint or finish the workbench as you choose. You may want to paint the shelves and drawers for protection, but leave the legs unfinished. To give the bench top a long working life, sand it and apply two coats of clear polyurethane.

Expect to spend some time sorting out and reorganizing your workshop. There are so many storage options that it may take some experimenting to find the most convenient place for everything.

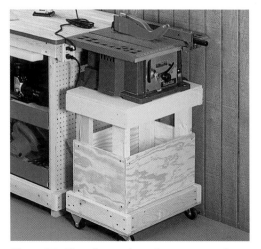

Photo 27. The roll-around stand can accommodate various tools mounted on lift-out tops. Locking casters on one pair of legs will keep it still when in use, but otherwise readily movable.

Photo 28. Make the roll-around tall enough to put a saw table or other tool work table 1/8 in. above the bench top. That way workpieces can slide onto the bench without dangerous binding or snagging.

Wiring Workbench Receptacles

A 4- x 4-inch electrical box can hold two duplex (dual-outlet) receptacles. The wiring of the receptacle depends on whether they are to be on the same or separate circuits, and whether they are standard or GFCI (ground fault circuit interrupt) receptacles.

BASIC CONNECTIONS

To prepare wire for a connection, strip 1/2 to 3/4 inch of the insulation away from the end. Use a wire-stripper to avoid damaging the wire.

To connect to a screw terminal, bend the end of the wire into a hook with needle-nose pliers. Slip the hook around the screw running clockwise, so that tightening the screw pulls the wire further around it **(Figure A).** Never place two wires under a single terminal screw.

To connect two or more wires together, use a twist-on connector. Lay the bare ends side by side and screw on a connector until it stops **(Figure B).** The screwing movement twists the wires together **(Figure C).**

TERMINALS

Standard duplex receptacles usually contain screw terminals of distinct colors: two brass (or unmarked) terminals to receive black or red wires; two silver (or marked "white") terminals to receive white wires; and a green or dark-colored terminal to receive a ground wire. GFCI receptacles have screw terminals or short wire leads, labeled "Line," "Load," and "Ground." Metal electrical boxes have a threaded hole for a #10-32 screw for attaching the ground wire.

Figure A

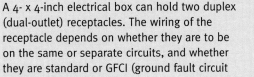

Figure B

Figure C

Figure D

PIGTAILS AND JUMPERS

Electrical codes forbid connecting more than one wire to a screw terminal. To connect one cable wire to two or more terminals, use a twist-on connector to attach short insulated wires called pigtails, one pigtail for each terminal **(Figure D).** A pigtail should be the same gauge and color as the wire to which it is connected.

Make terminal-to-terminal connections with short lengths of insulated wire called jumpers. Use only black or red jumpers between brass terminals; white jumpers between silver terminals. Never run a jumper between terminals of different colors (e.g., brass and silver) and never jumper between ground terminals.

WIRING TWO STANDARD RECEPTACLES

• **One 12-2 cable (single circuit)** Connect the cable black wire to one brass screw of receptacle **A** and the cable white wire to one silver screw of receptacle **A**. Connect a black jumper from the other **A** brass screw to one brass screw of receptacle **B**. Connect a white jumper from the other **A** silver screw to a **B** silver screw. Connect pigtails from the cable ground wire to the **A, B,** and electrical box ground terminals. Do not connect receptacle ground terminals with a jumper.

• **Two 12-2 cables (separate circuits)** Connect the cable #1 black and white wires to receptacle **A** brass and silver screws, as above. Connect the cable #2 black and white wires to receptacle **B** brass and silver screws in the same way. Connect both cable ground wires together with pigtails to the receptacle **A, B,** and electrical box ground terminals.

• **One 12-3 cable (separate circuits)** Connect the cable black wire to one receptacle **A** brass screw and the cable red wire to one receptacle **B** brass screw. Connect the cable white wire to an **A** silver screw. Connect a white jumper from the other **A** silver screw to a **B** silver screw. Connect

pigtails from the cable ground wire to the receptacle **A, B,** and electrical box ground terminals.

WIRING ONE GFCI AND ONE STANDARD RECEPTACLE

• **One 12-2 cable (single circuit)** Connect the cable black wire to the GFCI receptacle LINE brass terminal or black lead. Connect the cable white wire to the GFCI LINE silver terminal or white lead. Connect a black jumper or pigtail from the GFCI LOAD brass/black to the standard (STANDARD) receptacle brass terminal. Connect a white jumper or pigtail from the GFCI LOAD silver/white to the STANDARD receptacle silver terminal. Connect the cable ground wire with pigtails to the GFCI, STANDARD, and electrical box ground terminals.

WIRING TWO GFCI RECEPTACLES

• **Two 12-2 cables (separate circuits)** Connect cable #1 black and white wires to the GFCI **A** receptacle LINE terminals/leads, as above. Connect cable #2 black and white wires to the corresponding GFCI **B** receptacle LINE terminals/ leads. Connect the cable ground wires together with pigtails to the GFCI **A,** GFCI **B,** and electrical box ground terminals. Clip the bare wire off the LOAD leads of both receptacles. Fold the end of each lead back about 1/2 inch and wrap several times with 3/4 inch wide electrician's tape over the cut end.

• **One 12-3 cable (separate circuits)** Connect cable black wire to the LINE brass terminal or black lead of the GFCI **A** receptacle. Connect cable red wire to the LINE brass or black terminal/lead of the GFCI **B** receptacle. Connect cable white wire with pigtails to the GFCI **A** and GFCI **B** LINE silver/white terminals or leads. Connect cable ground wire with pigtails to the GFCI **A,** GFCI **B,** and electrical box ground terminals. Clip off and tape any LOAD leads on the receptacle, in the same way as described above.

Your eyesight is one of your most precious personal assets—

one that you should make every effort to protect.

Protect Your Sight

Your eyesight is also extremely vulnerable. Although your eyes are amazingly

flexible and adaptable, they are delicate, and even slight physical injury

can have a dramatic and long-lasting effect on your vision.

Do-it-yourself work poses continual hazards, because both materials and tools

throw off particles that can fly into unprotected eyes.

But 90 percent of all eye injuries can be avoided with proper safety

practices and protective eyewear.

There are many ways to protect your eyes, no matter what you are doing.

The best are described here. It's information you must not ignore.

Safety glasses, especially those with top and side shields, offer eye protection while still being comfortable and easy to slip on and off.

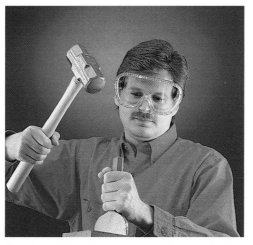

Goggles with safety lenses provide protection for the greatest variety of jobs. They should be the first type of eye protection you purchase.

A face shield provides both eye and full-face protection. However, additional eye protection is a must. Wear goggles or safety glasses as well.

EYESIGHT HAZARDS

Although it's possible to poke something in your eye with a careless gesture, the vast majority of eye injuries are caused by airborne particles, fumes, splashes, and both visible and invisible radiation.

▲ Saws, routers, shapers, lathes, and other power tools all throw sawdust and wood or metal chips into the air with great force and at very high speed. Sanders and sharpening wheels throw off grit, bits of workpiece material, and sparks. Chips of metal fly from a badly hit nailhead or cold chisel, or from a screw head when a power bit slips.

▲ Volatile liquids give off fumes whenever their containers are open, and can spatter when being poured or applied. Adhesives and similar materials give off fumes, too.

▲ Radiation hazards to eyesight are of two types. One is extreme brightness, which can lead to momentary dazzling or partial blindness during which accidents can occur. The other is infrared wavelengths, which can permanently injure the retina. Welding or brazing is the most common work source of this sort of danger.

Because some sort of hazard is present every time you undertake a project, you need to protect your vision when you work.

KINDS OF EYE PROTECTION

There are basically three kinds of vision-protecting devices:

▲ Glasses
▲ Goggles
▲ Face shields

All must provide a physical barrier without impeding your vision. The barrier material must not be a potential hazard in itself. Acceptable protective lenses, whether made from safety glass, polycarbonate, or other plastics, will be stamped by the manufacturer to indicate they have passed safety tests. The frames will bear a "Z 87.1" stamp to indicate they too have passed certain tests. By far the most impact-resistant lens material is polycarbonate; it's not unbreakable, but it's considered to be many times stronger than either glass or other plastic. Most off-the-shelf safety goggles and glasses sold these days are polycarbonate.

Whichever type of protective eyewear you choose, buy a product that's right for the job and comfortable to wear. If it's uncomfortable, chances are you won't wear it.

All three types of protection are available clear or shaded. Tinted or shaded eyewear is good for working outdoors. When welding or brazing, always wear specially shaded eye protection rated for welding use, to guard your eyes from the extreme brightness and infrared rays those processes give off.

Protective Equipment and Practices

SELECTING PROTECTIVE EYEWEAR

To help you choose the eye protection that will best fit your needs, here's some information about each kind of device.

Glasses

Ordinary eyeglasses do not offer adequate protection for most work. They are open at the top, bottom, and sides, and their lenses are not made of safety glass or plastic. In fact, everyday glasses can cause great injury if shards from a broken lens fly into the eye.

Only true safety glasses can offer working protection. Costing as little as $3, they are the most compact form of protective eyewear. Those with side shields will block particles from entering at the sides. Some also have brow shields across the top. A basic pair of safety glasses offers adequate protection when hammering or using hand tools and slow-moving electric tools.

Some safety glasses are designed with wide front frames (bows) to slip over prescription glasses. However, you can also get prescription safety glasses from most eyewear stores. Those with polycarbonate lenses and side shields offer the best protection. The frames, available in plastic or metal, are more rugged than ordinary eyeglass frames.

Goggles

Goggles are close-fitting devices that provide front, side, top, and bottom protection. Costing $5 to $15, they usually are secured with a band that fits snugly around the back of the head. Those with direct vents allow good air circulation, minimize internal fogging, and are adequate for sawing and hammering. Those with indirect vents offer added protection from fine particles or chemical splashes.

Goggles with pliable sides are more comfortable to wear than rigid molded shapes, and they provide a cushion against impact. Many can be worn over prescription glasses.

Goggles can be cumbersome to put on and take off, and some types can limit peripheral vision. However, if you're going to buy only one kind of protective eyewear, get goggles; they'll protect you in most situations.

Full-face shields

Face shields offer full-face protection and are ideal for blocking chips and shavings from lathes or routers. They have a brow band and one or two bands that pass over the top or around the back of the head. Prices for full-face shields with a headband start at about $10.

Face shields don't offer good protection against heavy impact or objects that fly up or around their edges. For that reason, always wear safety glasses or goggles as well.

Glasses

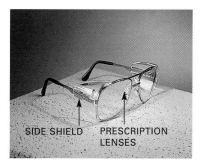

SIDE SHIELD   PRESCRIPTION LENSES

TINTED LENSES

OVERSIZE FRAME

Prescription safety glasses are ideal for those who need glasses all the time. Side shields are essential.

Tinted lenses in safety glasses are especially good for outdoor work. Special tinting is required for welding or brazing.

Large slip-over frames permit wearing safety glasses over most styles of ordinary eyeglasses.

Goggles

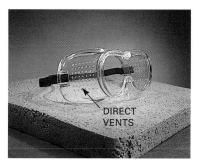

DIRECT VENTS

INDIRECT VENTS

EARMUFFS

Direct vent goggles, which protect eyes from chips and large particles, provide air circulation through small holes.

Indirect vent goggles guard against liquid splashes and fine particles. Baffled vents provide air circulation.

Combined goggles and noise-reducing earmuffs provide two important types of protection in a single unit.

Full-face Shields

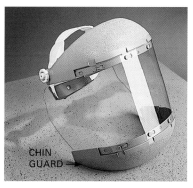

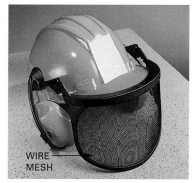

CHIN GUARD

SHADED LENS

WIRE MESH

Face shields with a chin guard offer extra protection from flying debris.

Specially shaded lenses are a must for welding or brazing.

Wire mesh shields are well ventilated and good for outdoor work.

WHEN TO WEAR EYE PROTECTION

Obviously, you should always wear eye protection when using power tools. You should also have protection whenever using hand tools in which force is involved: hammering, prying, splitting. Wear protection when using household paints, especially when painting ceilings, and chemicals such as solvents, thinners, and cleansers. Wear indirect vent goggles when using, mixing, or pouring any chemical that emits fumes. And wear eye protection when cleaning up, whether you use a broom, a vacuum, or a damp rag. Eye protection is important during other jobs around the house, including:

Lawn and garden work. Thousands of eye injuries occur when stones or sticks are hurled from mowers or when branches snap back during hedge trimming. Goggles offer the best eye protection for lawn and garden work. Always wear a face shield and glasses or goggles when using a chain saw.

Automotive work. Wear goggles when jump-starting a motor or working beneath a car where grime can fall into your eyes. Also, protect your eyes when working with anti-freeze, brake fluid, engine cleaners, and other volatile or caustic fluids.

Household paints and chemicals. Wear indirect vent goggles when using, mixing, or pouring oven cleaners, swimming pool chemicals, pesticides, and paint thinners.

Sports. Baseball, basketball, tennis, handball, and racquetball are all high-risk sports. Wearing safety goggles secured with an elastic "sports strap" is a wise precaution.

PREVENTIVE MEASURES

Risky situations can't be predicted. But you can take measures to minimize the risk by being aware of what's around you and having protective eyewear easily accessible. The place for protective eyewear is on your face, not on your workbench or in your toolbox. It makes sense to observe the following preventive measures:

Have an extra pair of safety goggles. Give them to workshop visitors or helpers to wear.

Keep eye protection handy. Keep a pair of safety glasses or goggles draped over the handle of frequently used tools. If they're handy, you'll wear them.

Keep it clean. Protection doesn't mean much if you can't see what you're doing clearly. Use an antifog, antistatic cleaning solution for best results.

Get your kids in the habit. This is important in any case, but especially if they're aspiring woodworkers or hobby crafters.

Think prevention. Anticipate possible problems and take care of seemingly small details. Many eye injuries are caused by lumber or broom handles carelessly left sticking out into a room.

There's a basic fact every do-it-yourselfer should know: Tools make noise,

and noise damages hearing.

Protect Your Hearing

Loud noise causes pain as real and damaging as whacking your thumb with

a hammer or dropping a brick on your toe. Noise also causes stress, which can induce

high blood pressure and headaches.

Worst of all, hearing damage is permanent.

To avoid that, protect your hearing whenever you work.

Here's what you can do to reduce the hazard of noise, so you can work safely

and continue to hear the good things in life.

TOOLS AND NOISE

Hearing loss is cumulative. Each bit of damage adds to what has gone before, so repeated exposure to loud noise slowly but surely erodes your hearing. To understand more about this process, see How You Hear (page 41). Because hearing loss from noise is cumulative and progressive, you need to protect your hearing every time you use a power tool or work with outdoor equipment.

HEARING PROTECTION

There are two basic modes of hearing protection: in the ear and outside the ear. Various kinds of earplugs provide in-the-ear protection; earmuffs of different designs provide outside-the-ear protection. Choose a protector with a noise reduction rating that brings the noise into the 85 db safe range.

For example, if you're working with a circular saw that screams at 110 db, you need a hearing protector rated at 25 NRR or more to bring the sound into the safe range (110 db minus 25 db equals 85 db). Extremely loud situations, such as shooting a firearm or working near a jackhammer, dictate using both earmuffs and earplugs.

Make certain to pick a hearing protector that is comfortable and convenient enough so you'll actually wear it. Don't try to use a substitute for a professional protector. Cotton and tissue paper don't offer the protection of true earplugs. Portable cassette player or radio headphones are not earmuffs, and if their device is turned on they only add to the noise level.

Pages 39 and 40 contain photographs of some of the various hearing protectors available, along with additional information about each type.

NOISE AND LOUDNESS

Noise is measured in units called decibels (db); the louder the noise, the higher the db rating.

Most experts say 85 db is the safe maximum noise level. Devices for hearing protection are rated in terms of their ability to block noise and reduce decibel levels; this is their noise reduction rating (NRR). Hearing protection with an NRR of 30 will reduce the noise reaching your ears by about 30 db.

Loudness Levels

Painfully Loud	140 db: Gunshot at close range; jet engine
	130 db: Jackhammer
Extremely Loud	120 db: Chain saw
	110 db: Circular saw; gas-powered mower
Very Loud	100 db: Router; vacuum cleaner; manufacturing plant
	90 db: Drill press; truck traffic
Acceptable	80 db: Typewriter; electric razor
	60 db: Normal conversation

A circular saw can be nearly as loud and nerve-wracking as a jackhammer. Routers, lathes, and sanders can be just as noisy. Don't ignore the hazard. Hearing that is lost can seldom be restored.

In the ear

Plugs for in-the-ear use are inexpensive yet offer extremely good protection. The best earplugs offer an NRR of 33. Their effectiveness lies in their ability to conform to the ear canal, blocking the sound path.

Foam earplugs are twisted, then inserted in the ear, where they expand to block the ear canal. Flange plugs have two or more flanges that act as sound baffles. Both types have a slight disadvantage—they do such a good job blocking noise that they can make normal conversation difficult.

Because these protectors go inside the ear, they pick up wax and oils and therefore are more likely to attract dirt and sawdust when removed. They must be replaced or cleaned frequently. Also, some people simply don't like putting things inside their ears.

Foam earplugs are available in corded and noncorded styles. Inexpensive and difficult to clean, they are considered disposable.

Flange earplugs are washable, reusable, and comfortable. They are available either corded or noncorded.

Banded earplugs provide in-ear protection with the convenience of a headband. Pads swivel for comfort.

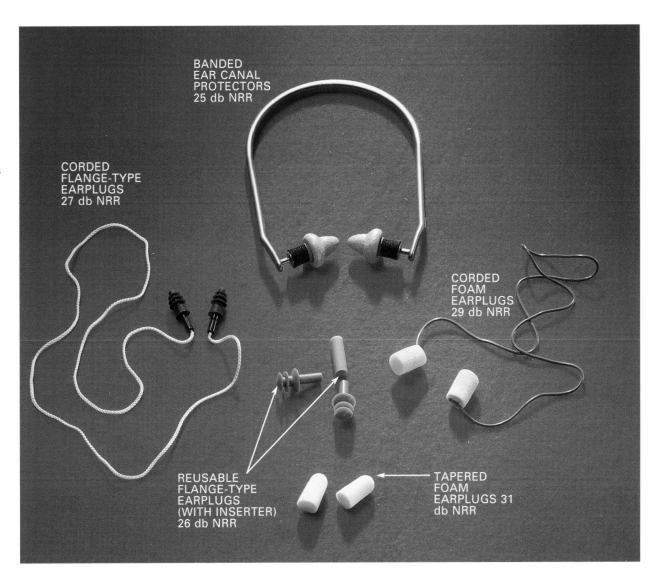

BANDED
EAR CANAL
PROTECTORS
25 db NRR

CORDED
FLANGE-TYPE
EARPLUGS
27 db NRR

CORDED
FOAM
EARPLUGS
29 db NRR

REUSABLE
FLANGE-TYPE
EARPLUGS
(WITH INSERTER)
26 db NRR

TAPERED
FOAM
EARPLUGS 31
db NRR

Outside the ear

Earmuffs for outside-the-ear protection cost more than earplugs but last longer and are harder to misplace. Most earmuffs have a fixed level of sound blocking; noise-activated muffs—the most expensive type—increase their blocking or sound-canceling level as noise grows louder.

The best earmuffs offer an NRR of around 30. Almost all types permit conversation better than earplugs do. Because they are connected to a headband, they can be looped down around the neck or perched atop the head when not in use. Unlike earplugs, they do not risk carrying dirt into the ear canal, they block the infiltration of airborne sawdust and similar waste, and they physically protect the outer ear from flying debris.

Noise-activated earmuffs can be either battery operated or nonelectronic. They gradually increase the amount of hearing protection as noise levels rise, yet permit (or amplify) normal conversation.

Wrap-around earmuffs with a neck strap permit wearing a hard hat or helmet. Other versions have muffs that attach directly to protective headgear.

Foam ear caps are ideal for those who don't like using in-ear earplugs or larger muff-style hearing protection. Worn with a connecting band that passes under the chin, they are lightweight and easy to use.

Combination goggle-muffs combine hearing and sight protection into an easy-to-use unit.

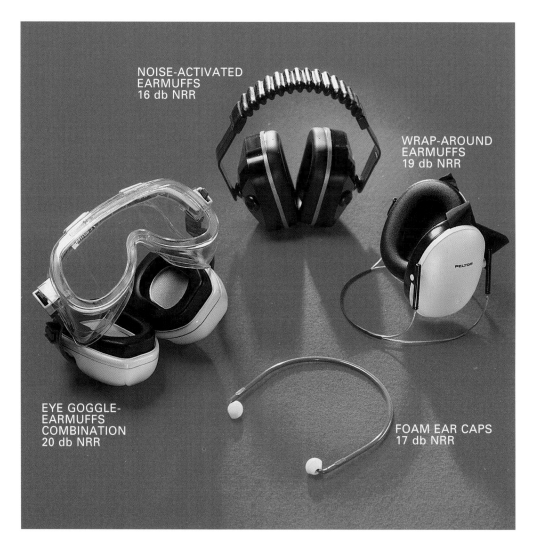

NOISE-ACTIVATED EARMUFFS
16 db NRR

WRAP-AROUND EARMUFFS
19 db NRR

EYE GOGGLE-EARMUFFS COMBINATION
20 db NRR

FOAM EAR CAPS
17 db NRR

WHEN TO WEAR PROTECTION

Ideally, you should wear hearing protection any time the noise level exceeds 85 db—the approximate volume of a drill or garbage disposal. Of course, wearing hearing protection isn't always practical, but be especially diligent about protecting yourself around the following noise sources:

Power tools. The high-pitched whine of a router or radial arm saw can be especially damaging. Even cleaning up afterward with a wet-dry vacuum can be painfully noisy.

Impact sounds. Hammering in a confined space can be painful, even with a small hammer. The crack and screech of pry bars during demolition can be amazingly loud.

Outdoor equipment. Chain saws, lawn mowers, and string trimmers all call for hearing protection. Hard hats with integral earmuffs and a face shield for eyesight protection are available for chain sawing.

GETTING USED TO PROTECTION

At first, hearing protection may make you feel uncomfortable or out of touch with the sound of your tools. The whirs and warning noises of your power tools will sound different, but after a while you'll relearn these sounds. In time, wearing hearing protection will become a habit and you will no more cut a board without your muffs than drive your car without a seat belt.

Use hearing protection even for short work periods. Remember that hearing loss is cumulative; a lot of short working spurts without hearing protection can add up to hearing loss. Also remember to keep an extra set of ear muffs or plugs around for visitors or helpers. It's a good idea to teach your family to use them, too.

Measures

There are other steps you can take to preserve your hearing:

Make sure the tools and machines you are using are well oiled and balanced.

Mount machines on carpet pads or rubber washers to reduce vibration and noise.

"Soften" the work area by lining it with sound-absorbing materials such as cork or fiberboard acoustical panels, or install acoustical tiles made from old indoor/outdoor carpeting.

Use sharp blades and bits; they'll cut faster and quieter.

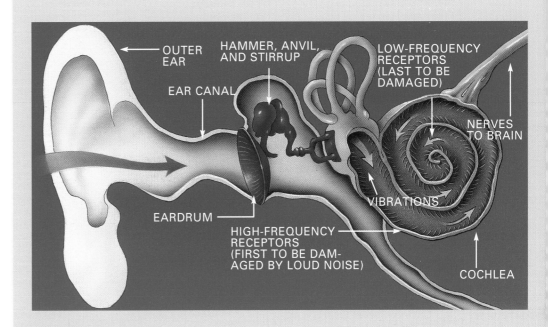

OUTER EAR

HAMMER, ANVIL, AND STIRRUP

LOW-FREQUENCY RECEPTORS (LAST TO BE DAMAGED)

EAR CANAL

NERVES TO BRAIN

EARDRUM

VIBRATIONS

HIGH-FREQUENCY RECEPTORS (FIRST TO BE DAMAGED BY LOUD NOISE)

COCHLEA

How You Hear

The intricate workings of the ear—how a sound wave is turned into a nerve impulse for the brain—are a small miracle.

Sound is channeled through the ear canal and eardrum, then on to the middle ear, which contains the hammer, anvil, and stirrup. It is in the cochlea of the inner ear that most noise-related hearing damage occurs.

The cochlea is lined with small hairs that move nerve impulses along to the brain. These hairs can be bent, broken, or literally blown away by loud noises. The hairs that line the first bend of the cochlea—the high-frequency receptors—are the most susceptible to damage from noise.

Damage to the high-frequency receptors means soft sounds like "s," "sh," and "f" or high-pitched voices cannot be heard as easily, while deeper voices or stronger sounds may still be understood. These receptors are also the first to go with age; many people begin to experience some level of natural hearing loss around the age of 50.

Tinnitus, a constant ringing in the ears, can be caused by long exposure to loud noise, or even by a single enormous impact noise. Woodworkers, musicians, and factory workers are often plagued by tinnitus.

The damaged nerve cells of an ear will never heal. Don't expose yourself to injury. Use hearing protection.

Living Room and Front Hall

A Graceful Side Table
Ideal for a hall, living room, or dining room, this table combines the beauty of natural wood details with a handsome painted base.
44

Here's a perfect table for use in a front hall, beside a living-room sofa,

or in a dining room as a buffet stand.

A Graceful Side Table

The table is narrow enough to fit in a variety of locations, and its two drawers

provide convenient space to store small items.

The tabletop and drawer knobs are solid oak, finished with Danish oil.

The base is birch, painted whatever color you prefer.

Graceful tapered legs lend an air of elegance to the overall simplicity of the design.

Half-overlay lip drawer fronts overlap their openings on all four sides.

The tabletop is secured to the base with steel fastening brackets that allow it

to expand and contract without splitting or damaging the base.

Materials List

Quantity	Size and Description
1	3/4" x 8" x 9' oak
1	1-1/2" x 4" x 6' birch
2	3/4" x 6" x 6' birch
2	3/4" x 4" x 6' birch
1	1/4" x 12" x 36" birch plywood
50	4d finish nails
16	3/8" dia. x 2" spiral dowel pins
2	No. 8 x 3/4" pan-head screws with washers
2	Oak drawer knobs
6	Tabletop fasteners
1 can	Wood putty
1 pint	Enamel paint
1 pint	Enamel underbody primer
1 pint	Danish oil finish, natural

Construction Plans

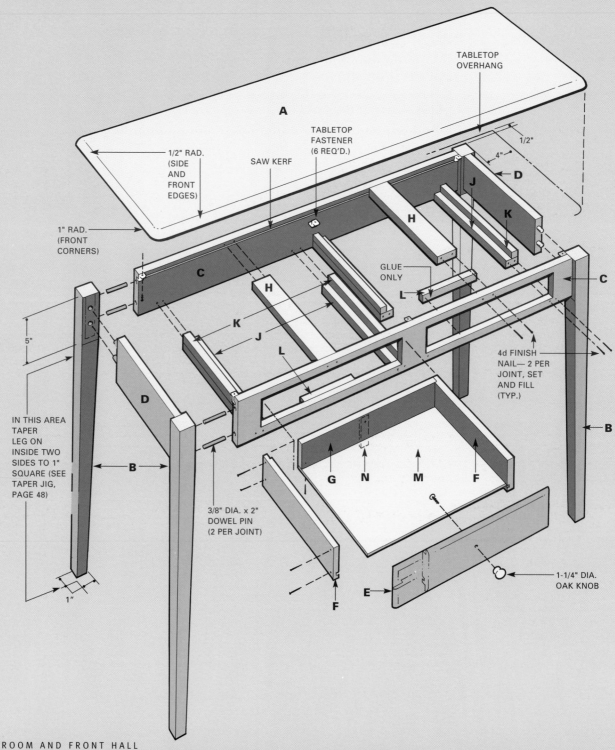

TABLETOP OVERHANG

A

TABLETOP FASTENER (6 REQ'D.)

1/2"

4"

D

SAW KERF

1/2" RAD. (SIDE AND FRONT EDGES)

J

K

H

1" RAD. (FRONT CORNERS)

C

GLUE ONLY

L

H

C

K

5"

J

4d FINISH NAIL— 2 PER JOINT, SET AND FILL (TYP.)

L

D

B

IN THIS AREA TAPER LEG ON INSIDE TWO SIDES TO 1" SQUARE (SEE TAPER JIG, PAGE 48)

G

N

M

F

B

3/8" DIA. x 2" DOWEL PIN (2 PER JOINT)

E

1-1/4" DIA. OAK KNOB

F

1"

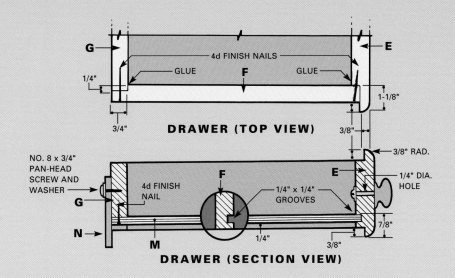

DRAWER (TOP VIEW)

G
E
4d FINISH NAILS
GLUE   F   GLUE
1/4"
1-1/8"
3/4"   3/8"

NO. 8 x 3/4"
PAN-HEAD
SCREW AND
WASHER
G
N
M
4d FINISH
NAIL
F
E
1/4" x 1/4"
GROOVES
3/8" RAD.
1/4" DIA.
HOLE
7/8"
1/4"
3/8"

DRAWER (SECTION VIEW)

Cutting List

Key	Pcs.	Size and Description
A	1	3/4" x 14" x 48" oak (top)
B	4	1-1/2" x 1-1/2" x 31-1/4" birch (legs)
C	2	3/4" x 4-1/2" x 37" birch (front and back aprons)
D	2	3/4" x 4-1/2" x 10" birch (side aprons)
E	2	3/4" x 3-5/8" x 15-1/2" birch (drawer fronts)
F	4	3/4" x 2-7/8" x 11" birch (drawer sides)
G	2	3/4" x 2-3/8" x 13-3/4" birch (drawer backs)
H	2	3/4" x 2" x 10-3/4" birch (upper drawer runners)
J	4	3/4" x 1-1/2" x 10-3/4" birch (drawer runners)
K	4	3/4" x 3/4" x 10-3/4" birch (drawer runners)
L	2	3/4" x 3/4" x 6" birch (stop blocks)
M	2	1/4" x 10-3/4" x 13-3/4" birch plywood (drawer bottoms)
N	2	1/4" x 1" x 3" birch plywood (drawer stops)

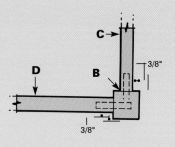

C
D
B
3/8"
3/8"

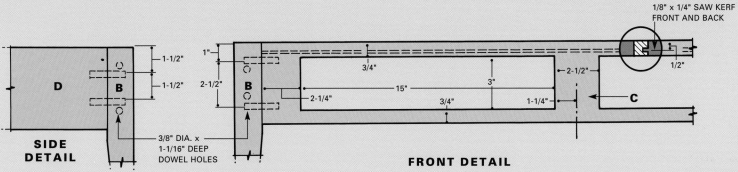

D
B
1-1/2"
1-1/2"
3/8" DIA. x
1-1/16" DEEP
DOWEL HOLES

SIDE DETAIL

1/8" x 1/4" SAW KERF
FRONT AND BACK
1"
2-1/2"
B
2-1/4"
3/4"
15"
3/4"
3"
1-1/4"
2-1/2"
C
1/2"

FRONT DETAIL

Construction Procedures and Techniques

CUTTING AND DRILLING THE PIECES

This table's legs are made of solid birch stock 1-1/2 inches thick. If you have trouble finding birch of this dimension, glue together two 3/4-inch pieces.

The taper on two sides of each leg is easy to cut with a homemade taper jig.

The drawers are boxes assembled with nails—very easy to make and align—and they ride on wooden runners.

Glue the top

To make the top (A), edge-glue together two 3/4 x 8-inch oak boards that are 49 inches long. Alternate the direction of the growth rings in the end grain of the boards to prevent the tabletop from warping. After the glue has dried, cut the top to its finished dimensions of 14 x 28 inches.

Make the initial cuts

Cut all the birch pieces (B) through (N) to the dimensions given in the cutting list. Glue the drawer runner pieces (J) and (K) together.

Draw the drawer openings in the apron front (C) and drill a 3/8-inch starter hole for your saw blade inside each marked area. Cut the openings with a saber saw (Photo 1). Smooth the sawn edges with a file.

Taper the legs

Make the leg-tapering jig by cutting a 3/4-inch thick piece of scrap plywood 5 inches wide by 33 inches long. Draw the angled side as shown in the diagram below left, and cut out the notch with a saber saw.

Tools You Need

Table saw with dado blade

Saber saw

Router

Electric drill

Hammer

Nail set

4' pipe clamp

18" pipe clamps (4)

Dowel jig (optional)

Natural-bristle brush

TAPER JIG

3-3/8"

MAKE JIG FROM 3/4" SCRAP PLYWOOD

SET LEG HERE TO TAPER

33"

SET FENCE 5" FROM BLADE; THIS EDGE AGAINST FENCE

1"

1-3/4"

5"

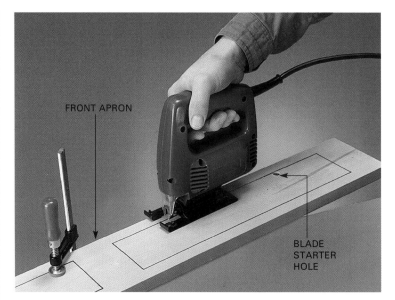

FRONT APRON

BLADE STARTER HOLE

Photo 1. Cut out the drawer openings in the apron front with a saber saw. Drill a 3/8-in. diameter starter hole for the saw blade inside each opening. File the edges smooth after cutting the opening.

To cut the legs, set the table saw fence 5 inches from the saw blade and set the blade slightly higher than 1-1/2 inches. You must cut a taper on two adjacent sides of each leg and leave the sides that fit against the aprons uncut. Place a leg (B) in the notch of the taper jig and slide the jig across the table, holding it tight to the fence (Photo 2). Use a push stick to hold the leg tight against the side of the notch as you cut the taper.

Rotate the leg 90 degrees in the jig so the tapered side you just cut is facing up, then cut the other tapered side of the leg. Repeat these steps for the remaining three legs.

Drill dowel holes

Drilling the dowel holes can be confusing unless you first mark which sides of the legs and ends of the apron pieces (C) go together.

The easiest way to do this is to place all the legs and apron pieces upside down on your worktable in the relative positions they'll assume when the base is assembled. Label each joint with a different identifying mark so you can assemble it the same way later.

Mark the positions of the dowel holes in the sides of the legs and the ends of the apron pieces (see Side Detail in the construction

plans). Offset the dowels slightly on each side of the legs so they won't interfere with each other. Drill the 3/8-inch diameter dowel holes. A dowel jig makes it easy to keep the drill bit perpendicular to the leg (Photo 3). Put a tape flag on the bit to mark the depth of the hole.

Finally, with your table saw blade set 1/4 inch high, cut the grooves for the tabletop fasteners 1/2 inch from the top edge of the front and back aprons (C) (see Front Detail in the construction plans).

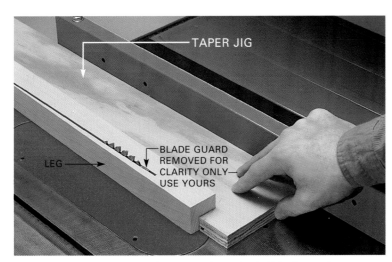

TAPER JIG

BLADE GUARD REMOVED FOR CLARITY ONLY— USE YOURS

LEG

Photo 2. Use a taper jig made from scrap plywood to hold the legs at the proper angle as you cut them. Taper two adjacent sides; leave the other two square. Use a blade guard for all table-saw cuts.

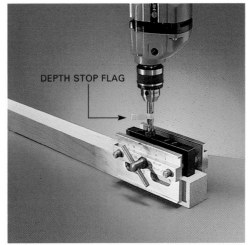

DEPTH STOP FLAG

Photo 3. Drilling the dowel holes in the legs and aprons is simpler and more accurate if you use a dowel-drilling jig. Place a piece of masking tape on the drill bit for a depth stop flag.

ASSEMBLING THE TABLE

There are three stages in assembling the table. First, construct the frame from the legs and apron pieces. Second, make the drawers. Third, complete the top, which has already been glued together and cut to size.

Construct the frame

Sand the legs and aprons with 120-grit paper, then smooth them all with 180-grit paper. Dowel, glue, and clamp the front legs to the front apron and the back legs to the back apron. Then dowel, glue, and clamp the side aprons to the assembled front and back.

Make the drawers

Drill the holes for the knobs in the drawer fronts (E). Shape the drawer front edges with a router and 3/8-inch round-over bit.

Cut rabbets 1-1/8 inches wide by 3/8 inch deep on the inside ends of the drawer fronts, using a dado blade on your table saw (Photo 4). Use the table saw's miter gauge to ensure square cuts. Clamp a stop block to the fence to hold the piece the correct distance from the blade. Cut rabbets 3/4 inch wide x 1/4 inch deep on the back ends of the drawer sides (F) in the same way (see Drawer Top View and Drawer Section View in the plans).

Cut the grooves for the drawer bottoms (M) in the drawer fronts and sides.

Sand all the drawer pieces, then glue and clamp all the pieces together except for the drawer bottoms. You'll push the bottoms into their grooves after finishing, to avoid having to wipe Danish oil out of the corners.

Drill pilot holes, and then drive finish nails through the drawer sides into the drawer fronts and backs. To make nailing easier, clamp the drawer front or back in a vise so that the drawer side is supported on the top edge of the vise jaw. Use a nail set to finish driving the nails into the drawer fronts past the lips of the fronts.

Align the upper drawer runners (H) between the front and back aprons. Use a clamp to hold them in place, then drill pilot holes and drive finish nails. Use a nail set to drive the heads below the surface. Fill the nail holes with wood putty. Then glue the stop block (L) in place at the bottom of each drawer opening in the front apron.

Complete the top

Cut the rounded corners of the top (A) and use a router with a 1/2-inch round-over bit to shape its sides and front edges. Sand the top on both sides and mount it to the base with tabletop fasteners (Photo 5). The end of a fastener fits into the groove cut into the apron, and is screwed to the underside of the top. Place one fastener in each corner and one in the center of the front and back aprons. Leave a 1/16-inch space between the fasteners and the aprons to allow for expansion of the top with humidity changes. Drill pilot holes for the screws. Once all the fasteners have been installed, unscrew them, remove the top, and set it aside.

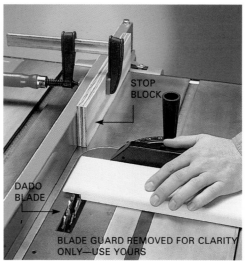

STOP BLOCK

DADO BLADE

BLADE GUARD REMOVED FOR CLARITY ONLY—USE YOURS

Photo 4. Cut rabbets on the ends of the drawer fronts and drawer sides using a table saw, dado blade, and miter gauge. A stop block clamped to the saw's fence positions the end of the workpiece.

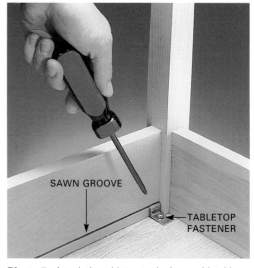

SAWN GROOVE

TABLETOP FASTENER

Photo 5. Attach the tabletop to the base with table fastener brackets. Leave a 1/16-in. space between the fasteners and the aprons to allow the top to expand.

Affix the lower runners

To mount the runners (J, K) that guide the sides and bottoms of the drawers, set the table base on its back and align the drawers in their openings. Set them tight to the bottom edge of the opening in the apron, with a 1/8-inch gap on each side.

Set the drawer runners in place and mark their outside edges on the front and back aprons (Photo 6). Hammer finish nails through the aprons and into the drawer runners to hold them in place. Use a nail set to drive the nailheads slightly below the surface. Fill the nail holes with wood putty.

FINISHING THE TABLE

Sand smooth all sharp edges of the base, drawers, and top. Apply tinted primer to the legs, aprons, and drawer fronts (Photo 7).

When the primer is dry, lightly sand it with 220-grit paper. Then apply two coats of finish enamel, sanding lightly between coats.

Apply three coats of Danish oil finish to the unpainted parts of the drawers and to both sides of the tabletop.

After the oil finish is dry, slide the drawer bottoms (M) into their grooves. Fasten them with finish nails driven into the drawer backs.

Attach the knobs to the drawer fronts and pivoted stops to the backs of the drawers. The stops are 1-inch x 3-inch pieces of 1/4-inch plywood. Attach them with a single pan-head screw and a washer (see Drawer Section View in the construction plans).

Reattach the top to the base with the metal fasteners. Turn the rear drawer stops horizontal so you can slide the drawers in place. Then turn the stops downward so the drawers won't fall out when you open them.

Finishing Tip

Covering light wood with dark paint can be difficult. Often, dark colors don't "hide" the surface below very well, so it's easy to get light-colored blotches where the paint is a little thinner.

To avoid this problem, have the paint store tint the white primer darker by adding the same color as your final coat. The primer will be lighter than the final color (because of the white base), but it will make the final finish look better, with fewer coats.

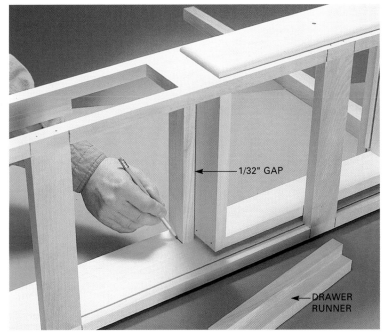

1/32" GAP

DRAWER RUNNER

Photo 6. Mark where the ends of the drawer runners join the front and back apron pieces. Leave a 1/32-inch gap between the runners and the sides of the drawers.

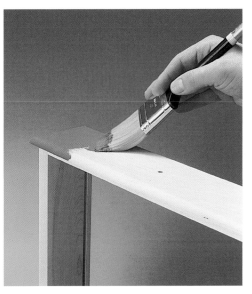

Photo 7. Apply tinted primer with a natural-bristle paint brush. Using a dark-tinted primer under a dark paint makes it easier to hide light-colored wood.

This hall stand features fancy brass coat hooks, a large mirror, and a seat that's a perfect place for changing shoes or removing boots.

Victorian Hall Stand

This classic is as practical today as it was 100 years ago, always ready at the entrance to serve anyone entering your home. Because it needs only a small amount of floor space, it can be set in almost any entryway.

This hall stand is made with red oak boards and crown molding, both available at most lumberyards.

Building requires moderate woodworking skills. The joints are either doweled, screwed, or nailed together.

Materials List

Quantity	Size and Description
25 board ft.	3/4" red oak
3 linear ft.	3-1/4" red oak crown molding
3 linear ft.	2" x 4" pine stud
22	3/8" x 2" spiral doweling pins
18	No. 6 x 2" flathead wood screws
36	No. 6 x 1-1/4" flathead wood screws
4	1/4" flat washers
20	1-1/2" finish nails
20	1" finish nails
2	Brass costumer coat hooks
1	1/4" x 20" x 41" mirror
1 quart	Tung oil or other finish

Construction Plans

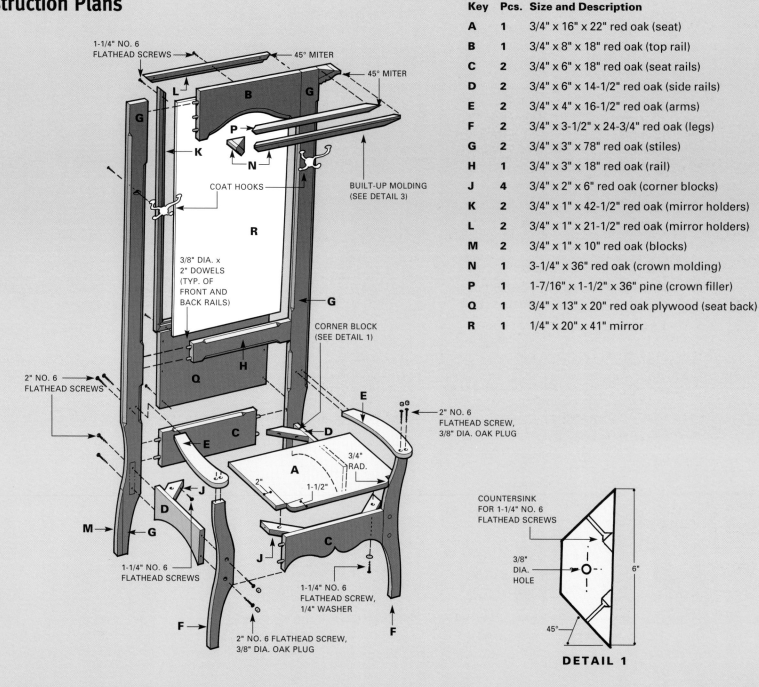

1-1/4" NO. 6 FLATHEAD SCREWS

45° MITER

45° MITER

L

B

G

G

K

P

N

COAT HOOKS

BUILT-UP MOLDING (SEE DETAIL 3)

R

3/8" DIA. x 2" DOWELS (TYP. OF FRONT AND BACK RAILS)

G

CORNER BLOCK (SEE DETAIL 1)

2" NO. 6 FLATHEAD SCREWS

Q

H

E

2" NO. 6 FLATHEAD SCREW, 3/8" DIA. OAK PLUG

C

E

D

A

3/4" RAD.

2"

1-1/2"

M

G

D

J

J

C

1-1/4" NO. 6 FLATHEAD SCREWS

1-1/4" NO. 6 FLATHEAD SCREW, 1/4" WASHER

F

2" NO. 6 FLATHEAD SCREW, 3/8" DIA. OAK PLUG

F

Cutting List

Key	Pcs.	Size and Description
A	1	3/4" x 16" x 22" red oak (seat)
B	1	3/4" x 8" x 18" red oak (top rail)
C	2	3/4" x 6" x 18" red oak (seat rails)
D	2	3/4" x 6" x 14-1/2" red oak (side rails)
E	2	3/4" x 4" x 16-1/2" red oak (arms)
F	2	3/4" x 3-1/2" x 24-3/4" red oak (legs)
G	2	3/4" x 3" x 78" red oak (stiles)
H	1	3/4" x 3" x 18" red oak (rail)
J	4	3/4" x 2" x 6" red oak (corner blocks)
K	2	3/4" x 1" x 42-1/2" red oak (mirror holders)
L	2	3/4" x 1" x 21-1/2" red oak (mirror holders)
M	2	3/4" x 1" x 10" red oak (blocks)
N	1	3-1/4" x 36" red oak (crown molding)
P	1	1-7/16" x 1-1/2" x 36" pine (crown filler)
Q	1	3/4" x 13" x 20" red oak plywood (seat back)
R	1	1/4" x 20" x 41" mirror

COUNTERSINK FOR 1-1/4" NO. 6 FLATHEAD SCREWS

3/8" DIA. HOLE

6"

45°

DETAIL 1

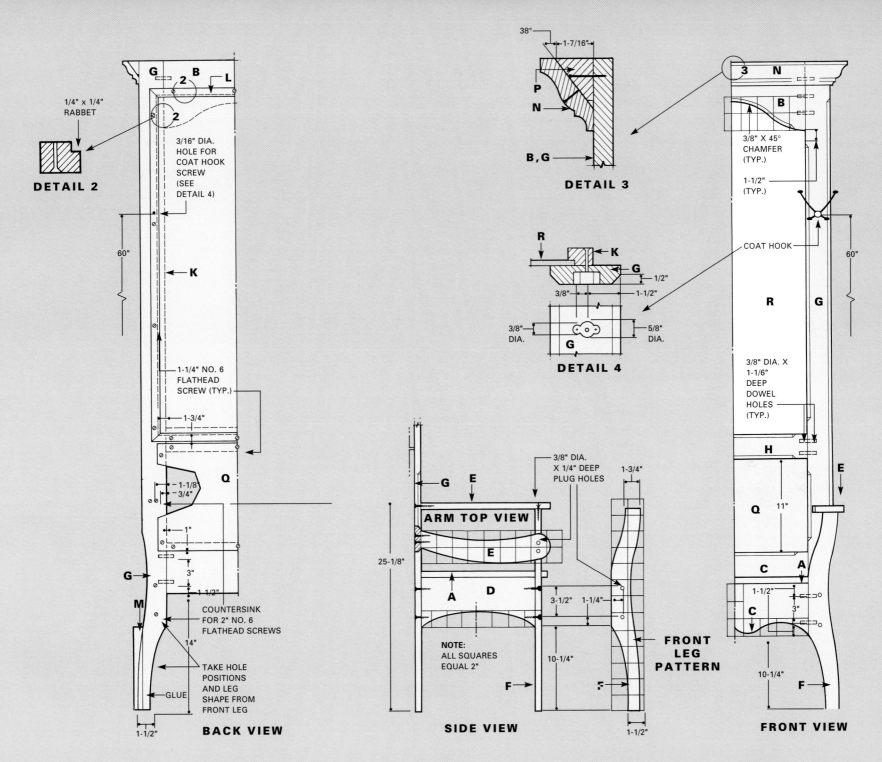

DETAIL 2

1/4" x 1/4" RABBET

G B 2 L

2

3/16" DIA. HOLE FOR COAT HOOK SCREW (SEE DETAIL 4)

60"

K

1-1/4" NO. 6 FLATHEAD SCREW (TYP.)

1-3/4"

Q

1-1/8"
3/4"

1"

3"

1-1/2"

G

M

COUNTERSINK FOR 2" NO. 6 FLATHEAD SCREWS

14"

TAKE HOLE POSITIONS AND LEG SHAPE FROM FRONT LEG

GLUE

1-1/2"

BACK VIEW

38°
1-7/16"

P

N

B,G

DETAIL 3

R

K

G
1/2"

3/8"
1-1/2"

3/8" DIA.

5/8" DIA.

G

DETAIL 4

3/8" DIA. X 1/4" DEEP PLUG HOLES

1-3/4"

G E

ARM TOP VIEW

E

25-1/8"

A D

3-1/2"
1-1/4"

NOTE: ALL SQUARES EQUAL 2"

F

10-1/4"

F

FRONT LEG PATTERN

1-1/2"

SIDE VIEW

3 N

B

3/8" X 45° CHAMFER (TYP.)

1-1/2" (TYP.)

COAT HOOK

60"

R G

3/8" DIA. X 1-1/6" DEEP DOWEL HOLES (TYP.)

H

E

Q
11"

C A

1-1/2"
3"

C

10-1/4"

F

FRONT VIEW

Construction Procedures and Techniques

CUTTING AND DRILLING THE PIECES

This project requires careful transfer of curved shapes from a grid provided in the plans. To ensure symmetry, trace and cut one side of each type of piece, then use it to trace the shape onto the partner piece for the other side of the stand.

Glue the seat boards

You will have to edge-glue at least three boards to make the seat (A). Cut these boards long so the seat can be trimmed to its finished dimensions after it's been glued. Be sure to alternate the direction of the growth rings in the end grain of the boards so the seat won't warp.

Cut the pieces

Cut the seat to its finished dimensions of 16 inches by 22 inches.

Cut the remaining 3/4-inch oak pieces (B to M) to the dimensions given in the cutting list. Also cut the oak plywood seat back (Q) to size. You'll cut the oak crown (N) and the pine crown filler (P) later.

Prepare the stiles (G) for shaping by edge-gluing the blocks (M) to the bottoms of the stiles. These blocks widen the legs where needed (Photo 1). This is easier and more economical than trying to cut them from a single long, wide board.

Transfer the grid

Draw a grid of 2-inch squares on the top rail (B), front seat rail (C), and one side rail (D), arm (E), and leg (F). Transfer the shapes from the grids on the construction plans to the grids on your wood by following the curved lines on the plans, marking off where they intersect the corresponding grid lines on the wood (Photo 2). After you have enough points on the grid, connect them to make the curve.

Cut the curved pieces

Cut out pieces D, E, and F with a saber saw or band saw. Then use them as templates for tracing the shapes of the opposite-side rail, arm, and leg. The stiles (G and M glued together) are the same shape as the front legs.

Use a band saw or saber saw to cut out the top rail (B), front seat rail (C), and the remaining side rail (D), arm (E), and leg (F). Sand the edges with a sanding drum attached to a drill (Photo 3).

Tools You Need

- Table saw or radial arm saw
- Router with chamfer bit
- Drill with twist bits and drum sander
- Saber saw or band saw
- Pipe clamps
- Torpedo level
- Miter box
- Backsaw
- Plug cutter
- Block clamp
- Hammer

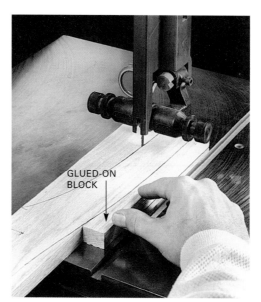

Photo 1. Cut legs on the stiles after gluing on a block to make them wider. This is easier than cutting them from a single long, wide board.

GLUED-ON BLOCK

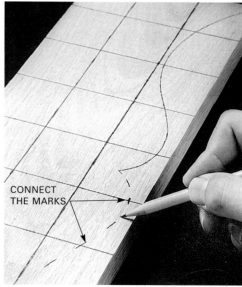

Photo 2. Transfer shapes for curved parts from the plans to grids you've drawn on the wood pieces. Cut them with a band saw or saber saw.

CONNECT THE MARKS

Drill assembly holes

Lay out and drill the dowel holes in the back frame pieces B, C, G, and H and the front pieces C and F. Next, lay out and drill the plug and screw holes in the arms and legs (see Front View, Side View, and Back View details in the construction plans).

Lay out, countersink, and drill the screw holes for the arms, seat, and side rails in the stiles, and the holes in the seat back (Q).

Drill a practice mortise for the coat hook on a piece of scrap wood (see Detail 4 in the plans). The hook should fit snugly in its mortise so it doesn't rotate. When the pattern is correct, drill the mortises in the stiles.

ASSEMBLING THE HALL STAND

Put together the back and front frames

Sand the inside edges of the stiles (G), both edges of the rail (H), and the top edge of the back seat rail (C). Glue and dowel one stile to the rails (Photo 4).

Dry-fit the other stile—don't glue it yet—and clamp the back frame together. When the glue has cured in the other pieces, remove the dry-fit side and then glue, dowel, and clamp it to the rails. Now dowel and clamp the legs and front seat rail together.

Rout a chamfered edge

Put a chamfering bit in your router and set it to cut 3/8 inch deep. Mark the points on the frame back where the chamfers end. Clamp stop blocks to the face of the back frame to limit how far the router can travel; their location will vary with the dimensions of your router (Photo 5). Cut the chamfers.

Support the mirror and seat

Use a table saw or radial arm saw to cut the 1/4-inch by 1/4-inch rabbets in the mirror holders (K, L) (Detail 2 in the plans).

Cut 45-degree miters in the ends of the corner blocks (J) and the mirror holders. Lay out, countersink, and drill the screw holes in the corner blocks and mirror holders.

With the back frame resting on its face, position the mirror, mirror holders, and seat back, then screw them on. Now unscrew the holders and back for finishing separately and place the mirror safely out of the way until the entire piece is finished.

Working Tip

Here's an easy way to dry-fit dowel joints accurately while leaving them easy to disassemble.

Make test-assembly dowels by sawing a slot along the length of each dowel reaching almost to the center. Rotate the dowel a quarter-turn and saw a second slot in the same way. This will leave a pie-shaped wedge along one side of the dowel, attached at the center.

Dowels slotted in this way will slide in and out of the holes easily. For final assembly, replace the test dowels with ordinary pieces. Be sure to use scrap wood or pieces of cardboard on clamping surfaces during final assembly to protect the work.

Photo 3. Use a sanding drum as a quick way to smooth curved edges. Start with a coarse sanding sleeve, then finish-sand with fine grit.

Photo 4. Join frames with dowels. Put a small amount of glue in the dowel holes and clamp the frame so that it is flat and square.

Photo 5. Rout stopped chamfers on the inside edge of the frame, using a clamped-on block to keep your router from going too far.

PLUG

Photo 7. Glue in oak plugs to cover the screws that hold the arms. Align the grain of the plugs parallel with the grain of the arm.

Assemble the stand

Finish-sand all faces that show on the back frame, side rails, seat back, and both sides of the front arms. Drill pilot holes where the screws hold the side rails (see Side View in the plans). Screw the back frame, the side rails, and the front together.

Set the hall stand upright on a flat surface, such as a few pieces of 3/4-inch plywood, and check that all four feet rest firmly on the floor. Trim legs that are too long.

Screw the corner blocks (J) to the inside joints of the assembled hall stand (Detail 1 in the plans; Photo 6).

CORNER BLOCK

HOLE FOR ATTACHING SEAT

Photo 6. Screw on corner blocks to reinforce the joints. They also keep everything square and provide a way to screw on the seat.

Attach the arms and seat

Clamp a scrap board across the back frame 25-1/16 inches above the floor to support the arms (E) while they're being attached. Use a level to ensure that the arms are level before drilling the holes.

Insert the screws in their holes through the stiles (G) and the top of the arms (E). Tap them lightly with a hammer to mark where pilot holes will be drilled in the back edges of the arms (E) and legs (F). Drill the holes, reposition the arms, and screw them on.

Use a band saw or saber saw to cut the notches and rounded corners on the front of the seat. Cut the notches so there will be a 1/16- to 1/8-inch space between the seat and the inside of the front legs. This lets the seat expand with humidity changes.

Finish-sand the seat and slip it on. Attach it with screws through the back frame, then screw from underneath through predrilled holes in the corner blocks (J).

Plug the screw holes

Chuck a 3/8-inch plug cutter in a drill press or drill guide and cut out eight plugs 3/8 inch long. Place a small amount of glue on the plugs, align the grain so it is parallel with the grain of the arms, and gently tap them into the plug holes (Photo 7).

Allow the glue to cure, then trim and finish-sand the plugs flush with their surfaces.

Cut the crown filler

Draw the shape of the crown filler (P) on the end of a 2x4, so you can see the shape you'll need to cut out (Detail 3, plans). Tilt your table saw blade to 38 degrees and cut the angled edge. Now adjust the blade angle to 90 degrees. Set the fence so when the square edge rides against it, the crown filler will be cut off. Now make your cut.

Attach crown molding

Use a miter box to cut the crown filler (P) and molding to the dimensions shown in the cutting list (page 54).

The crown molding (N) requires a compound miter cut. Place it in the miter box upside down and backwards at the angle it will take when installed, resting against the bottom and side of the miter box. Start by mitering the front crown filler piece to fit. Glue and nail it to the top of the back frame (Detail 3 in plans).

Miter the ends of the side crown filler pieces (N) the same way, set them in position, mark their lengths, and cut the square ends. Glue and nail these side pieces to the top edges of the back frame (Photo 8). Drill pilot holes, then nail and glue the mitered corners together so they can't separate.

Miter, fit, and attach the crown molding (N) as you did with the crown filler.

Use a nail set to drive the nailheads just below the surface of the molding. Fill the nail holes with putty and finish-sand the molding.

FINISHING

The hall stand shown on these pages is finished with tung oil because it's easy to apply and durable. Remember: Test any finish on scrap wood first to see how it looks and applies. This is especially important if the finish you are using is new to you.

Apply the finish

Unscrew and remove the seat. Finish-sand any remaining unsanded surfaces and sand smooth all sharp corners and edges. Apply the finish equally to all exposed surfaces. Follow the manufacturer's instructions exactly to ensure good results.

Reassemble the hall stand

After the finish is dry, reattach the seat, the bottom mirror holder (L), and one side mirror holder (K).

Carefully rest the mirror in the rabbet of the bottom mirror holder. Then slide the mirror over into the rabbet in the side mirror clip (Photo 9). Now reattach the other two mirror holders, then the seat back.

Drill holes for the coat hook bolts in the center of the hook mortises and through the back frame and side mirror holders (Detail 4 in plans). Countersink the holes on the back of the mirror holders. The hook bolts are a little long, so cut 3/16 inch off their length before bolting on the hooks.

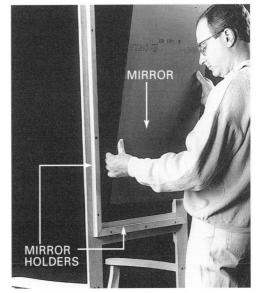

Photo 9. Insert the mirror when the finish is dry. Screw on two of the rabbeted holders, slip the mirror in, and screw on the last two holders.

Using the Stand

Keep in mind that this hall stand is a tall piece of furniture. Place it against a wall where it can't tip over backwards.

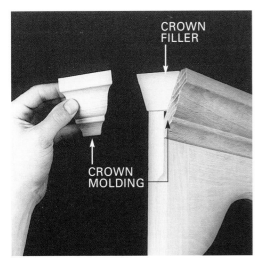

Photo 8. Glue and nail crown molding to a filler piece. A couple of nails through the corners will help keep the joints closed tightly.

This mahogany drop-leaf end table is based on one commissioned by Welsh royalty more than 200 years ago.

Drop-Leaf End Table

Its tapered legs, oval top, and hinged side leaves capture the refined elegance of the original.

These same qualities make this project a classic woodworker's challenge.

It features rule joints between the top and side leaves.

These require special drop-leaf hinges and careful planning.

When properly crafted, however, the joints move gracefully, making the table equally attractive with the leaves raised or resting folded at the sides.

The table shown on these pages is made with mahogany for a traditional look, but other woods could be used with equally handsome results.

Materials List

Quantity	Size and Description
5 board ft.	8/4 mahogany
25 board ft.	4/4 mahogany
2 pairs	Drop-leaf hinges
1	Brass pull
20	3/8" x 2" dowel pins
5	No. 10 x 1-1/4" pan-head screws with washers
2	No. 6 x 2" drywall screws
8	No. 6 x 1-1/2" drywall screws
24	1-1/4" finish nails
1/2 pint	Dark mahogany stain
1 pint	Varnish

Construction Plans

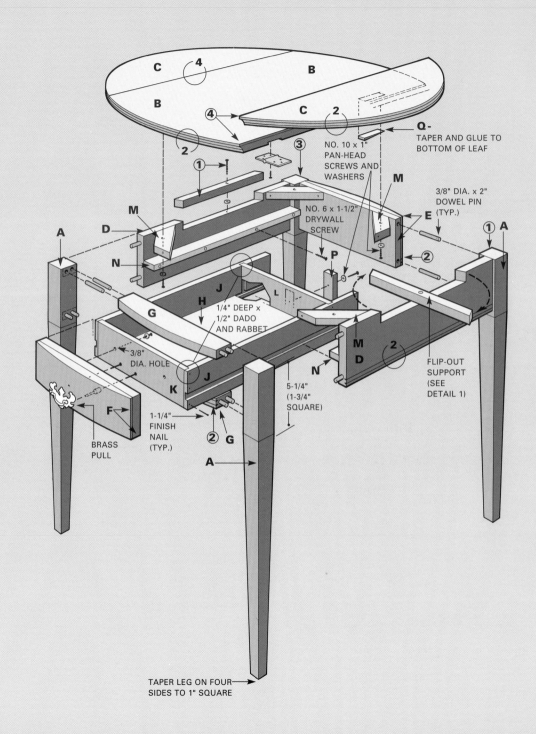

C 4

B

B

C 2

4

2

Q-
TAPER AND GLUE TO
BOTTOM OF LEAF

NO. 10 x 1"
PAN-HEAD
SCREWS AND
WASHERS

3

1

M

M

3/8" DIA. x 2"
DOWEL PIN
(TYP.)

NO. 6 x 1-1/2"
DRYWALL
SCREW

D

M

E

1 A

A

N

P

2

1

H

J

G

L

N

M
D

J

1/4" DEEP x
1/2" DADO
AND RABBET

2

FLIP-OUT
SUPPORT
(SEE
DETAIL 1)

3/8"
DIA. HOLE

J

K

5-1/4"
(1-3/4"
SQUARE)

F

1-1/4"
FINISH
NAIL
(TYP.)

2

G

BRASS
PULL

A

TAPER LEG ON FOUR
SIDES TO 1" SQUARE

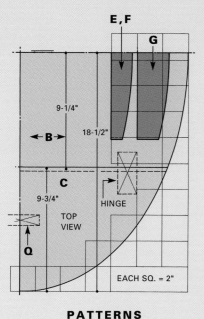

DETAIL 1

11"

C

NO. 10 x 2" FLATHEAD SCREW AND WASHER

FLIP-OUT SUP-PORT (CUT OUT OF APRON D)

30°   3/4"

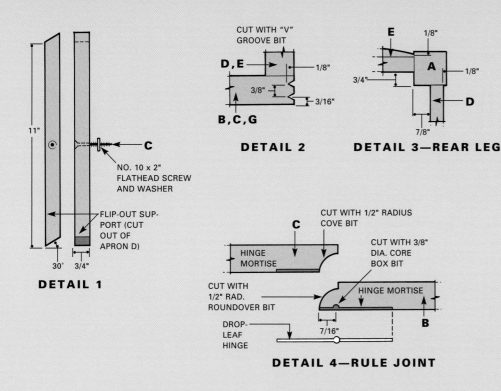

CUT WITH "V" GROOVE BIT

D,E   1/8"

3/8"   3/16"

B,C,G

DETAIL 2

E   1/8"

A   1/8"

3/4"

D

7/8"

DETAIL 3—REAR LEG

CUT WITH 1/2" RADIUS COVE BIT

C

CUT WITH 3/8" DIA. CORE BOX BIT

HINGE MORTISE

HINGE MORTISE

CUT WITH 1/2" RAD. ROUNDOVER BIT

DROP-LEAF HINGE

7/16"   B

DETAIL 4—RULE JOINT

Cutting List

Key	Pcs.	Size and Description
A	4	1-3/4" x 1-3/4" x 23-1/4" (legs)
B	1	3/4" x 18-1/2" x 26-1/2" (top)
C	2	3/4" x 9-3/4" x 26-1/2" (leaves)
D	2	3/4" x 4-3/4" x 19-1/4" (side aprons)
E	2	3/4" x 4-3/4" x 13-1/4" (back aprons)
F	2	3/4" x 3-1/8" x 13-1/8" (drawer face)
G	2	3/4" x 2-1/4" x 13-1/4" (drawer rails)
H	1	1/2" x 12-3/8" x 17-3/4" (drawer bottom)
J	2	1/2" x 3" x 20-3/4" (drawer sides)
K	1	1/2" x 3" x 12-1/2" (drawer front)
L	1	1/2" x 2-1/2" x 12-1/2" (drawer back)
M	4	1/2" x 1-1/2" x 5-1/2" (corner blocks)
N	2	1/2" x 1-1/8" x 19-1/4" (drawer guides)
P	1	1/2" x 1-1/8" x 3" (drawer stop)
Q	2	1/8" x 3/4" x 3" (leaf wedges)

E,F

G

9-1/4"

18-1/2"

B

C

9-3/4"

HINGE

TOP VIEW

Q

EACH SQ. = 2"

PATTERNS

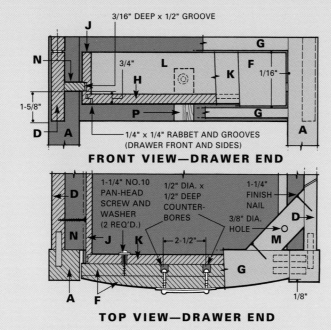

3/16" DEEP x 1/2" GROOVE

J   G

N   3/4"   L   F

H   K   1/16"

1-5/8"

P   G

D   A   A

1/4" x 1/4" RABBET AND GROOVES (DRAWER FRONT AND SIDES)

FRONT VIEW—DRAWER END

D

1-1/4" NO.10 PAN-HEAD SCREW AND WASHER (2 REQ'D.)

1/2" DIA. x 1/2" DEEP COUNTER-BORES

1-1/4" FINISH NAIL

3/8" DIA. HOLE

N   J   K   2-1/2"   M

D

A   F   G

1/8"

TOP VIEW—DRAWER END

Construction Procedures and Techniques

CUTTING AND DRILLING THE PIECES

This project requires advanced woodworking skills. A minor error in measurement or cutting will result in a poor fit or gaps between the leaves and tabletop.

A band saw is essential for this job, as several of the pieces are too thick or tall to be cut with a jigsaw or saber saw.

Make the initial cuts

Prepare the wide top (B), leaves (C), and drawer bottom (H) by edge-gluing narrow boards together. Choose these boards carefully so their color and grain match. Glue the boards together so the completed piece is slightly wider and longer than the dimensions given in the cutting list, and be sure to alternate the direction of the growth rings in the end grain to avoid warping of the wood.

Cut the two side apron pieces (D) oversize (about 5-1/4 inches by 20-1/4 inches for now). The pivoting leaf supports and the end pieces will be cut from these boards in the next step (see Detail 1 in the construction plans).

Cut the remaining pieces A, E, F, G, and J through Q to size.

Cut the leaf supports

Draw center lines dividing the length of both side aprons (D). Mark all your length measurements relative to these center lines.

Rip one 7/8-inch wide strip from each oversized side apron for constructing the flip-out leaf supports. Cut these 7/8-inch wide strips into three pieces: the 11-inch leaf support (with parallel 30-degree angles at each end of the cut) and the two shorter end pieces.

Rip the leaf supports (but not the end pieces) one more time, to 3/4 inch thickness, so that they can pivot freely when in place. Rip the remaining sections of the side aprons to 3-7/8 inches and countersink and drill the pivot screw holes so they are exactly on the center line. Then screw the leaf supports to the side aprons.

Glue the 7/8-inch wide end pieces back on the side aprons so their parallel angled ends act as stops for the leaf supports (Photo 1). Cut the side aprons to their finished length of 19-1/4 inches.

Drill dowel holes; glue-up parts

Lay out and drill the dowel holes in the two side aprons (D), four legs (A), top and bottom drawer rails (G), and the inner back apron piece E (Photo 2).

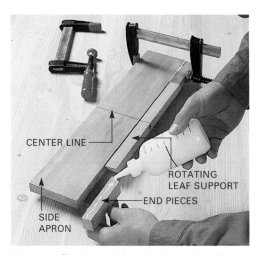

Photo 1. Glue the end pieces back onto the side aprons after ripping and angle-cutting the rotating leaf supports. The supports are secured with screws.

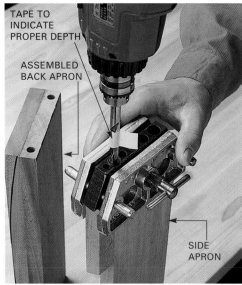

Photo 2. Drill dowel holes using a dowel jig for straight, centered holes. The piece on the left shows the assembled back apron before cutting the curve.

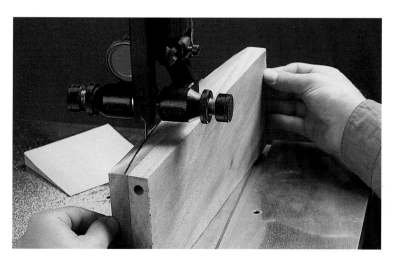

Photo 3. Cut the curved back apron and drawer face and rail using a band saw. Use templates made from the plans to trace the shape onto the edge of each piece.

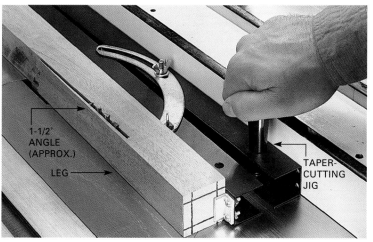

1-1/2° ANGLE (APPROX.)

LEG

TAPER-CUTTING JIG

Photo 4. Use a taper-cutting jig to cut the leg tapers. Cut two adjoining sides, re-adjust the jig, then cut the remaining two sides.

Cutting Tip

Cutting the taper for the table legs and the rule joint for the table top can be tricky—and expensive if you make a mistake in mahogany. It's a good idea to practice cutting these parts on scrap wood of the same dimensions until you feel comfortable making the cuts.

Glue together the two back apron pieces (E) and the two drawer face pieces (F). Countersink and drill the drawer face for the brass pull (see the Top View—Drawer End diagram in the construction plans).

Cut the curves

Transfer the grids and shapes from the plan drawings to 1/4-inch scrap plywood, then cut out the shapes. Set aside the oval pattern for the top for later use.

Trace the curved template shapes onto the edges of the back apron and drawer face pieces (E, F) and the face of the two drawer rails (G). Cut out the shapes with a band saw (Photo 3), then sand smooth.

Taper the legs

Mark the taper-cut starting points on the sides of the legs and mark the ending points on the legs' ends. You can make two taper-cutting jigs, one with a slant of 1-1/2 degrees and the other with a slant of 3 degrees (see page 48). However, it's worthwhile to invest about $20 in an adjustable taper jig, available from many woodworking supply outlets and from tool dealers.

Set the taper jig to 1-1/2 degrees, place a scrap test leg in the jig, and with the jig against the saw fence, make a trial run. Adjust the position of the fence as necessary and mark that position on your saw top with masking tape. When the adjustments

are correct, cut the taper on two adjacent sides on each leg (Photo 4).

Set the taper jig to 3 degrees and run your trial scrap leg through. Adjust the saw fence and mark with tape, then cut the two remaining sides of each leg. Sand the legs smooth, starting with coarse paper and working through finer grits.

Cut the rule joint

For your rule joint to look good and operate smoothly, the profiles of the top and side leaves must mesh exactly (Detail 4—Rule Joint in the plans).

First rout the profile on the two parallel edges of the tabletop (B) that will join the leaves (C). Mount a 1/2-inch-radius round-over bit in a router table and adjust the cutting depth so that a 1/16-inch squared-off lip remains (Photo 5). Run both edges of the top through.

Mount a 1/2-inch radius cove bit in the router. Set the depth so the cut mates perfectly with the rounded-over edges of the top, then rout the cove along the edge of each leaf (C) where it joins the top.

Position the drop-leaf hinges

Before beginning work on your actual piece, test the procedure for hinge mortising and alignment on the scrap rule-joint pieces you previously routed. When the leaf is lowered, its edge should hide the hinge mortise on the underside of the top (B). As the leaf is raised, there should be no binding in the joint, and when completely up, there should be no gap between the leaf and tabletop. Even a slight dislocation of the hinge knuckle will significantly offset the joint.

Start by routing a groove for the hinge knuckle, using a 3/8-inch diameter core box bit set to cut 1/4 inch deep. With an edge guide on your router, cut the grooves 7/16 inch in from the top's rounded-over edge (Detail 4—Rule Joint). Butt the rule-joint sections of the top and leaves together, center the hinge knuckle in its groove, then temporarily screw the hinge in place.

Mark the outline of the hinge mortises (Photo 6), remove the hinges, rout or chisel out the mortises, then fasten the hinges.

Cut the oval top

Set the opened, hinged top good side up across two sticks to provide clearance for the protruding hinge knuckles. Sand flat any unevenness that may exist at the rule joints on the top surface.

Lightly draw lines splitting the top into four equal sections. Align the plywood quarter-oval template that you made earlier with the lines and trace the oval shape onto both the top and leaves.

Disassemble the top, then cut the curved edges of the top and two leaves on a band saw. Reassemble the top and sand it into a smooth oval shape.

Rout decorative V-grooves

Remove the hinges and disassemble the tabletop entirely so that you can edge-rout the top and leaves.

Set the rear fence of the router table 3/16 inches away from the center of the V-groove router bit, then add an extra front fence.

Photo 5. Rout the profile for the tabletop rule joint along two edges and the cove on the leaf edges.

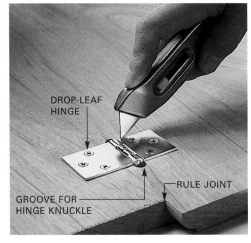

Photo 6. Score the hinge outline onto the top and leaves with a utility knife, then rout the mortise.

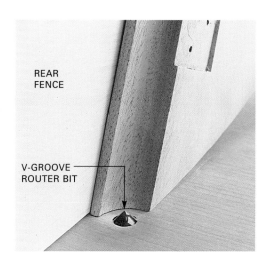

Photo 7. Route the V-grooves on the edges of the top, leaves, and drawer rails using a router table. Use fences to hold the pieces straight and true.

Keep the edge perpendicular to the router bit as the cuts are made (Photo 7). Make several passes, checking your progress as you go. You want grooves of a uniform 1/8-inch depth along the curved edges (see Detail 2 in the plans). Rout along the front and back edges of the top (B); the rounded leaf edges (C); and the bottom drawer rail edge (G).

Remove the front fence of the router table and rout the grooves along the bottom of the back and side aprons (E and D).

Shift the fence back 3/8 inch to cut the second groove in pieces B, C, D, E, and G.

ASSEMBLING THE TABLE

Miter the ends of the corner blocks (M) and drill clearance holes through them for the screws that secure the top.

Finish-sand all the table base pieces. Glue and dowel together the legs (A), side aprons (D), back apron (E), and drawer rails (G). Glue and nail the corner blocks (A), then glue and screw the drawer guides (N).

Cut the rabbets and dadoes in the drawer sides (J), drawer front (K), and drawer bottom (H) (see the Drawer End front and top views in the plans). Check the fit of the drawer guide dadoes and the drawer guides and widen the dadoes as needed.

Drill the holes in the drawer front (K) for the screws that attach the drawer face (F), then fasten them together. Finish-sand and assemble the drawer.

Drill the screw hole in the drawer stop (P). Place two washers over the drawer-stop screw so it doesn't penetrate the inside of the drawer back, then screw it in place.

Finish-sand the top and leaves, then rejoin them with the hinges. Align the top and the base, and then screw them together.

Glue the leaf wedges (Q) to the underside of the leaves. Taper the leading edges of the wedges with a disc grinder (Photo 8) or sander so the leaf supports ride under the wedges when turned to support the leaves.

FINISHING

Disassemble all the parts that can be unscrewed. Sand and smooth any sharp edges. Apply stain and then two coats of varnish. Be sure to varnish the underside of the top to seal it against unequal expansion and contraction with changes in humidity. Consider giving the upper side of the tabletop a third coat for durability. Reassemble the table and install the brass pull.

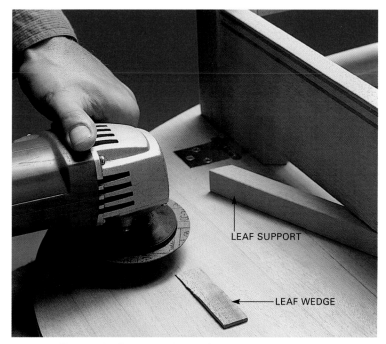

Photo 8. Taper the leading edges of the leaf wedges. A disc grinder (shown), belt sander, or sanding disc in a drill work equally well.

This is a modern version of the classic Morris chair, which was popular

in the late nineteenth century.

Classic Comfort Chair

It was one of the first chairs designed with an adjustable back, and it characteristically

was large and square, with slats along the sides.

This chair is a good beginner's project. There is no need to cut exacting joints,

and the chair is assembled using only dowels and screws.

Material for the cushions is available at most fabric stores. The chair uses a brass rod—

the kind used to hold carpet on stairs—to support the adjustable hinged back.

To adjust the angle, simply move the rod to one of three sets of slots

behind the back.

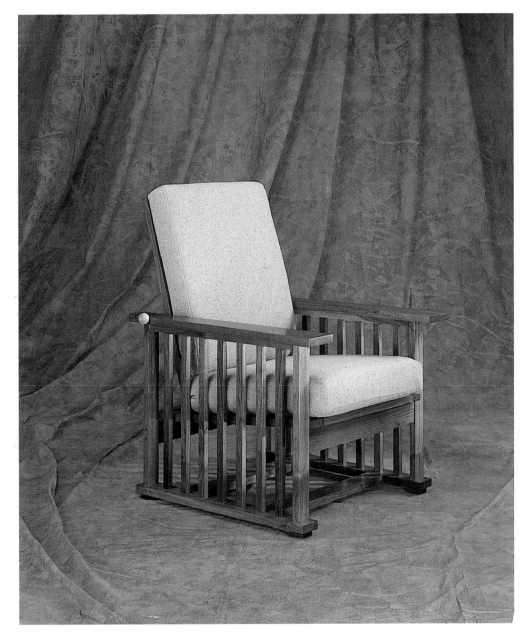

Materials List

Quantity	Size and Description
20 board ft.	5/4 walnut
5 board ft.	4/4 walnut
2	1-1/2" diameter birch balls
100	3/8" x 1-1/2" spiral doweling pins
1	1-1/2" x 36" brass-plated piano hinge
1	1/4" diameter x 30" brass-plated carpet rod
4	No. 6 x 1-1/4" flathead wood screws
1 pint	Natural Danish oil
	Epoxy glue

Construction Plans

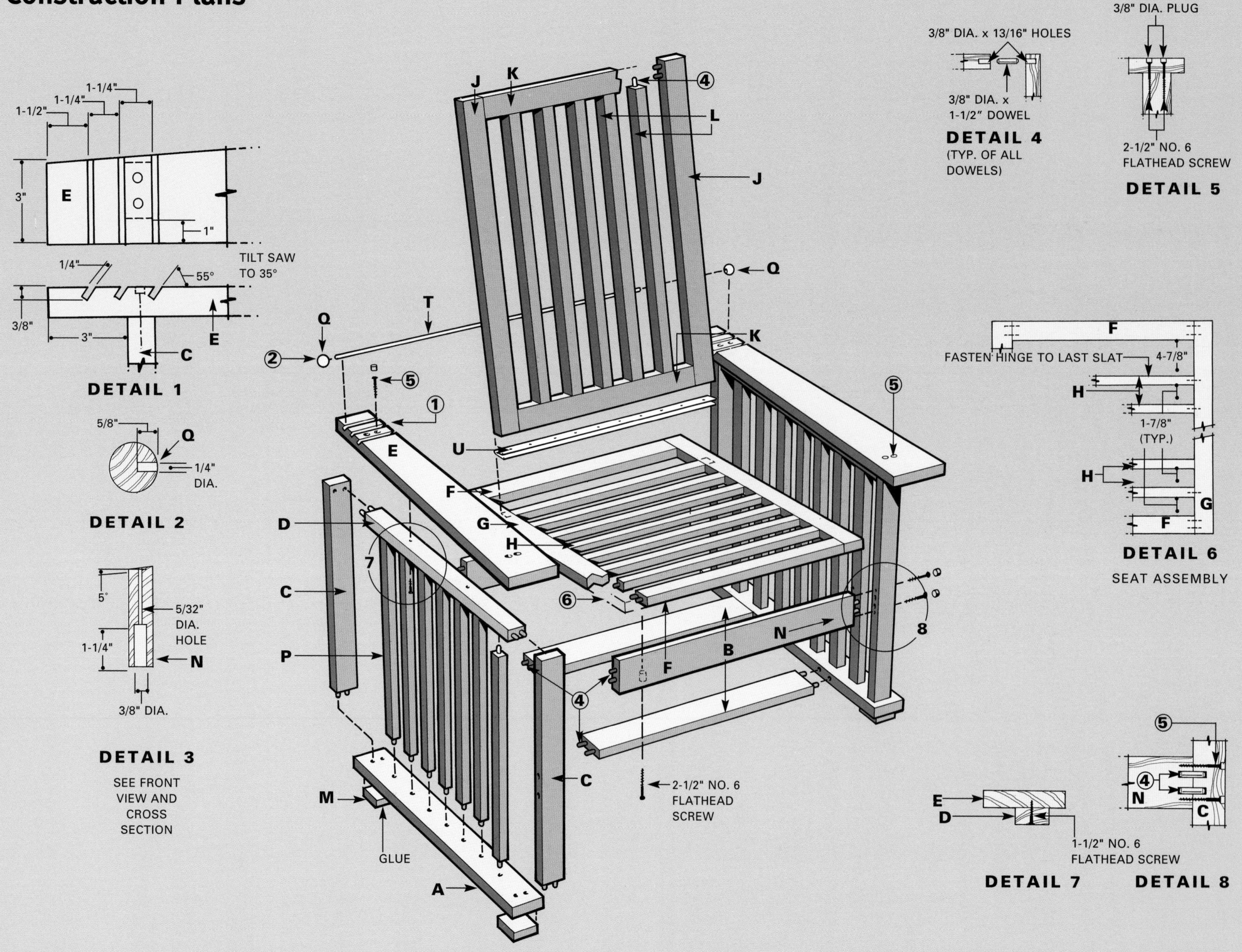

DETAIL 1

1-1/2"
1-1/4"
1-1/4"
3"
E
1"
1/4"
55°
3/8"
3"
C
E
TILT SAW
TO 35°

DETAIL 2

5/8"
Q
1/4"
DIA.

DETAIL 3

5°
5/32"
DIA.
HOLE
1-1/4"
N
3/8" DIA.
P
C
D

SEE FRONT
VIEW AND
CROSS
SECTION

3/8" DIA. x 13/16" HOLES

3/8" DIA. x
1-1/2" DOWEL

DETAIL 4
(TYP. OF ALL
DOWELS)

3/8" DIA. PLUG

2-1/2" NO. 6
FLATHEAD SCREW

DETAIL 5

F
FASTEN HINGE TO LAST SLAT
4-7/8"
H
1-7/8"
(TYP.)
H
G
F

DETAIL 6

SEAT ASSEMBLY

J   K
L
J
Q
T
Q
K
E
U
F
G
H
N
B
F
M
GLUE
A
C
P
C
D
7
6
4
8
5
5
1
2
4

2-1/2" NO. 6
FLATHEAD
SCREW

E
D
1-1/2" NO. 6
FLATHEAD SCREW

DETAIL 7

N
C
4
5

DETAIL 8

Cutting List

Key	Pcs.	Size and Description
A	2	1" x 3" x 29" walnut (side bottoms)
B	2	1" x 3" x 23" walnut (cross supports)
C	4	1" x 2" x 21-1/4" walnut (side ends)
D	2	1" x 1-1/2" x 25" walnut (side tops)
E	2	1" x 5" x 33" walnut (arms)
F	2	1" x 2" x 20" walnut (seat rails)
G	2	1" x 2" x 29" walnut (seat stiles)
H	7	1" x 1" x 20" walnut (seat slats)
J	2	1" x 2" x 28" walnut (back stiles)
K	2	1" x 2" x 17-3/4" walnut (back rails)

Key	Pcs.	Size and Description
L	5	1" x 1" x 24" walnut (back slats)
M	4	3/4" x 2" x 2" walnut (feet)
N	2	3/4" x 3" x 24" walnut (seat supports)
P	14	3/4" x 1" x 20-1/4" walnut (side slats)
Q	2	1-1/2" diameter birch balls (rod ends)
R	1	4" x 22" x 24" upholstered cushion (seat)
S	1	4" x 21-3/4" x 24" upholstered cushion (back)
T	1	1/4" diameter x 30" brass-plated carpet rod (seat back adjuster)
U	1	1-1/2" x 21-3/4" brass-plated piano hinge (seat back)

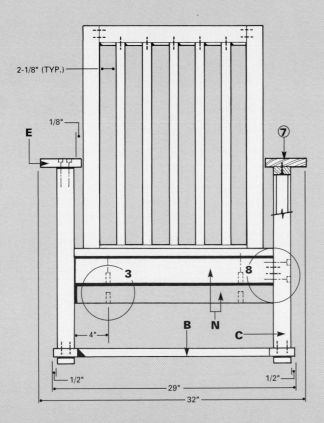

FRONT VIEW

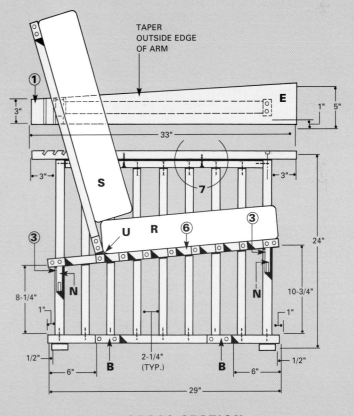

TAPER OUTSIDE EDGE OF ARM

CROSS SECTION

Construction Procedures and Techniques

CUTTING AND DRILLING THE PIECES

Several parts of this chair are made with 5/4 (five-quarter or 1-1/4 inch thick) lumber, planed to a thickness of 1 inch.

Precut and predrill the parts

Begin by cutting the pieces to size (Photo 1). Follow the dimensions given in the cutting list with the construction plans.

Lay out the locations of the dowel holes and drill them, using a dowel jig, drill press, or drill guide (Photo 2). Drill the holes 13/16 inch deep—1/16 inch deeper than the dowel will go—to leave room for excess glue to be squeezed out. This arrangement makes the joints tighter and easier to assemble.

Cut the slots in the arms

Lay out and cut the angled slots for the seat back adjuster rod (T), using a dado blade on your table saw or radial arm saw (Photo 3).

Because the arms (E) are mirror images, you should double-check to be sure you cut the slots in the upper faces of both. (See Detail 1 in the construction plans.)

Finish-sand all the slats before assembling. On a coarse-grained wood like walnut, use 180-grit paper for final smoothing.

Tools You Need

Table saw or radial arm saw

Saber saw or band saw

Planer

Drill press or drill guide

Plug cutter

Drill

Dowel jig

Pipe clamps

Wood hand screws

Screwdrivers

Hacksaw

Jack plane

Files or chisel

Tabletop vise

Photo 1. Cut all parts to width and length and sand them smooth. This chair uses both 3/4 in. and 1-in. thick walnut and is joined with dowels and screws.

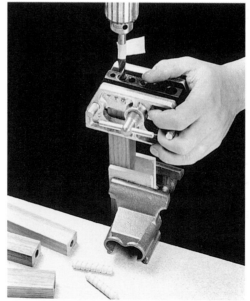

Photo 2. Use a dowel jig and a brad point drill bit for straight, clean dowel holes. Use a drill press or drill guide for holes that can't be drilled with the dowel jig.

Photo 3. Angled slots in the arms hold the brass rod to support the adjustable back. Cut them with a dado blade in your table saw or radial arm saw.

Cut the arms to shape

Lay out the tapered sides of the arms, then use a saber saw or band saw to cut the waste away. Now smooth the sawn edges with a jack plane, working "downhill" with the grain to avoid tearing out the wood (Photo 4).

Follow the assembly directions exactly; the parts of this chair must be glued together in a specific order.

During assembly, drill pilot holes for all screws to avoid splitting the wood.

Construct the sides

Begin by doweling the side slats (P) to the side tops (D) (see the Cross Section in the plans). Dry-fit (no glue) the side bottoms (A) to the slats to help position the slats and provide a flat clamping surface. Now clamp together the side slats and the side tops.

Glue and dowel the side ends (C) to the side tops (D). Once again, dry-fit the side bottoms (A) to the side assemblies, then clamp the side ends and side tops together (Photo 5). When the glue has cured, remove the bottoms from the side assemblies.

Glue and clamp the feet (M) to the underside of the side bottoms. Finish assembling the sides by gluing, doweling, and clamping the side bottoms (A) to the side assemblies.

Photo 5. Glue and clamp the doweled joints together in the exact order described in the text. Use pieces of scrap wood on the clamp faces to avoid damaging the wood of the chair.

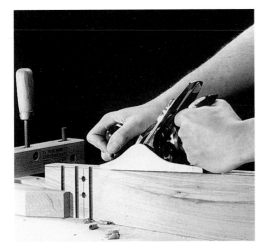

Photo 4. Use a jack plane to smooth the tapered sides of the arms. Plane from the wide end to the narrow end, "downhill," with the grain.

Assemble the seat and back

Glue and dowel the seat slats (H) and seat stiles (G) to one of the seat rails (F) (plans, Detail 6). Dry-fit the other seat rail clamp and the seat assembly together. When the glue has cured, remove the dry-fit seat rail, then glue, dowel, and clamp it to the assembly.

Assembling the back is similar to the seat, except that the back stiles (J) are glued on last. Glue, dowel, and clamp the back slats (L) to the back rails (K) and the back stiles (J) to the back assembly.

Build the chair base

Cut a five-degree taper on the top edge of the seat supports (N). Then drill 5/32-inch screw holes and 3/8-inch countersinks in them (plans, Detail 3). Glue and dowel the seat supports and the cross supports (B) to one of the assembled sides (plans, Detail 8). Make sure the angled tops of the seat supports slope toward the back of the chair. Dry-fit the other side and clamp the chair base together.

Check that the chair base is square by measuring from each corner to the diagonally opposite corner on both sides of the frame. The distance should be the same for both measurements. Make adjustments by lightly pulling the frame one way or the other.

When the glue has cured, remove the dry-fit side, then glue it on.

Attach the arms

Predrill the screw holes in the arms (see Detail 1 and Cross Section in the plans).

Attach the arms by placing them on the chair base in the correct positions. Make sure they hang over the side pieces (C) by 1 inch on the inside so there will be room for the back.

Loosely place screws in the holes and lightly tap the screw heads to mark the location for the pilot holes in the side ends (C) (Photo 6).

Complete the seat base by filling the screw holes with walnut plugs that you cut out with a plug cutter (Photo 7). Glue and lightly hammer the plugs into the screw holes. When the glue has cured, trim the protruding plugs flush with the wood's surface with a file, sandpaper, or chisel. If you use a chisel, go slowly and cut with the grain of the plug so you don't break it off below the surface.

Attach the seat and back

Position the seat on the chair base and align it so it overhangs the front and back equally. Then screw the seat to the chair base.

Cut the piano hinge to its finished 21-3/4 inch length (Photo 8) and attach it with just two screws in each leaf for now (Photo 9).

Photo 6. Position the arms on the sides and insert screws. Tap the screws lightly to mark the top ends of the sides. Then drill pilot holes in the sides.

Photo 7. Use a plug cutter in a drill press or drill guide to cut wood plugs. Pop each plug out by sticking a screwdriver next to it and twisting.

Set the brass seat adjuster rod (T) in the arm slots and check that the seat back rests evenly against the rod. Adjust as necessary by adjusting hinge screws. When everything aligns properly, drive the remaining screws in both leaves of the hinge.

Complete the adjuster rod

The final step before applying finish is to attach the rod ends (Q). Drill holes in the birch balls (Photo 10 and plan Detail 2) and glue them to the seat back adjuster rod (T) with epoxy glue.

FINISHING

There are two separate phases to finishing this project. One is to apply a suitable finish to the wood. The other is to make cushions for a comfortable seat.

Apply an oil finish

Unscrew the seat and back from the chair base. Complete the finish-sanding and soften all sharp edges with sandpaper. Apply the finish. The chair shown here is finished with Danish oil; it is easy to apply to all the slats and crevices at the joints. When the finishing is completed, reassemble the chair.

Make the cushions

The materials list (page 69) shows what is needed for the cushions, and the cutting list with the construction plans shows the finished dimensions of the cushions.

The cushions are box-edge, with the foam cut square to the finished size and wrapped in 1/2-inch batting for a compression fit. Use high-density foam in the seat and medium density in the back. You can also have an upholsterer make the cushions. Be sure the oil finish is completely dry before putting the cushions in position on the chair.

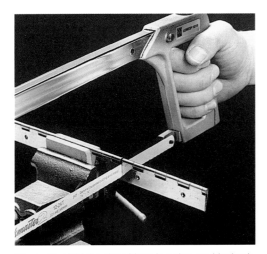

Photo 8. Hold the piano hinge in a vise, cushioning it with pieces of cloth or foam to avoid marring the surface. Cut the hinge with a hacksaw. File the ends to remove any burrs and round the corners.

Photo 9. Screw the hinge to the seat and back with two screws at opposite sides of the seat and two in the back. Check for alignment, then drill holes and insert the rest of the screws.

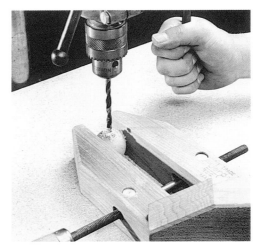

Photo 10. Drill holes in the birch balls for the ends of the adjuster rod; hold them steady for drilling with wood hand screws clamped to a workbench. Glue the balls to the brass rod.

Walls remodeled with wood-paneled wainscoting can change the entire character of a room.

Paneled Wainscoting

An unused bedroom can become a warm study. A cold basement can be converted to a friendly family room, and a so-so dining room can be transformed into a handsome space.

In a breakfast nook or eating alcove, wainscoting that mimics the cabinet doors in the adjoining kitchen can pull the whole area together.

These pages show how to install a wainscoting constructed of plywood paneling covered with trim fashioned from ordinary boards and molding.

This is a project well suited to the moderately skilled woodworker.

Planning the Project

There are three basic matters to decide in planning to install wainscoting:

▲ The height of the paneling
▲ The kind of wood and its appearance
▲ The detailed layout

Height

Wainscoting in a room with 8- or 9-foot ceilings looks and feels best when it's run about a third of the way up the walls. This 32- to 36-inch height is usually enough: Wainscoting shows over the top of a couch or provides a bumper rail for dining room chairs. Anything taller than that begins to look like partial-height wall paneling. (If that's what you want, you can install it as you would wainscoting.)

Choosing a wainscoting height of 32 inches is economical, because you can cut three sections of wainscot paneling from one standard 48- by 96-inch sheet of plywood with no waste.

Wood and appearance

The wainscoting shown on these pages is made from oak veneer plywood, which is widely available, isn't too expensive, and holds stain well. The veneer on the plywood used in the project is called "plain" or "flat sliced." It costs more than "rotary sliced" veneer but provides an even appearance—more like solid wood than thin veneer. The solid oak trim, cut from 1x4 and 1x6 boards, and the oak moldings are available at most lumberyards and home centers.

If you plan to paint the wainscoting, consider using birch, a smooth wood that accepts paint without much preparatory sanding or sealing. Pine is affordable and easy to find, but it will stain or paint unevenly unless it's properly prepared by sealing knots and priming it completely.

Whatever kind of wood you choose, applying a dark paint or stain will make the wainscoting look somewhat formal and the room smaller. Lighter colors will call more attention to the wainscoting as decor and may give a more casual, open feel to a room. Consider how you want the room to look and how you'll use it. Test several different patterns of wall-covering or shades of paint for the areas above the wainscoting. The right wall treatment will enhance the paneling greatly.

Detailed layout

Once you've settled on a style, measure the room and make an accurate sketch of each wall on graph paper. Also make drawings of various panel layouts scaled to the length of your walls. The three designs on the opposite page show the fundamental possibilities. The panel layout should be the same on all walls, if possible. In any case, the panels that meet at corners should be the same width for the best appearance.

You need to figure out exactly how the individual panels will fit and look on your walls in order to know how much material to order, where to place extra studs, and how the room will look and feel once the paneling is completed. Taking the time to map out the project carefully is as important as working carefully when you install the wainscoting.

Design Samples

Centered-stile layout

This wainscoting begins with a vertical stile at the center and works toward the corners. This will result in narrow panels at the ends on some walls, as here. How good the narrow panels look depends on the character of the room and the style of the furniture and decor. In general, a width that is less than one-third of the full-panel width tends to look crowded and skimpy.

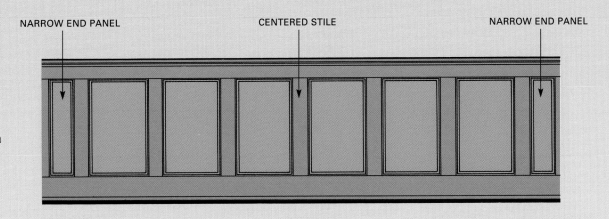

NARROW END PANEL   CENTERED STILE   NARROW END PANEL

Balanced panel layout

This wainscoting layout begins with a full-width panel at the exact center, then works toward the corners. Compared to the centered-stile layout above, it has fewer full panels (five instead of six), but the panels at the ends are wider and closer in size to those along the rest of the wall. This is generally more pleasing to the eye and is the way to avoid excessively narrow end panels.

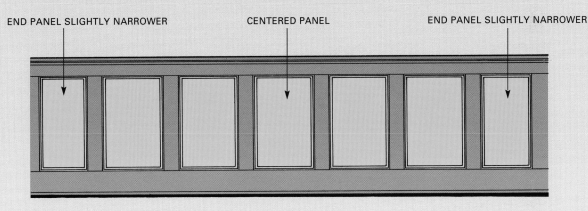

END PANEL SLIGHTLY NARROWER   CENTERED PANEL   END PANEL SLIGHTLY NARROWER

Uniform panel layout

This kind of layout is carefully mapped out so that all the panels are the same width. It may require cutting each sheet of plywood to a specific width and adding more studs to support the edges, but it gives a consistent look. However, unless the other walls in the room are the same length, they may well divide up into different-sized panels, which can look awkward.

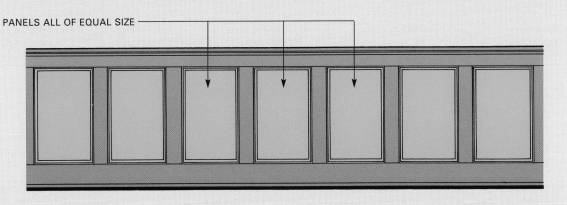

PANELS ALL OF EQUAL SIZE

Construction Plans

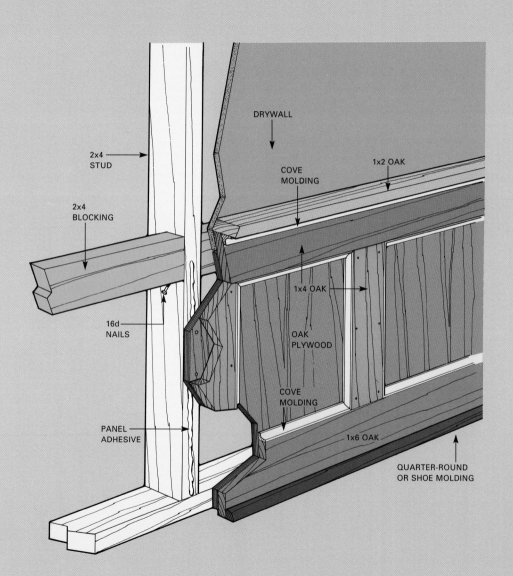

2x4
STUD

2x4
BLOCKING

16d
NAILS

PANEL
ADHESIVE

DRYWALL

COVE
MOLDING

1x2 OAK

1x4 OAK

OAK
PLYWOOD

COVE
MOLDING

1x6 OAK

QUARTER-ROUND
OR SHOE MOLDING

Materials List

Size and Description

4' x 8' oak plywood (panels)

1x4 oak (top rail and stiles)

1x6 oak (bottom rail)

1x2 oak (wainscot cap)

Oak cove molding

2x4 studs and blocking

Quarter-round or shoe molding

Panel adhesive

Wood glue

16d nails

10d finish nails

1-1/2" finish nails

1" brads

3" drywall screws

Stain

Colored wood putty

Satin-finish polyurethane

Note: The quantities required of the above materials and the cutting sizes of the various pieces will depend on the size of the room and the height of the wainscoting.

Construction Procedures and Techniques

PREPARATION

Don't rush this job. Plan on working over several days or three or four weekends. Use the first days to plan, estimate, and purchase materials; to prestain the plywood and moldings; and to remove the door trim, window trim, and drywall. It will take another few days to cut and install the oak plywood, boards, and moldings. Reserve the final days for filling nail holes with wood putty, applying a finish coat of polyurethane, cleaning up, and rearranging the furniture.

Prepare the work area and materials

Before beginning the actual work, cover your floor with drop cloths. Remember to turn off the power at the circuit or fuse box anytime you're cutting into walls or working near electrical switches or outlets.

Consider prestaining the plywood and moldings before installing them, to ensure a more uniform color and save the hassle of staining hard-to-reach inside corners where the cove moldings meet. If you prefer to leave the wood unstained, that has one advantage—you can sand smooth any uneven surfaces before staining or painting.

Success relies on accurate measuring and cutting; if you're comfortable with these tasks, you should feel comfortable with the rest of the project.

Prepare the walls

Pry off trim around the doors and windows (Photo 1). Remove the baseboard, as well as electrical cover plates, heating grilles, or anything else on the wall surface where the wainscoting will be installed.

If your wainscoting will be the same height as that shown in the photos—32 inches, producing three panels from each 8-foot sheet of plywood—make a mark 32-1/2 inches up from the floor at both ends of each wall that will be wainscoted. If your wainscoting will be a different height, mark the walls high enough for a 1/2-inch gap between the paneling and the drywall or plaster above. Snap a chalk line between the marks on each wall.

Cut with a drywall saw along the chalk lines (Photo 2), but use a utility knife where the drywall abuts other walls so you will have clean edges all around. Remove the drywall in large chunks in order to minimize the mess. Most modern houses have walls covered in 1/2-inch drywall; in such a case, you can replace the drywall with 1/2- inch thick oak plywood nailed directly to the studs. If you encounter 5/8-inch or 3/4-inch drywall or plaster, attach furring strips of wood to the studs thick enough to bring the 1/2-inch plywood flush with the existing wall surface.

Tools You Need

Circular saw with plywood blade

Saber saw

Backsaw and miter box or power miter saw

Hammer

Nail set

Putty knife

Drill with twist bits

Drywall saw

Utility knife

Pry bar

Framing square

Tape measure

Compass

Block plane

Chalk line

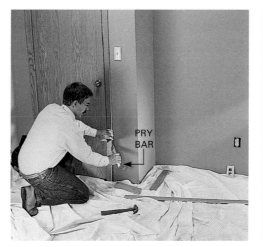

Photo 1. Remove the trim from doors, windows, and the base of the wall. Work carefully with a pry bar to avoid damage. Also remove switch and receptacle covers and any heating grilles.

Photo 2. Use a drywall saw to cut along a line marked 1/2 in. above the wainscoting panel height. Turn off electrical power before sawing; use a utility knife for clean cuts at corners.

Install 2x4 horizontal blocking at the top of the wainscoting area, between the exposed studs. Half the width of the blocking should go behind the drywall; the other half should be exposed to support the top edge of the plywood panels (Photo 3 and construction plan). Drive two 16d nails or 3-inch drywall screws from the accessible side of each stud into the end of a piece of blocking. Toenail or screw the other end where previously installed blocking is in the way.

Next, use your graph paper sketch as a guide to determine where the side edges of the plywood panels will fall. Your plan should have worked out the spacing so that the edges will be covered by the vertical trim (stiles). Make a tick mark on the lower edge of the existing drywall at each point where the panels will meet.

Install additional short studs wherever necessary to back up the butt joints between adjacent panels. Use 2x4 stock for the studs, turned broad side out, and toenail them from both edges, top and bottom (Photo 4).

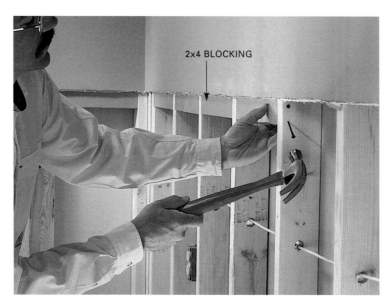

Photo 3. Install 2x4 blocking to support the cut edge of the drywall and the upper edge of the wainscoting plywood. Secure the blocking by toenailing with 16d nails or 3-in. drywall screws.

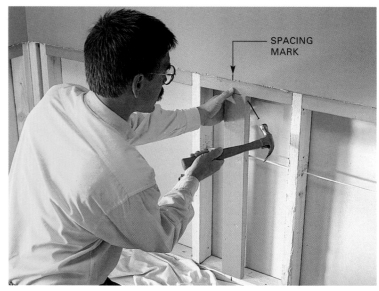

Photo 4. Add short studs where necessary to provide support for joints between the plywood panels. Mark the panel spacing on the drywall to position the studs accurately.

INSTALLING THE WAINSCOTING

There are four stages to the process of installing the wainscoting:

1. Cut and install the plywood.
2. Add the rails and stiles to frame the panel areas.
3. Add molding to dress up the inside edges of the stiles and rails.
4. Install the cap across the top of the wainscoting, and finish the floor line if desired.

Cut and install the plywood

Cut an 8-foot plywood panel into three 32-inch pieces (Photo 5) or into other lengths if your wainscoting is to be a different height. Make sure the panel is face down so any splintering will be on the back; support both sides of the cut line to avoid binding. Clamp a straightedge to the panel to guide the saw.

If any panels are not to be used full width (48 inches), rip them to the required size now. Mark them clearly on the back to avoid putting them in the wrong position.

Fasten the plywood paneling to the wall using panel adhesive and 1-1/2-inch finish nails (Photo 6). The adhesive prevents bowing and nail popping and requires fewer nails. Drive the nails where they will be covered by the base, moldings, rails, or stiles.

When you come to a space where there is an electrical receptacle, measure carefully to mark the hole position and cut the hole for a clean, close fit (Photo 7). An easy method is described at right.

Marking Receptacle Openings

Make sure power is off in the receptacle by turning off the circuit breaker or removing the fuse at the service panel and testing with a voltage tester. Insert drywall screws or sharp nails, points facing out, in the receptacle mounting tabs of the box. Get the plywood panel exactly in position on the wall and then press it firmly against the box; the screw or nail points will make indentations in the panel.

Lay the panel face side down, then place an extra electrical box of the same type with its mounting tabs aligned with the indentations on the back. Trace the shape of the box, drill access holes at the corners, and cut out the shape of the box with a saber saw.

Photo 5. Cut the plywood into panel-height sections using a circular saw with a fine-tooth blade. Support the panel well and cut with the good side facing down to minimize splintering.

STRAIGHT-EDGE

Photo 6. Secure the plywood to the studs with panel adhesive and 1-1/2 in. finish nails. The adhesive holds fast and allows you to use fewer nails. Drive nails where trim will hide them.

PANEL ADHESIVE

Photo 7. Cut out holes for electrical receptacles and other openings with a saber saw. Measure and mark hole positions carefully—a mistake in quality veneer plywood is expensive.

HOLES DRILLED AT CORNERS

Add rails and stiles

Because the horizontal upper rail and the baseboard—which is also the bottom rail—will butt against window and door trim, install the casings around the windows and doors after fastening the plywood panels in place (Photo 8).

Glue and nail the horizontal 1x4 upper rail in place (Photo 9), covering the 1/2-inch gap between plywood and drywall. Then install the 1x6 base. Fasten both the upper rail and the baseboard securely through the plywood and into the studs with 10d finish nails.

Mark the center positions of the vertical stiles that stand between the upper and lower rails. Use a framing square to ensure they're square, then angle-nail and glue the stiles to the plywood (Photo 10).

Add molding to the rails and stiles

To complete each panel section, add cove molding to the edges of the rails and stiles. You can cut the molding with a backsaw and miter box, but a power miter saw with a 60-tooth carbide blade will make the job go much faster (Photo 11). You can rent such a miter saw if you don't have one. Measure carefully before cutting the cove molding.

Use carpenter's glue to provide a tight bond between the molding and the paneling, and secure it with 1-inch brads (Photo 12).

Install the wainscot cap and shoe molding

The cap is constructed of oak 1x2 and cove molding. You might have to shave parts of the 1x2 to conform to slight bulges and dips in the wall. You can mark the cap by scribing, using the following methods.

Set the 1x2 on the top rail, make sure it is level, and tack it in place temporarily with a partially driven finish nail in the middle and at each end. Inspect the joint between the back edge of the 1x2 and the wall surface. Identify the widest gap and set a compass to that width. Now run the compass lightly along the wall, scribing the contours of the wall surface on the top of the cap.

Remove the wainscot cap and use a block plane or sandpaper along the inside edge of the cap to remove small amounts of wood to conform to the line you scribed. Replace the cap from time to time to check the fit. When the joint is tight along the entire length, glue and nail the cap in place. Then add cove molding under the front edge (Photo 13).

Finally, install quarter-round or shoe molding over the joint, to cover any gaps where the base rails meet the floor. This is especially important with wood, tile, and vinyl floors but may not be necessary with well-installed wall-to-wall carpeting.

Photo 8. Install door and window casings before the wainscoting rail and base. Use 1x4 stock that matches the wainscoting. Corner blocks provide a finished look without your having to cut miters.

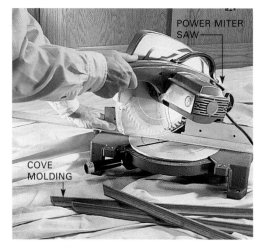

Photo 11. Cut trim moldings with a power miter saw for speed and accuracy. A 60-tooth carbide blade gives the smoothest cut with the least splintering of prestained wood.

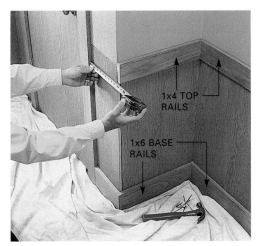

Photo 9. Measure and install the top rail and the base rail on each wall. The top rail covers the seam between the plywood and drywall. Secure with carpenter's glue and 10d finish nails.

Photo 10. Secure 1x4 stiles with 1-1/2 in. finish nails and carpenter's glue. Measure and cut each stile separately for an exact fit. Predrill and angle-nail for the greatest holding power.

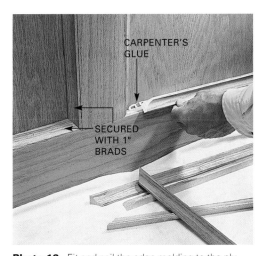

Photo 12. Fit and nail the edge molding to the plywood using 1-in. brads and carpenter's glue. Tap the final piece of molding into place using a small block of wood to protect the surface.

Photo 13. Install the two-part wainscot cap. Scribe and plane or sand the back edge of the 1x2 to conform to any dips or bulges along the wall. Then install cove molding along the underside.

FINISHING THE JOB

If you did not prestain the paneling and trim, apply the stain now. Be especially careful where the wood meets the wall or floor, and be sure to catch and wipe up any excess stain that gathers in the many crannies and corners of the paneling. If you did prestain the materials, inspect the wainscoting carefully and touch up any nicks, cut edges, or other exposed wood with stain and a small brush.

When the stain is dry, wipe the surface clean with a tack cloth and apply a coat of clear polyurethane. A satin finish will look better than a glossy surface. Let the first coat dry according to the manufacturer's instructions.

Go over the wainscoting and fill any nail holes with colored wood putty. Then apply a final coat of polyurethane.

When the finish has dried completely, reinstall electrical cover plates and heating and cold air return grilles.

A wood beam-and-panel ceiling is rich, warm, and ornate. It can turn a living room,

family room, or study into a space that is both impressive and inviting.

Wood-Beam Paneled Ceiling

The design explained here may look like one only a gifted craftsperson could build.

In fact, the ceiling is made from ordinary oak boards, moldings, and plywood.

While it requires careful work, it really calls more for patience

than great woodworking skill.

This beam-and-recessed-panel ceiling design is versatile.

You can alter it by using different moldings, by building deeper or wider beams,

or by crafting different corner blocks.

You can even eliminate the plywood panels and let the painted drywall

or plaster ceiling show between the beams.

Construction Plan

Materials List

Size and Description

2x4 pine (framework)

1x4 oak (beam bottom)

1-1/2" x 1-1/2" stair railing balusters (corner blocks)

3/4" x 1-1/4" oak cove molding

1x3 oak (beam sides)

4' x 8' oak plywood (ceiling panels)

2" finish nails

1" finish nails or 1" brads

4" drywall screws

Construction adhesive

Colored wood putty

Stain

Clear finish

Note: The quantities required of the above materials and the cutting sizes of the various pieces will depend on the size of the room and the beam spacing you choose.

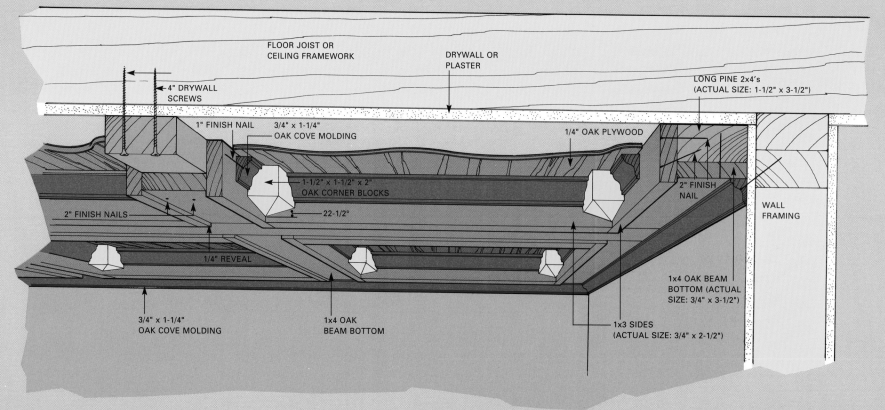

FLOOR JOIST OR CEILING FRAMEWORK

DRYWALL OR PLASTER

LONG PINE 2x4's (ACTUAL SIZE: 1-1/2" x 3-1/2")

4" DRYWALL SCREWS

1" FINISH NAIL

3/4" x 1-1/4" OAK COVE MOLDING

1/4" OAK PLYWOOD

1-1/2" x 1-1/2" x 2" OAK CORNER BLOCKS

2" FINISH NAILS

22-1/2°

2" FINISH NAIL

WALL FRAMING

1/4" REVEAL

1x4 OAK BEAM BOTTOM (ACTUAL SIZE: 3/4" x 3-1/2")

3/4" x 1-1/4" OAK COVE MOLDING

1x4 OAK BEAM BOTTOM

1x3 SIDES (ACTUAL SIZE: 3/4" x 2-1/2")

Construction Procedures and Techniques

GETTING READY

Before beginning this project, you need to get a clear understanding of the scope of the work—what skills are required and how long it will take—and you need to select the materials you'll be using.

Scope

Building this ceiling requires close attention to detail, combined with patience. Begin by reading through all the instructions so you have a clear idea of what is involved.

The ceiling is constructed of a grid of box beams built around 2x4's fastened to the existing ceiling. Plywood panels fill the recessed spaces between the beams. All joints are concealed with molding or other trim. Although the finished installation looks very complex, it does not require hundreds of 45-degree angle cuts. Instead, the boards and moldings are butted together with square-cut ends. However, all the joints must be snug and tight—gaps or rough-cut ends would look especially out of place on a refined project like this.

Plan on taking several days to build this ceiling. Staining and finishing will add at least two more days. Keep in mind that this is a major project, one that will put the room out of commission for the duration of the work, so be realistic in your planning.

Materials

The ceiling shown in this project is made with oak. You could use birch instead, for a lighter, more contemporary look, or pine painted to create either a formal or country feel. The cost won't vary that much. A painted version, using pine or birch, might cost 10 percent less than oak, but any high-quality wood free of knots and other defects is expensive. Whatever wood you decide on, you should build a small, 4- by 4-foot mockup to get a feel for how your finished ceiling will look and fit together.

The 1x4 and 1x3 oak boards, cove moldings, and 2x4 pine boards are all standard items at most large home centers or lumberyards. Remember that the actual lumber sizes are smaller than the nominal sizes given in the materials list. All the layout and cutting measurements in the following instructions are for precise actual sizes. So make certain the oak 1x4's actually measure 3/4 x 3-1/2 inches and the 1x3's measure 3/4 x 2-1/2 inches. Also check to make sure your pine 2x4's are straight and measure 3-1/2 inches wide. If you can't find materials in these exact sizes, you'll need to have them special-ordered or cut to width at a full-service lumberyard.

The ceiling panels shown in the photographs are made from special-ordered plywood with a surface layer of "plain sawn" oak rather than the more common "rotary cut" surface. The plain sawn veneer produces panels that look more like real boards.

It's a good idea to stain and finish the oak before putting it up. It is difficult to stain overhead, and with all the joints and angles it's tough to get a uniform color after the ceiling is assembled. The ceiling on these pages was finished with a cherry stain covered by a clear water-based finish. Stain and finish some test pieces before tackling the entire pile of oak so you can be certain you'll get the color and sheen you desire.

Tools You Need

- Circular saw
- Power miter saw
- Hammer
- Power nailer (optional)
- Stepladder
- Chalk line
- Drill
- Caulking gun
- Drill with twist bits and Phillips bit
- Putty knife
- Nail set
- Framing square
- Tape measure
- Stud finder
- Surface-forming tool or rasp
- Compass
- Coping saw

BUILDING THE CEILING

Chances are slim that your room dimensions are such that you'll be able to use panels of one size to cover the entire ceiling. More than likely, you'll need to find a place for smaller, partial panels. Plan to distribute these panels equally at the perimeter of the room—not just on one side—and let the full panels flow across the main part of the ceiling.

Draw a plan

Measure the length and width of the room at the ceiling level, not down at the floor. Because walls often are not plumb, floor and ceiling-level measurements might differ by a few inches or more. Using this information, sketch the ceiling dimensions on graph paper, then try two different layouts.

Start your first layout with two beams centered between opposite walls, so that they cross in the center of the ceiling. Mark the positions of the beams on either side of these center beams all across the ceiling. The beam spacing shown here is 29-1/2 inches on center—that is, from the middle of one beam to the middle of the next. Allowing for the width of the 2x4's that form the structural grid for the beams, the full-panel space between the beams is 26 inches.

Draw the second layout starting with 26-inch panel widths centered on each wall and mark the corresponding beam positions across the entire ceiling. Compare the two layouts and choose the one that yields the largest-size panels around the perimeter of the room. This is your working plan.

Mark the beam grid on the ceiling

To get panel sections that are truly square, you must first mark off parallel beam positions running one way across the ceiling, then mark off a second set of beam positions running exactly at right angles to the first.

Do this by finding the center points of two opposite walls and measure outward in both directions, marking the beam centers every 29-1/2 inches (Photo 1). Then snap chalk lines on each side of these marks to show the 3-1/2 inch width of each 2x4 (Photo 2).

29-1/2" BETWEEN BEAM CENTERS

Photo 1. Mark out the spacing for the 2x4 ceiling framework. Work from a plan for a visually balanced ceiling with the largest possible partial-size panels around the perimeter of the room.

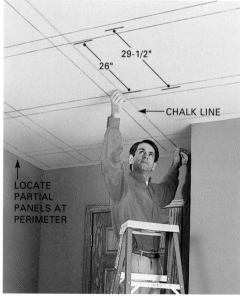

29-1/2"

26"

CHALK LINE

LOCATE PARTIAL PANELS AT PERIMETER

Photo 2. Snap chalk lines to divide the ceiling into a gridwork. Be meticulous; taking care here will allow you to mass-produce many parts of the ceiling later.

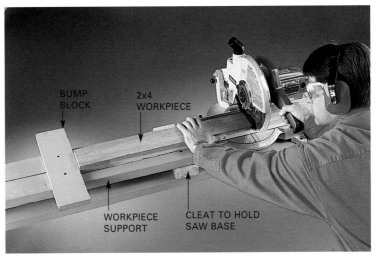

Photo 3. Secure the framework to the ceiling. First screw the long 2x4's perpendicular to the joists above, then add 26-in. blocks in between. Faces of all the 2x4's should be flush.

Photo 4. Use a bump block and power miter saw to cut blocks quickly. Set a block 26 in. from the blade, butt a 2x4 against it, and cut. Add cleats to a workpiece support to hold the saw in place.

Mark the center points of the other two walls, stretch a string between them, and place a carpenter's square at the intersection of the string and one of the existing chalk lines. If the room isn't square (a common situation), adjust the string until it is square with the chalk line. Use this as your new center line to mark off 2x4 beam centers. This way your panels can be cut perfectly square rather than one or two degrees off. Snap pairs of chalk lines as you did in the other direction to finish the gridwork.

Assemble the 2x4 framework

Use a stud finder to determine the location and direction of the ceiling's structural framework—the joists or ceiling crossties that normally run perpendicular to an exterior wall. After finding one joist, mark its location with a pencil and measure over 16 inches; joists generally are positioned every 16 or 24 inches on center. If you cannot find another joist after 16 or 24 inches, move back to the pencil mark and measure out in a line perpendicular to the first attempt.

After finding and marking the spacing of the ceiling joists, install full-length 2x4's running at right angles to this underlying framework (Photo 3). Use 4-inch drywall screws (or longer if your ceiling is plaster) to secure the 2x4's firmly to the ceiling framing along the chalk lines. The finished ceiling will be heavy—don't skimp on screws.

Next, install the shorter 2x4's between the long ones to complete the gridwork. Tap them into place with a hammer if necessary. Except for those along the perimeter, these should be 26 inches long. Use a bump block (Photo 4) to mass-produce them quickly.

Because there is no ceiling framework above the short pieces, secure them with 8d nails or 2-inch drywall screws driven into the long 2x4's at an angle (toe-nailed or screwed). Take care to keep these short pieces exactly on the chalk lines. The bottom surfaces of all the 2x4's facing the floor must be flush. The importance of this will become clear when you begin applying trim to the ceiling.

Box the beams

The oak beams are actually boxes built around the 2x4's on the ceiling. You first cover the bottom faces with oak 1x4's, then cover the sides with 1x3's.

Use 2-inch finish nails, staggered every 8 inches, to secure the long 1x4 oak boards to the 2x4's. Run them along the lines of the short 2x4's, crossing the long ones at a right angle (Photo 5). This locks the framework together and helps create a gridwork of beams with a smooth, flat bottom surface.

Now cut and secure the shorter oak 1x4's between the long ones. They should measure 26 inches long for the full-panel spaces and shorter for the partial-panel spaces around the perimeter. Measure carefully in case there are any slight variations, and make square cuts. Keep the side edges of the 1x4 oak boards aligned directly with the edges of the 2x4 framework above and be sure the intersecting joints butt together tightly.

Next install the 1x3 oak side pieces (see construction plans). They will extend 1/4 inch below the horizontal oak boards. Use a 1/4-inch thick spacer as a guide to create a consistent "reveal" below the beam bottoms (Photo 6). Don't worry about unevenness along the ceiling; the cove molding will cover it.

Cut the 1x3's long enough so they fit snugly when lightly tapped into place. Secure them with 2-inch finish nails staggered along the 2x4 framework. Don't try to nail into the sides of the 1x4 oak beam bottom—it's difficult to drive nails through two layers of oak, even if you predrill or use a power nailer.

Photo 5. Nail the long 1x4 oak beam bottoms running along the lines of short 2x4's in the framework. Then cut and nail the short 1x4 oak filler pieces running the other way across the ceiling.

Photo 6. Position the 1x3 oak beam sides using a 1/4-in. spacer so they extend a consistent 1/4 in. below the beam bottoms. Fasten them with staggered 2 in. finish nails driven into the 2x4's.

Create the corner blocks

The blocks at the inside corners of each panel space are both decorative and functional. They contribute to the elaborate look of the ceiling, cover small gaps where 1x3's meet, and eliminate the need for 45-degree cuts on the cove molding that runs between the beams. You will fasten the corner blocks in place when you install the plywood panels, so you need to cut them ahead of time.

To make the blocks, cut a 22-1/2 degree angle on one end of a 1-1/2 x 1-1/2 inch square baluster (Photo 7), then rotate the baluster 90 degrees toward you and cut a second 22-1/2 degree angle (Photo 8). This creates a point that ends at one corner of the baluster. Adjust the miter box to 0 degrees and cut the block to its finished 2-inch length (Photo 9). For safety, never cut a block from a baluster shorter than 6 inches.

Use sandpaper to slightly round over the front corner of each block, the one that will protrude into the panel space.

Work Tip

When making the corner blocks, eliminate a lot of the measuring and marking by using a cutoff line on the miter saw fence as a length guide.

This project uses a lot of blocks, so gear up for mass production. With the miter saw set at 22-1/2°, cut the points on both ends of 8 to 10 balusters first, then readjust the saw angle to 90° and cut all those pieces to length. This will eliminate switching between angled and square cuts on every block.

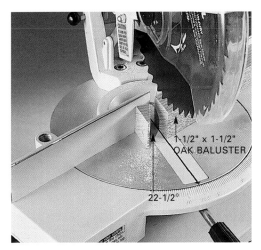

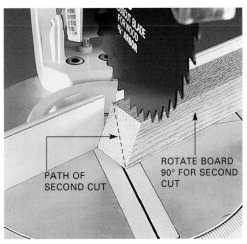

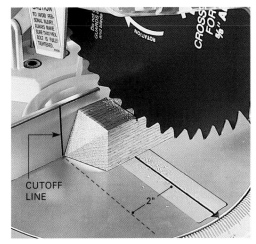

Photo 7. Cut corner blocks with a miter saw. First cut a 22-1/2 degree angle on one end of a 1-1/2 x 1-1/2 in. square oak stair railing baluster.

Photo 8. Rotate the baluster top 90 degrees toward you and make a second 22-1/2 degree cut from corner to corner across the first cut.

Photo 9. Cut the corner block to final length with the blade set at 90 degrees. Use a 2-in. cutoff line marked on the miter saw fence as a guide.

Cut and install the panels

Install all the full-size panels in the ceiling first, leaving the partial-size panels around the perimeter until later.

Cut eight 2-foot by 2-foot panels from each 4x8 sheet of oak plywood, using a straightedge and circular saw (Photo 10). Cut the full sheet in half lengthwise first, then cut each half into four 2-foot squares.

Make sure that the plywood is well supported on both sides of the cut line, and place the good side down to avoid splintering the prestained surface.

Apply construction adhesive to the back of a panel in an X and fit it into place against the ceiling (Photo 11). Temporarily hold it in place with finish nails wedged between the top of the oak beam and the drywall or plaster ceiling. The panel is slightly smaller than the area between the beams, so get it centered in the space.

Install the four corner blocks to hold each panel firmly in place before installing the panel in the next grid. Don't use a power nailer; securing the blocks requires angle nailing through two layers of oak, and there's not much room to hold each block. Position

one block, pushing that corner of the plywood firmly up against the ceiling. Drill two angled holes through the block and into the 1x3 material (Photo 12). Remove the block and apply 1/4-inch dots of wood glue to the back side. Position it in the corner again and secure it with 4d finish nails driven through the predrilled holes. Sink the heads 1/8 inch below the surface with a nail set.

Install the other three blocks in the same way. When they are all in place, remove the nails that were temporarily holding the plywood panel in place.

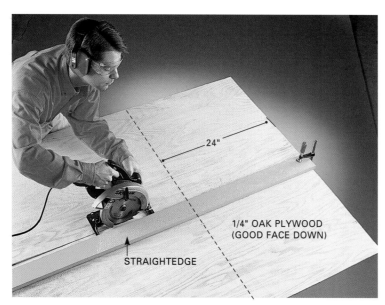

Photo 10. Cut the 1/4-in. oak plywood panels using a straightedge and circular saw. Cut with the good side down to prevent splintering and damage to the stained face of the panel.

Photo 11. Install each panel with construction adhesive on the back. Hold it temporarily in place with finish nails wedged between the tops of the beam sides and the existing ceiling.

Cut and install the molding

Measure and cut the cove molding to fit between the corner blocks. Most pieces will be the same length—21-1/2 inches—so set your bump block accordingly.

Test-fit each piece, then apply a thin bead of wood glue along the back of the molding (Photo 13). Reposition it tightly against the plywood panel and secure it to the 1x3 side piece with a 1-inch finish nail two inches from each end, and one in the middle.

Do the perimeter

After completing the entire center portion of the ceiling, measure, cut, and install the pieces for the perimeter of the ceiling. Don't assume all pieces will be the same dimension from one end of the wall to the next; corners are rarely perfectly square, so you might find your perimeter pieces getting slightly wider or narrower as you proceed along the wall. This will be tedious work, but it must be done this way to avoid awkward gaps along the edge of the ceiling.

Install 3/4 x 1-1/4 inch cove molding where the ceiling meets the wall (Photo 14). On long stretches of ceiling, cut scarf joints to join pieces of molding (see sidebar).

Cut inside corners first, using coped joints. Cut the end of one piece of molding square, butt it into the corner, and nail it in place. Hold the adjacent piece next to the first and use a compass to trace the profile of the first piece on the face of the adjacent piece. Cut away that profile with a coping saw, angling the blade toward the back of the molding. This allows the second piece to overlap the first. You'll no doubt have to do some trimming and adjusting with a surface-forming tool or rasp to get a good fit.

Cut 45-degree miters where the molding meets at an outside corner. Because corners are rarely a perfect 90 degrees, test-fit the pieces before nailing. You might have to shave away part of the back of one piece or do some slight filling with putty.

Making a Scarf Joint

Use a scarf joint to extend a length of molding in a straight line. Set the miter saw for a cut 22-1/2°, insert one piece of molding from the left, and cut the end. With the saw in the same position, insert a second piece of molding from the right and cut the end.

Overlap the angled ends to present a finished front surface when you install the molding. Prestain the cut end of the rear piece of molding, so if a slight misalignment occurs or the joint opens slightly no light-colored wood will be visible.

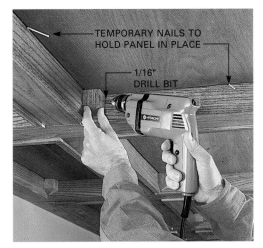

Photo 12. Predrill holes for the nails that secure the corner blocks in place. Use wood glue and two 4d finish nails to secure each block in place. Use a hammer and nail set, not a power nailer.

Photo 13. Fasten the cove molding along the beam and panel joint with wood glue and 1-in. finish nails or brads. Cut the molding to create a snug fit between the corner blocks.

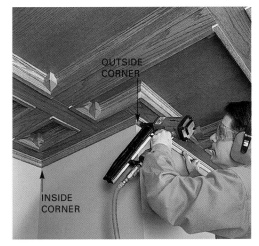

Photo 14. Install cove molding to cover gaps between the ceiling and wall. Make tight-fitting mitered joints at outside corners, coped joints at inside corners.

FINISHING THE CEILING

When all the woodworking is complete, apply stain to any exposed cut ends and fill nail holes and gaps with colored wood putty (Photo 15). Confine the putty to nail holes and gaps; any putty residue or thumbprints will mar the wood and resist a second coat of finish. You applied the first coat of clear, water-base finish when you prestained the wood. Now wipe everything clean and apply the final, second coat.

APPLY THINNED
STAIN TO
CUT ENDS

COLORED
WOOD
PUTTY

Photo 15. Fill nail holes with colored wood putty. Apply thinned stain to the cut ends of the beam sides exposed by the reveals. Then give the entire ceiling a final coat of clear finish.

Power Nailing

This project uses a lot of nails; consider using a pneumatic (air-powered) finish nailer for most of the work. With one squeeze of the trigger, the nail is driven in place with its head sunk to the proper depth. This not only allows you to work faster and with less effort, but more accurately too. You can hold a piece exactly in position with one hand and drive a nail with the pneumatic nailer in the other hand.

You also get cleaner looking results with a pneumatic nailer. The finish nails used in a pneumatic nailer have smaller heads than the conventional kind so the wood is less likely to split, and you eliminate damage from any misdirected hammer blows and nail sets that slip.

You can rent everything you need, especially if you choose a rental center that caters to contractors. Get a good finish nailer, a 1-horsepower air compressor, about 50 feet of hose, oil, and miscellaneous connections. The dealer can make sure you have everything required.

Be sure to have someone at the store give you a quick demonstration of the nailer. Then try it yourself while the demonstrator supervises. Bring along some scrap 3/4-inch oak to try out the equipment beforehand, to make sure it can handle the job you are undertaking.

USING A PNEUMATIC NAILER

There are almost as many varieties of trim nails for air nailers as for hand nailing. A variety of nail clips or strips are used in pneumatic nailers. The nails are bonded with a coating to hold them together. Spring tension within the magazine feeds them to the driving pin.

When you are ready to go to work, load a clip of nails into the magazine and grasp the handle firmly before connecting the air hose.

Place the nose of the nailer against the piece to be fastened and aim it so the nail will be driven at the angle you wish. Push the nailer against the workpiece until you feel the nose depress, then squeeze the trigger. You probably won't even realize the nail has penetrated because of the nailer's quick action. It will take time to develop a feel for the tool.

As long as you hold the trigger depressed, the nailer will fire each time the nose piece is depressed. However, don't try this "bounce" technique with solid oak. Set the nose of the nailer firmly in place and then pull the trigger for each nail you drive.

Pneumatic nailers may drive the nails too deeply into soft wood trim such as cedar and pine. To remedy this problem, lower the air pressure. The nail should be set just below the surface of the trim.

If you have a tough time penetrating hardwoods such as oak or maple, turn up the air pressure or choose the next shortest nail to do the job, if possible.

When nailing small pieces of trim, be sure to aim the nailer so the nail enters perpendicular to the body of the workpiece. That way you avoid splitting the wood.

SAFETY AND MAINTENANCE

• Keep the nailer oiled. Add a few drops of No. 10 nondetergent oil (No. 30 nondetergent oil in warm temperatures) in the air inlet before use.
• Never load the nailer with the air hose attached to the tool.
• Never leave the nailer unattended. Children are fascinated by gunlike tools, and these machines can be deadly.
• If the nailer isn't firing, disconnect the air hose before attempting any repairs.
• Keep your mind on your work. Hold the material with your hand well out of the nail path.

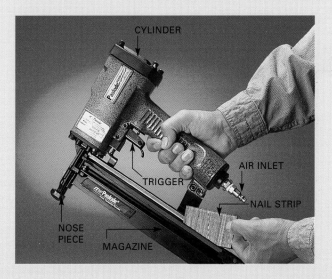

Kitchen and Dining Room

These two pieces of furniture are traditional but still casual.

They feature simple, old-fashioned details and a natural finish that lets

the clear pine darken gracefully on its own.

Early American Sideboard and Plate Rack

The sideboard is perfect for serving buffet meals and holding dishes

that won't fit on the table during family meals. The plate rack is great for practical

storage as well as decorative display.

The pieces shown are made from sugar pine, a wood that is free of knots. It is kiln

dried so the furniture won't split or warp from uneven drying.

You can substitute dimension pine lumber, but store it indoors for at least a month

to let it dry out a bit more.

Both pieces are constructed with simple joints to make them easy and fast to build.

Materials List

Quantity	Item
40 board ft.	4/4 pine
5 board ft.	8/4 pine
6 linear ft.	2" pine cove molding
16	3/8" x 1-1/2" dowels
14	No. 8 x 2" pan-head screws
14	1/4" flat washers
50	1-1/2" finish nails
20	1" finish nails
1 pint	Stain
1 quart	Semigloss clear varnish
	Heavy paper or thin hardboard
	Wood glue
	Glue sticks for hot-glue gun

Construction Plans

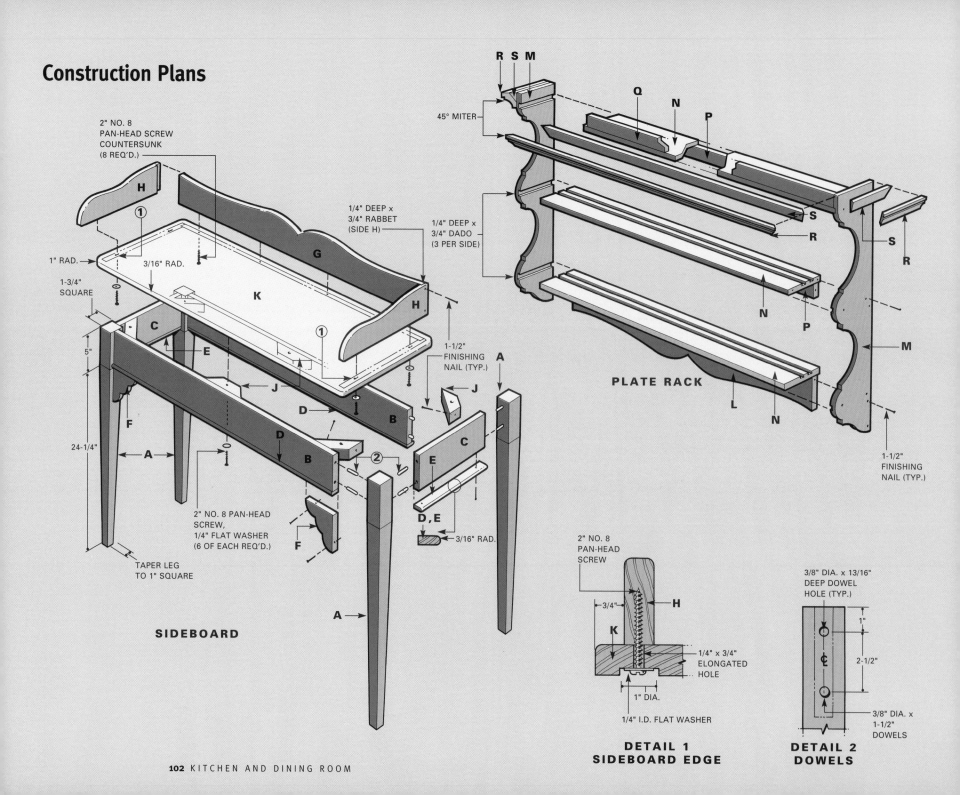

2" NO. 8 PAN-HEAD SCREW COUNTERSUNK (8 REQ'D.)

1/4" DEEP x 3/4" RABBET (SIDE H)

1/4" DEEP x 3/4" DADO (3 PER SIDE)

45° MITER

R S M

Q

N

P

S

R

S

R

H

G

H

K

1" RAD.

3/16" RAD.

1-3/4" SQUARE

C

E

K

J

1

1

1-1/2" FINISHING NAIL (TYP.)

A

J

A

F

24-1/4"

A

D

D

B

B

2

E

C

A

J

D, E

3/16" RAD.

A

2" NO. 8 PAN-HEAD SCREW, 1/4" FLAT WASHER (6 OF EACH REQ'D.)

F

TAPER LEG TO 1" SQUARE

5"

SIDEBOARD

N

P

L

N

M

1-1/2" FINISHING NAIL (TYP.)

PLATE RACK

DETAIL 1
SIDEBOARD EDGE

2" NO. 8 PAN-HEAD SCREW

3/4"

H

K

1/4" x 3/4" ELONGATED HOLE

1" DIA.

1/4" I.D. FLAT WASHER

DETAIL 2
DOWELS

3/8" DIA. x 13/16" DEEP DOWEL HOLE (TYP.)

1"

2-1/2"

3/8" DIA. x 1-1/2" DOWELS

Cutting List

Key	Pcs.	Size and Description

SIDEBOARD

Key	Pcs.	Size and Description
A	4	1-3/4" x 1-3/4" x 29-1/4" pine (legs)
B	2	3/4" x 4-1/2" x 43" pine (front and back skirts)
C	2	3/4" x 4-1/2" x 13" pine (side skirts)
D	2	3/8" x 15/16" x 43" pine (front and back skirt beading)
E	2	3/8" x 15/16" x 13" pine (side skirt beading)
F	2	3/4" x 4-1/2" x 4-1/2" pine (bracket)
G	1	3/4" x 5" x 45-1/2" pine (top back)
H	2	3/4" x 4" x 16-1/2" pine (top sides)
J	6	1-1/2" x 2" x 6" pine (corner blocks and cleats)
K	1	3/4" x 18" x 48" pine (tabletop)

PLATE RACK

Key	Pcs.	Size and Description
L	1	3/4" x 6" x 45" pine (scrolled bottom)
M	2	3/4" x 7" x 32-3/4" pine (sides)
N	3	3/4" x 7" x 45-1/2" pine (shelves and top)
P	2	3/4" x 2" x 45" pine (shelf supports)
Q	1	3/4" x 1-1/2" x 45" pine (cove supports)
R	1	1/2" x 2" x 72" pine (cove molding)
S	1	3/4" x 1-1/2" x 72" pine (cove filler)

1-1/2"
3/4"

12"

3/4"

12"

3/4"

5"

EACH SQUARE = 2"

PATTERN—SIDE, M

R
S

1" FINISHING NAIL

Q

3/8" DEEP x 1/2" GROOVES (TWO SHELVES ONLY)

1-1/4"   1-1/4"

TOP, N   **SHELF, N**

SECTION VIEW   **P,L**
TOP AND
SHELVES

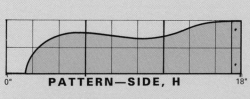

0"   PATTERN—SIDE, H   18"

EACH SQUARE = 2"

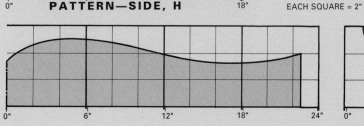

0"   6"   12"   18"   24"

PATTERN—BACK, G; BOTTOM, L

SAND SIDE TO MATCH LEG TAPER

0"   6"

BRACKET, F

Construction Procedures and Techniques

CUTTING AND DRILLING THE PIECES

There are quite a few curves in these two projects. You'll need templates to trace and cut the curves accurately.

Make templates

Make templates from heavy paper, thin hardboard, or plywood. Mark off grids on the template material, and transfer the shapes from the plans to the templates. The pattern grids in the plans have 2-inch squares.

You need full-size templates for the brackets (F), top sides (H), plate rack sides (M), and the profile of the legs (A). Note that the leg taper begins 5 inches from the top of the leg.

Make a half-template for the top back (G) of the sideboard and for the scrolled bottom (L) of the plate rack. Flipping a half-template at its center point to continue the pattern across the piece of wood guarantees that both sides of a symmetrical part will be uniform.

Make the sideboard tabletop

Choose the boards for the tabletop (K). If you are using No. 2 pine (in Canada, So2S or So1S pine), keep the widths less than 4 inches to minimize warping. Also be sure to alternate the direction of the growth rings in the end grain. Glue and clamp the boards together (Photo 1).

When the glue is dry, cut the tabletop to size: 18 inches wide by 48 inches long.

Lay out and drill the holes for the screws that hold the top back and sides (G, H) to the tabletop (see Detail 1, Sideboard Edge, in the plans). Elongate the holes by drilling three 3/16-inch holes next to each other, then flatten the sides with a small file. These elongated holes allow the top to expand and contract with indoor humidity changes without being restrained by the pieces G and H.

Round the four corners of the tabletop with a 1-inch radius. Round over the top edges of the tabletop with a 3/16-inch round-over bit in a router, then finish-sand the top.

Photo 1. Glue and clamp boards to get the width required for the tabletop. Alternate the clamps, top and bottom, to help keep the top flat as it dries.

Cut the other sideboard pieces

Using the template, trace the shape of the top back and sides (G, H) onto the pine. Place a dado blade in a radial arm saw or table saw, and cut the rabbets on the ends of the top sides. Then cut out the curved profiles with a band saw or saber saw.

Transfer bracket shapes (F) from the template to your wood, and cut them out with a band saw or saber saw.

Cut all remaining pieces for the sideboard (parts A through K) except the skirt beading (D, E) and the corner blocks and cleats (J) to the lengths and widths shown in the cutting list. Pieces D, E, and J require shaping before they can be cut to their finished dimensions. Don't cut any of the parts for the plate rack (parts L through S) yet.

Tools You Need

Pipe clamps

Band saw

Hot-glue gun

Heat gun or hair dryer (optional)

Drill with twist bits and brad-point bits

Hammer

Router

Router table (optional)

Saber saw

Backsaw

Miter box

Radial arm saw with dado blade

File

Dowel center

Cut the tapered legs

You'll need to use a trick with a hot-glue gun to cut the taper on all four sides of the sideboard legs. Trace the profile of the leg to the four sides of all four legs.

Using a band saw, cut off two opposite tapered sides of each leg. Number each of the cut-off pieces with its respective side as it is cut from the leg.

Place three or four small dabs of hot glue on the cut side of the waste pieces and reattach them temporarily. This provides a flat surface to ride on the band saw table as you cut the other sides (Photo 2).

Photo 2. Cut the taper on two sides of the legs, then spot-glue the cut-off pieces back on to provide a square surface against the band saw table when you cut the other two sides.

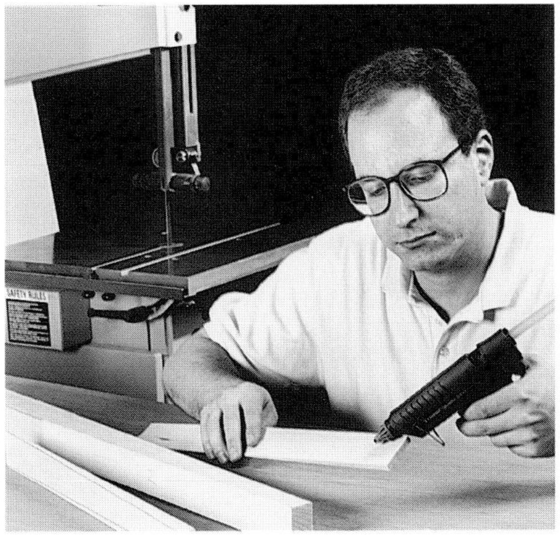

Cut off the remaining two tapered sides of all four legs, then pop off the glued-on sides. Use a heat gun or hair dryer to soften the hot glue, if needed. Sand the cut sides smooth.

Drill the dowel holes

Lay out and drill the dowel holes in the legs and skirts, using dowel centers to transfer the hole locations from one piece to another (see plans, Detail 2, Dowels). A brad-point drill bit will keep the dowel holes on their marks. Finish-sand the legs and skirts.

ASSEMBLING THE SIDEBOARD

Check the sizes of the sideboard legs and skirts against the plans and cutting list. Wipe off all sanding dust with a tack cloth before gluing any of the parts.

Assemble the base

The base consists of the legs and skirts. Glue, dowel, and clamp the legs to the side skirts first and allow them to dry. Dry-fit the front and back skirts to the assembled sides and check to see that everything fits properly. Then glue, dowel, and clamp the front and back skirts to the assembled sides.

Plane or cut the corner blocks and cleats (J) to a thickness of 1-1/2 inches, then cut them to width and length as shown in the cutting list. Miter both ends of all six pieces. Drill 1/2-inch holes in the cleats and corner blocks for the screws that hold the tabletop to the base (Photo 3).

Glue and nail the corner blocks and cleats to the insides of the skirts. Be careful not to nail completely through the skirts.

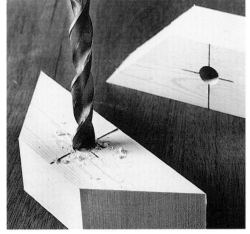

Photo 3. Drill oversized holes for the screws that hold the sideboard top to the base. They will allow the top to expand and contract as the humidity changes without splitting the wood.

Work Tips

Because routers and router bits vary in size, always use the set-and-check method when setting the fence (photo 8, page 107). Measure from the outside of the bit to the inside of the fence when adjusting the fence. Then make a test run on a scrap piece of wood before cutting into your project.

To sand long pieces such as the sideboard legs, clamp a belt sander upside down in a vise and run the pieces across it.

Add skirt beading and leg brackets

Plane or rip the skirt beading boards (D, E) 3/8 inch thick, 2 inches wide, and to the lengths shown in the cutting list. Use a 3/16-inch round-over bit in a router table with a fence to round both edges (Photo 4). Then rip the beading to final width and finish-sand the edges. Glue and nail the skirt beading to the bottom edges of the skirts.

Finish-sand the brackets (F) and attach them to the base with glue and nails (Photo 5). Because the leg tapers, you must sand one side of each bracket to conform to the taper.

Complete the sideboard assembly

Finish-sand all sides and edges of the back and sides (G, H) of the top, then glue, clamp, and nail them with 1-1/2 inch finish nails.

Screw the top, back, and side assembly to the tabletop. Use spacer blocks to align the tabletop with the proper overhang as you screw it to the sideboard base (Photo 6).

BUILDING THE PLATE RACK

The plate rack is easier to build than the sideboard but requires careful fitting.

Cut the parts

Trace the plate rack patterns from the templates onto the sides (M) and scrolled bottom (L). Set up a dado blade in a radial arm saw or table saw and cut the dadoes in the sides. Then cut out the shapes with a band saw or saber saw. First make relief cuts from the edge in to the marked curves to prevent the saw blade from binding (Photo 7).

Mark the plate grooves on the shelves (see Section View in the plans). Mount a 1/2-inch straight bit in a router, attach a fence to the router base, and rout the plate grooves in the shelves (Photo 8).

Finish-sand the shelf supports (P), the shelves, the top (N), and the inside surfaces of the two sides (M).

Assemble the plate rack

Dry-fit the shelves and top to the sides, and glue the plate rack together (Photo 9).

Glue and clamp the shelf supports (P), cove support (Q), and scrolled bottom (L) to the shelves and top. Drive 1-1/2 inch finish nails through the sides into the shelves and the other horizontal pieces.

Set the blade angle on a table saw to 45 degrees and rip off the cove filler (S) from the 1-1/2-inch wide board. Cut the cove filler to seven inches to fit the sides and 45 inches for the front; miter the front corners where they meet. Measure, glue, and nail the cove filler to the top of the plate rack.

Because of minor discrepancies in board thicknesses and previous cuts, measure the plate rack carefully before cutting the cove molding (R). Cut the corners with a miter cut (Photo 10). First cut the miters for one corner, then measure, mark, and cut the other end. Be sure to put the molding in the miter

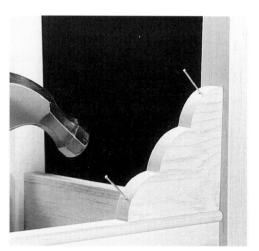

Photo 5. Attach the leg–skirt brackets with glue and 1-1/2 inch finish nails. One side of each bracket must be sanded to match the leg taper.

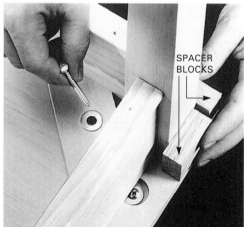

Photo 6. Screw the top to the base with washers and pan-head screws. Use temporary spacer blocks to position the top for an equal overhang on all sides.

Photo 4. Round over both edges of the skirt beading on a router table. Then rip the beading to width on a table saw and nail it to the skirt boards.

box upside down. If you have never cut molding for a headband or crown before, cut a trial corner joint or two with scrap pieces before you attempt to cut a piece to final size.

Attach the cove molding to the top and cove filler with glue and 1-inch finish nails.

FINISHING THE TWO PIECES

Disassemble the screwed-together components of the sideboard. Using a small nail set, hammer the heads of all exposed finish nails to slightly below the surface of the wood in both the sideboard and the plate rack. Fill the holes with wood putty.

Finish-sand any unsanded surfaces and smooth any sharp edges. Wipe all surfaces and edges clean with a tack cloth or a cloth dampened with mineral spirits. Finally, apply a semigloss clear varnish or stain the pieces and apply a finish of your choice.

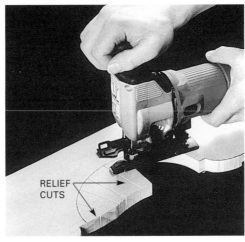

Photo 7. Cut the sides of the plate rack with a band saw or saber saw. Make relief cuts first to prevent the saw blade from binding as you cut the marked curves.

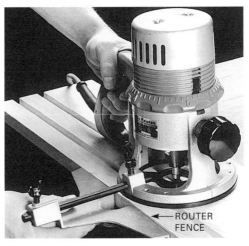

Photo 8. Guide the router against the back edge of a shelf to cut the rear plate groove nearest the back. Readjust the fence and cut the front groove.

Photo 9. Glue the shelves and top of the plate rack to one side piece. Check that they're square as you clamp them together. When the glue has dried, glue and clamp the other side.

Photo 10. Make miter cuts with the cove molding upside down in the miter box. The molding is installed around the top of the plate rack the same way crown molding would be affixed to a wall.

This handsome sideboard looks like something it's not—

a difficult, advanced woodworking project. In fact, it is really rather simple.

Contemporary Walnut Sideboard

This sideboard is made of plywood joined together almost entirely with screws; the exposed

edges are finished with easy-to-use, iron-on veneer edging.

The metal drawer slides and European-style hinges look and feel very professional,

but they are actually easier to work with than traditional all-wood drawers and leaf hinges.

The shelf surfaces are covered with plastic laminate.

If you have never worked with laminate before, this is an excellent beginning project, because

there are no seams or difficult corners. A special section takes you through the process of

cutting and applying the laminate.

Materials List

Quantity	Size and Description
1	1" x 4" x 48" walnut
2 sheets	4' x 8' x 3/4" walnut plywood
7 rolls	13/16" x 8' iron-on walnut veneer edging
1 sheet	4' x 8' x 3/4" industrial-grade particleboard
1	1/2" x 24" x 48" no-void birch plywood
1	1/4" x 11-3/4" x 26-1/2" birch plywood
1 sheet	49" x 97" Imperial Green plastic laminate
1 quart	Nonflammable contact cement
1 set	12" full extension box drawer slide
2	35 mm 95° free-swinging inset hinge
2	35 mm 95° snap-closing inset hinge
4	Pin-style shelf supports
52	No. 6 x 1-1/2" drywall screws
19	No. 6 x 1-1/4" drywall screws
3	No. 10 x 1" pan-head screws with 1/4" washers
8	3/8" x 1-1/2" dowel pins
4	1/4" x 1-1/2" dowel pins
1 quart	Black walnut Danish oil finish

Note: Drawer and shelf hardware and specialty hinges are available from specialty woodworking stores.

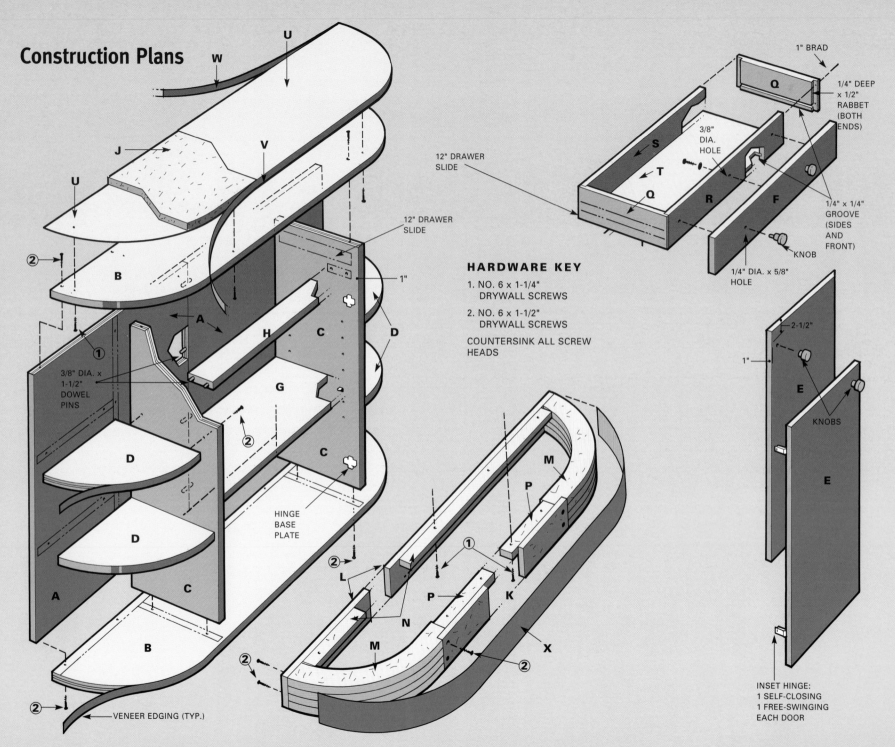

Construction Plans

U

W

V

J

U

B

② ①

3/8" DIA. x
1-1/2"
DOWEL
PINS

A

A

D

D

B

② VENEER EDGING (TYP.)

H

A

C

G

C

C

② ②

HINGE
BASE
PLATE

L

N

P

M

P

K

② ②

X

M

12" DRAWER
SLIDE

12" DRAWER
SLIDE

1"

D

1

HARDWARE KEY

1. NO. 6 x 1-1/4"
   DRYWALL SCREWS

2. NO. 6 x 1-1/2"
   DRYWALL SCREWS

COUNTERSINK ALL SCREW
HEADS

1" BRAD

Q

1/4" DEEP
x 1/2"
RABBET
(BOTH
ENDS)

3/8"
DIA.
HOLE

S

T

Q

R

F

1/4" x 1/4"
GROOVE
(SIDES
AND
FRONT)

KNOB

1/4" DIA. x 5/8"
HOLE

2-1/2"

1"

E

KNOBS

E

INSET HINGE:
1 SELF-CLOSING
1 FREE-SWINGING
EACH DOOR

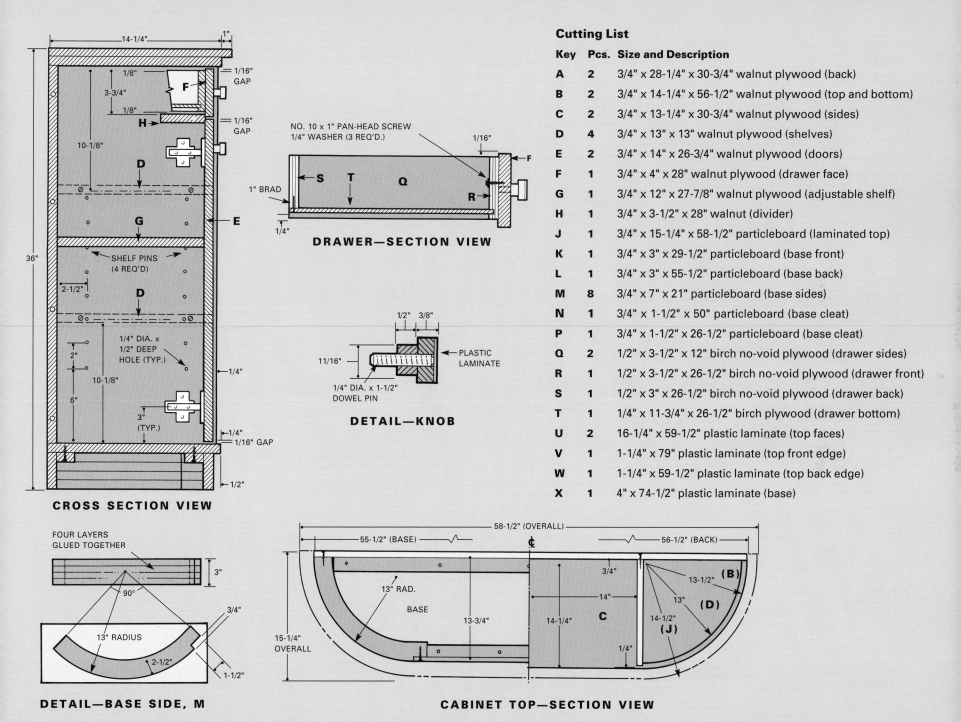

Cutting List

Key	Pcs.	Size and Description
A	2	3/4" x 28-1/4" x 30-3/4" walnut plywood (back)
B	2	3/4" x 14-1/4" x 56-1/2" walnut plywood (top and bottom)
C	2	3/4" x 13-1/4" x 30-3/4" walnut plywood (sides)
D	4	3/4" x 13" x 13" walnut plywood (shelves)
E	2	3/4" x 14" x 26-3/4" walnut plywood (doors)
F	1	3/4" x 4" x 28" walnut plywood (drawer face)
G	1	3/4" x 12" x 27-7/8" walnut plywood (adjustable shelf)
H	1	3/4" x 3-1/2" x 28" walnut (divider)
J	1	3/4" x 15-1/4" x 58-1/2" particleboard (laminated top)
K	1	3/4" x 3" x 29-1/2" particleboard (base front)
L	1	3/4" x 3" x 55-1/2" particleboard (base back)
M	8	3/4" x 7" x 21" particleboard (base sides)
N	1	3/4" x 1-1/2" x 50" particleboard (base cleat)
P	1	3/4" x 1-1/2" x 26-1/2" particleboard (base cleat)
Q	2	1/2" x 3-1/2" x 12" birch no-void plywood (drawer sides)
R	1	1/2" x 3-1/2" x 26-1/2" birch no-void plywood (drawer front)
S	1	1/2" x 3" x 26-1/2" birch no-void plywood (drawer back)
T	1	1/4" x 11-3/4" x 26-1/2" birch plywood (drawer bottom)
U	2	16-1/4" x 59-1/2" plastic laminate (top faces)
V	1	1-1/4" x 79" plastic laminate (top front edge)
W	1	1-1/4" x 59-1/2" plastic laminate (top back edge)
X	1	4" x 74-1/2" plastic laminate (base)

CROSS SECTION VIEW

DRAWER—SECTION VIEW

NO. 10 x 1" PAN-HEAD SCREW
1/4" WASHER (3 REQ'D.)

1" BRAD

DETAIL—KNOB

11/16"

1/4" DIA. x 1-1/2"
DOWEL PIN

PLASTIC
LAMINATE

DETAIL—BASE SIDE, M

FOUR LAYERS
GLUED TOGETHER

90°

13" RADIUS

CABINET TOP—SECTION VIEW

58-1/2" (OVERALL)

55-1/2" (BASE)

56-1/2" (BACK)

13" RAD.

BASE

15-1/4"
OVERALL

13-3/4"

14-1/4"

14"

(B)

13-1/2"

13"

(D)

14-1/2"

(J)

Construction Procedures and Techniques

CUTTING THE PIECES

For efficiency and accuracy lay out and cut all the parts for the sideboard before beginning assembly. Refer to the cutting list with the construction plans for the size and number of each piece (to avoid confusion, no pieces are labeled I or O).

Cut the pieces in the order in which they are listed in the instructions. Some pieces must be cut first because they are used as templates for laying out other pieces.

Cut the doors and drawer front

To get a good match between the grain patterns of the two doors (E), find the seam where the walnut veneers are glued together, and lay out the doors so that the gap between them falls right on the seam.

Cut the doors and drawer front (F) 1/2 inch wider and 1 inch longer than the dimensions that are given in the cutting list. You'll trim these pieces to fit later.

Cut the remaining wood pieces

Cut the plywood pieces (A–D), the particleboard pieces (J–L, N, P), the drawer pieces (Q–T), the adjustable shelf (G), and the divider (H) to their finished dimensions. Note that pieces B, D, and J have different lengths and that their curved ends have different radiuses; see the Cabinet Top Section View in the plans. Cut the rounded corners of these pieces using a band saw or jigsaw. Sand the edges smooth.

To cut the base sides (M) glue together two sets of four pieces of particleboard. Use a shelf (D) as a template to draw the shape of the sides. Cut them out on a band saw and sand the outside edges smooth (Photo 1). Alternatively, cut out eight single pieces with a jigsaw and glue them up in sets of four. This will require more sanding to achieve smooth, uniform base sides.

Cut the knobs from solid walnut (Photo 2). Cut two 1-1/4 inch wide strips of walnut. Plane or resaw one strip 1/2 inch thick; use a 1-1/8 inch hole saw to cut the knob faces from this piece. Plane or resaw the other strip 3/8 inch thick for the knob stems; cut the stems with a 3/4-inch hole saw.

Cut the plastic laminate pieces

All the plastic laminate dimensions given in the cutting list allow enough overhang for trimming. Use a carbide-tip saw blade or a metal-cutting blade in a jigsaw to cut the laminate pieces (U–X) to the dimensions given in the cutting list. Round the ends of the laminate pieces for the top faces (U), allowing them to overhang the particleboard 1/2 inch on all sides.

Use a band saw or jigsaw to cut four 1-1/2 inch diameter pieces of laminate. These will form the faces of the knobs.

Tools You Need

Table saw with plywood finish and carbide-tip blades

Jigsaw with metal-cutting blade

Band saw

Drill press with 1/4", 3/8", 35 mm bits

3/4" hole saw

1-1/8" hole saw

Router with piloted flush- and bevel-cutting carbide-tip laminate bits

Phillips and blade screwdrivers

Hand file

Spring clamps

Two 3" disposable rollers and trays

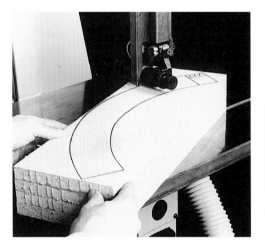

Photo 1. Cut the base sides, which are glued up from particleboard, with a band saw. Use a shelf as a template for marking out the curve.

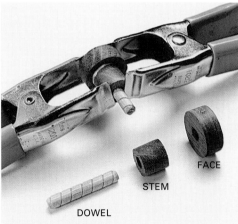

Photo 2. Cut the knobs with hole saws, finish-sand them, and glue them together with a dowel through the middle for mounting.

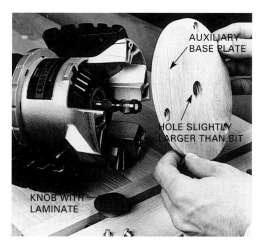

Photo 3. Add an auxiliary base to your router, to help keep it steady while trimming the laminate, especially on the knobs.

For trimming laminate during assembly, make an auxiliary router base of scrap 1/4-inch plywood for your router (Photo 3). Drill the center hole in the base slightly larger than the diameter of your router bit.

ASSEMBLING THE PIECES

Follow the assembly instructions exactly. Some parts are temporarily assembled early in the project, then taken apart for further work before final assembly and finishing.

Drill the assembly holes

Drill the assembly holes in the two back pieces (A). Glue and dowel the pieces together. Drill the remaining dowel holes, but don't glue any more pieces together, because the case will be disassembled later to apply edge veneer.

Drill the assembly screw holes in pieces A, B, C, K, L, N, and P. Drill the 3/8-inch diameter holes in the drawer front (R), and drill the shelf-pin holes in the sides.

Assemble the base

Sand the outside edges of the base sides (M) smooth. Glue and screw the base front and back to the base sides (drill pilot holes for the screws) and then glue the base cleats (N, P) to the base.

Assemble the case

Screw one side (C) to the back. Insert dowels (without glue) into the ends of the divider (H). Attach the divider to the other side (C), then to the side which is screwed to the back. Screw the back to the remaining side, then screw on the top and bottom.

Cut two 9-3/4 inch x 9-3/4 inch alignment blocks from scrap wood to help position the shelves (D) relative to the top and bottom, then screw the shelves to the case. Set the assembled case aside.

Make the knobs

Finish-sand the knob stems and faces. Glue them together, using 1/4 inch x 1-1/2 inch dowels. Clamp the parts until the glue sets.

Apply the plastic laminate

See the Quick Guide, Applying Plastic Laminate (page 115) for detailed instructions.

Glue the plastic laminate to the knobs and let them dry overnight so the small pieces of laminate won't slip as they're trimmed. Hold the knobs in a woodworking vise and trim the laminate edges with your router fitted with the auxiliary base.

Apply the plastic laminate to the top (J) in this order: first the underside face (U), then the back edge (W), the front edge (V), and finally the remaining face (U). Apply the base laminate piece (X), making a dry run first and marking where the middle of the laminate must go. If the ends of the laminate on the curved front edge won't stay down, put a long clamp across the back of the base overnight to bond the contact cement securely.

Assemble and mount the drawer

Cut dadoes and rabbets in drawer pieces Q and R, then finish-sand the drawer pieces (Q–T). Glue and nail the drawers together.

Screw the slide sections to the case and the drawer. Drive screws only through the slotted holes at this time (Photo 4).

Photo 4. Mark the center line for the drawer slide screws with a combination square. Put screws through the slotted holes for the first mounting.

Mount the drawer face and doors

Determine the final size of the doors and drawer face by measuring the openings in the case and subtracting an allowance for the thickness of the iron-on edging that will be applied to each edge, plus a 1/16-inch clearance all around. Cut the drawer faces and doors to size, then screw each face to its corresponding drawer.

The hinges require 35 mm holes. Test your hinge mounting on scrap wood before drilling into the doors (Photo 5). Remember that the drawer front and doors are set 1/4 inch back into the opening of the case. Mount the hinges, base plates, and doors.

Remove the drawer and doors, unscrew the drawer face, and detach the slides. Drill the 1/4-inch holes for the knobs.

FINISHING THE SIDEBOARD

If any laminate edges have not been finished, trim them now with a piloted bit in your router, then smooth the edges with a hand file. Finish the wood as follows.

Apply the iron-on veneer edging

Disassemble the case and apply the veneer edging to all the exposed plywood edges. Use a household iron (Photo 6).

Finish-sand the overhanging edges and all exposed surfaces. The edging has been sanded at the factory, but you still might need to sand it lightly to remove any hot glue or ironing marks.

Trim the dowels in the knobs to final length, then glue them in place.

Apply the finish

Apply an oil finish. A black-walnut Danish oil will give the sideboard a rich color.

Reassemble the case except for the shelves (D), and screw on the base. Align and clamp the top to the case, then attach the top. Screw on the shelves.

Remount the hinges, drawer slide, drawer face, and doors. Loosen the screws in the slotted holes to adjust the drawer for a proper fit, then tighten them and install the remaining screws to lock the slide in position. Set the adjustable shelf (G) on its pins and your sideboard is done.

Veneering Tip

Before using a steam iron to apply veneer edging, drain out all the water and operate it for a few minutes at the highest temperature and the Steam setting—to drive out all moisture.

Change to the No Steam setting and the temperature recommended in the veneer instructions. Wait for the temperature to adjust, then iron on the veneer.

Photo 5. Clamp a fence on the drill press table to drill the 35 mm hinge holes in the doors. Test your setup on scrap wood first.

Photo 6. Use a household iron to heat the iron-on veneer edging, then apply pressure with a steel roller or a wood block until the glue cools.

Applying Plastic Laminate

Photo A. Apply contact cement with a disposable roller and roller tray. Put two coats on the particleboard and one on the laminate.

DISPOSABLE ROLLER

Photo B. Hold large pieces of laminate off the contact cement with dowels while you align them, then remove the dowels one by one and press down.

DOWEL

Photo C. Press down laminate with light hammer taps and a wood block. As you tap, keep back from the overhanging edges so they won't break.

Photo D. Trim the overhanging laminate with a carbide-tip laminate trimming bit. This one also bevels the laminate edge.

BEVEL-TRIMMING ROUTER BIT

Photo E. Finish the edge with a file after trimming with the router. Always move the file so it pushes the laminate downward.

FILING DIRECTION

Laminate is brittle, so handle it carefully to avoid cracking.

1. Cut laminate with a jigsaw and a metal-cutting blade, or with a table saw or radial arm saw with a carbide-tip blade. If you use a table saw, clamp a board to the rip fence to keep the laminate from sliding between it and the table. Support the laminate well.

Cut the laminate to overhang the surface it will be mounted on by 1/4 to 1/2 inch, to allow for trimming and alignment.

2. Make sure both surfaces to be joined are clean and dust-free before applying the contact cement. Apply contact cement to the wood surface (usually industrial particleboard) and to the back of the laminate. Use a nonflammable cement, either solvent- or water-based. Particleboard needs two coats. The easiest way to apply contact cement is with a disposable roller and tray **(Photo A)**, which are available at most paint stores.

3. When the cement is dry, press the laminate onto the wood surface. Once the laminate and surface are cemented together, they can't be separated, so line them up perfectly. To help with larger pieces, lay clean dowels or venetian blind slats on the dry cement, place the laminate on top, line it up, then remove the dowels or slats one at a time, pressing the laminate firmly in place **(Photo B)**.

4. Apply plenty of pressure to get the contact cement to bond. Use a rubber-faced mallet, or hit a wood block with a hammer **(Photo C)**. Work over the entire surface of the laminate while tapping it with the mallet or wood block and hammer. Be careful near the edges so you don't break them. Whenever the wood block overlaps the piece you're applying pressure to, you run the risk of breaking or cracking the overhanging laminate. On narrow pieces, such as the edges of the top, apply pressure with your fingers.

5. Trim the overhanging laminate edges with a router and a ball-bearing piloted, carbide-tip laminate trimming bit. Use a straight, flush-cutting bit when another piece of laminate will be applied over the trimmed edge. Use a bevel-cutting bit when trimming finished edges **(Photo D)**.

6. Smooth the trimmed laminate edges with a hand file **(Photo E)**. File at the same angle as the beveled edge and ONLY in the direction that pushes the laminate down, not lifts it up. Be careful not to scratch the adjacent laminate.

7. Use contact cement solvent to remove any contact cement on the surface of the laminate. Lightly sand the sharp edges smooth to give them a final finish.

This functional, elegant, and easy-to-build table displays all the best features

of the traditional trestle table—clean lines, a simple sliding top, and,

with an extra leaf in place, plenty of leg room for six people.

Oak Trestle Table

The table shown is made from oak that has been finished with Danish oil,

but you could use any hardwood.

The only part that requires gluing and clamping is the edging around the tabletop.

The base is assembled with joint connector bolts, threaded steel rods, and cap nuts.

The two sections of the tabletop and leaf are held tightly together

with table locks—cam-type window sash locks available at hardware

stores and home centers.

Materials List

Quantity	Size and Description
24 sq. ft.	3/4" oak
1 sheet	3/4" x 4' x 8' oak plywood
24	No. 6 x 1-5/8" drywall screws
24	No. 6 x 2" drywall screws
8	No. 6 x 2-1/2" drywall screws
36 in.	1/4"-20 threaded steel rod
8	2" joint connector bolts
16	Cap nuts
10	Wood table pins
8	Rubber cushion glides
2	Table locks (cam-type sash locks)
1 sheet	Poster board
1 pint	Danish oil finish

Note: Connector bolts, cap nuts, table pins, and cushion glides are available from specialty woodworking stores.

Construction Plans

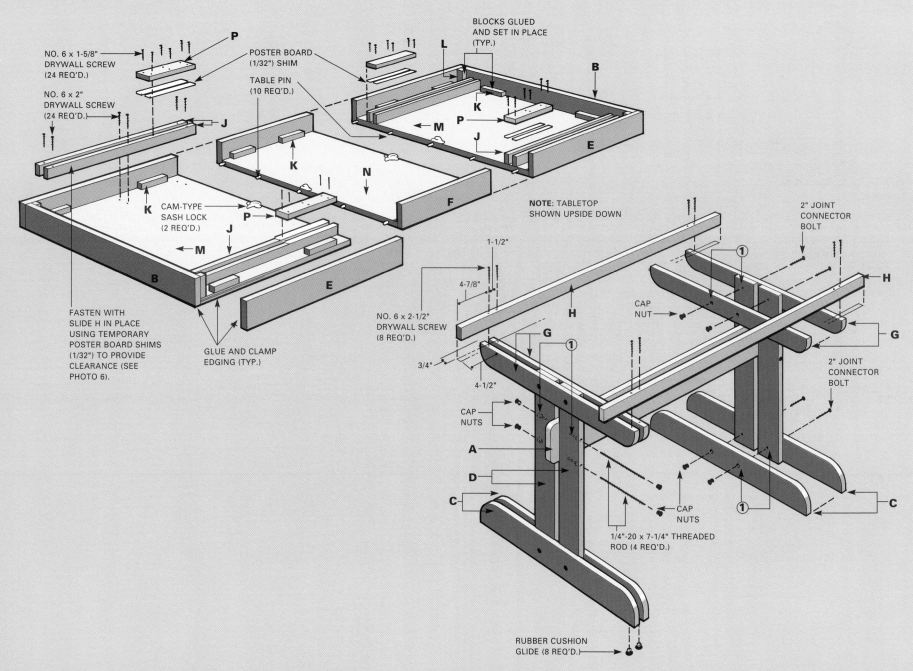

NO. 6 x 1-5/8"
DRYWALL SCREW
(24 REQ'D.)

NO. 6 x 2"
DRYWALL SCREW
(24 REQ'D.)

P

POSTER BOARD
(1/32") SHIM

TABLE PIN
(10 REQ'D.)

BLOCKS GLUED
AND SET IN PLACE
(TYP.)

L

B

K

M

P

J

E

J

CAM-TYPE
SASH LOCK
(2 REQ'D.)

K

P

M

J

K

N

F

E

B

E

FASTEN WITH
SLIDE H IN PLACE
USING TEMPORARY
POSTER BOARD SHIMS
(1/32") TO PROVIDE
CLEARANCE (SEE
PHOTO 6).

GLUE AND CLAMP
EDGING (TYP.)

NOTE: TABLETOP
SHOWN UPSIDE DOWN

2" JOINT
CONNECTOR
BOLT

1-1/2"

4-7/8"

NO. 6 x 2-1/2"
DRYWALL SCREW
(8 REQ'D.)

3/4"

4-1/2"

H

H

G

①

CAP
NUT

①

H

2" JOINT
CONNECTOR
BOLT

G

CAP
NUTS

A

D

C

①

C

1/4"-20 x 7-1/4" THREADED
ROD (4 REQ'D.)

CAP
NUTS

RUBBER CUSHION
GLIDE (8 REQ'D.)

Cutting List

Key	Pcs.	Size and Description
A	1	3/4" x 5-1/2" x 42-1/2" oak (cross support)
B	2	3/4" x 3-1/2" x 35" oak (end edging)
C	4	3/4" x 3-1/2" x 30" oak (feet)
D	4	3/4" x 3-1/2" x 27" oak (legs)
E	4	3/4" x 3-1/2" x 26" oak (side edging)
F	2	3/4" x 3-1/2" x 18" oak (leaf edging)
G	4	3/4" x 2-1/2" x 30" oak (top supports)
H	2	3/4" x 1-1/2" x 50" oak (slides)
J	8	3/4" x 1-1/2" x 25-1/4" oak (slide blocks)
K	16	3/4" x 3/4" x 4" oak (glue blocks)
L	4	3/4" x 3/4" x 2-3/4" oak (glue blocks)
M	2	3/4" x 35" x 25-1/4" oak plywood (top)
N	1	3/4" x 35" x 18" oak plywood (leaf)
P	4	3/4" x 2-1/4" x 8-1/2" oak (slide covers)

3/4"

3/8" DIA.
HOLE FOR
CAP NUT

17/64" DIA.
HOLE FOR
THREADED
ROD AND
CONNECTOR
BOLTS

DETAIL 1

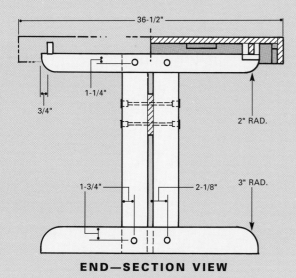

END—SECTION VIEW

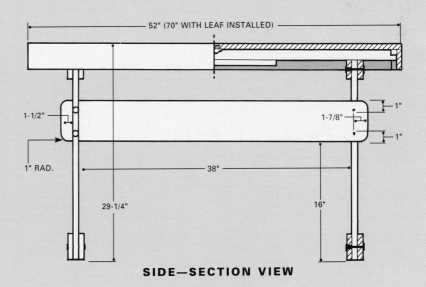

SIDE—SECTION VIEW

Construction Procedures and Techniques

CUTTING AND DRILLING THE PIECES

Choose only a hardwood such as oak to build this table; the pressure of the joint connector bolts used to assemble the base would crush softwood. All the solid pieces are 3/4 inch thick. Buy smooth-planed 3/4-inch boards, or have thicker stock planed by a lumberyard if you don't have a thickness planer.

Cut the tabletop

The tabletop is made from 3/4-inch oak veneer plywood with a glued-on edging of solid oak. Cut the plywood with a table saw with a sharp carbide-tip saw blade having 60 to 80 teeth. If you don't have a table saw, use a circular saw with a carbide-tip blade, or a high-quality saber saw with a fine-tooth blade. When using either of these hand-held saws, cut with the good side of the plywood facing down to avoid splintering the top surface, and use a clamped-on straightedge to ensure straight cuts.

Cut the plywood to 68-1/2 x 35 inches. Then cut out a section 18 x 35 inches exactly in the middle. This is the leaf (N). The two pieces on either side are the tabletop halves (M); they will measure 25-1/4 x 35 inches. This method of cutting ensures that the grain of the entire top will match exactly when the leaf is used.

Cut the remaining pieces

Cut all the pieces (A through P) to the sizes given in the cutting list. Cut the edging pieces as you did the top, removing the center piece (F) from between the two side pieces (E) to ensure a consistent grain pattern along the finished edges.

Drill the pin and bolt holes

Lay out and drill the holes for the joint connector bolts, cap nuts, and threaded rods in pieces A, C, and G.

Use a framing square to draw a line across the legs (D) where the threaded rods will be inserted. Use a dowel jig to ensure straight holes (Photo 1). When boring the holes in the legs, first drill the 3/8-inch holes for the cap nuts centered on the drill line (see Detail 1 in the construction plans). Then drill a 1/4-inch hole from inside the 3/8-inch hole and from the other side so the holes meet in the middle. Finally, drill through with a 17/64-inch bit to widen the holes so the threaded rods can be inserted easily.

Tools You Need

- Table saw or circular saw
- Saber saw
- Framing square
- Drill
- Drill press
- Doweling jig
- Hacksaw
- Metal file
- Hexagonal key wrenches
- Power sander
- 4' pipe clamps

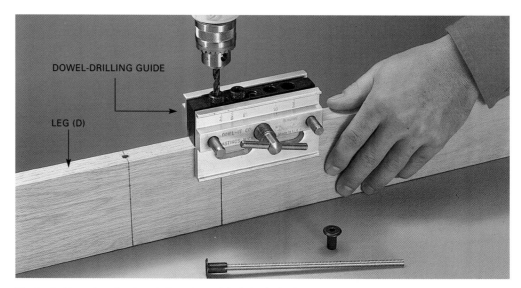

DOWEL-DRILLING GUIDE

LEG (D)

Photo 1. Use a doweling jig to help make straight holes in the legs for the threaded rods and joint connector bolts. Also use it to drill the table pin holes in the top pieces and the leaf.

Dry-assemble the tabletop pieces (M and N) and lay them face down with their edges perfectly aligned. These pieces must have matching holes and dowels (hardwood table pins) in their edges to align them in use. To ensure precise alignment of the holes, use a framing square to mark five evenly spaced positions across the gaps between all three pieces. Drill holes on these marks in the inside edges of each tabletop half and both edges of the leaf. Make the holes the same diameter as the table pins, and use a doweling jig to bore them perpendicular to the edges of the pieces.

Lay out, countersink and drill the screw holes in pieces H, J, and P.

Draw and cut the rounded corners of pieces A, C, and G (Photo 2). The four corners of the cross support (A) have a 1-inch radius. The top corners of the feet (C) have a 3-inch radius. The bottom corners of the top supports (G) have a 2-inch radius.

With a hacksaw, cut four pieces of threaded rod 7-1/4 inches long. File the cut ends smooth so the cap nuts thread on easily.

ASSEMBLING THE TABLE

The table is assembled with joint connector bolts and threaded rods. Slide blocks and covers are fastened with drywall screws. Only the tabletop edging is glued.

Attach the edging

Glue and clamp the edging pieces (B, E, F) to the tabletop halves (M) and the leaf (N), as shown in Photo 3. Glue the end pieces (B) first, then the sides (E). Align the edging with the face of the plywood.

Work Tip

Place pieces of cardboard or scrap wood on the faces of the pipe clamps to avoid marring the edging when you glue it to the tabletop and the leaf sections.

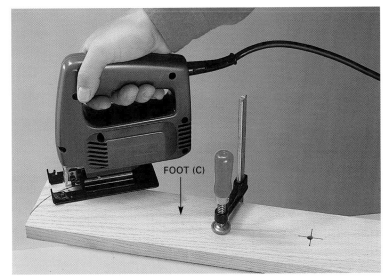

Photo 2. Cut the rounded corners with a saber saw. Use a fine-tooth saw blade, and follow the drawn lines closely to reduce the amount of sanding later.

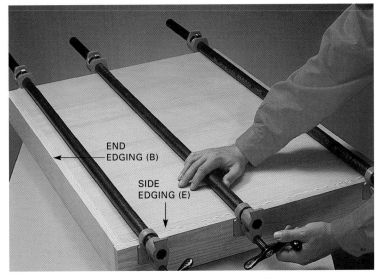

Photo 3. Glue and clamp the solid edging pieces to the tabletop and leaf sections. Do one section at a time. On the tabletop halves, attach the end edging pieces first, then the side pieces.

Construct the table base

Bolt the legs to the cross support with the threaded rods and cap nuts (Photo 4). Next, bolt the feet to the legs with the joint connector bolts and cap nuts. Then bolt the top supports to the legs (Photo 5). You will need hexagonal key wrenches to tighten the cap nuts and joint connector bolts.

Position the slides (H) on top of the top supports (G). Drill pilot holes through the slides into the top supports for the screws, then screw the slides in place.

Complete the tabletop

Tap table pins into the holes in the inside edge of one top half. They should line up exactly with the holes in the other top half, and the holes in the leaf when it is in place. Also tap table pins into the holes in one edge of the leaf. When the leaf is used, its pins engage the holes in one top half, and its holes receive the pins from the other top half. The table pins should fit tightly enough so they do not need glue, but if they do pull out use glue to secure them.

Put the tabletop halves together without the leaf; make sure the joint is snug. Assemble the two halves of one table lock and place it across the joint on the underside of the two tabletop halves; this means that when it is closed, it will pull the halves together tightly. Screw the lock into the underside of the top.

Separate the top halves, insert the leaf, and mount the top of the second table lock so it aligns with the bottom of the first. Repeat this step on the other side of the leaf, aligning the bottom to the top.

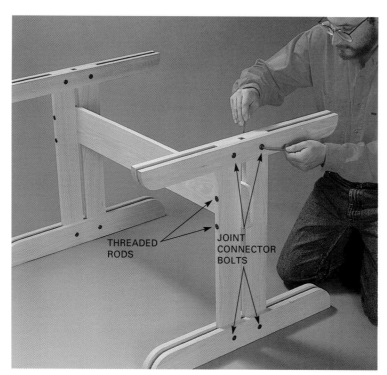

Photo 4. Join the base pieces together with the joint connector bolts, threaded rods, and cap nuts.

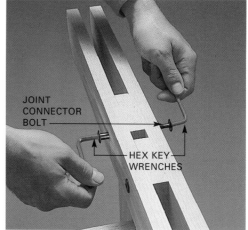

Photo 5. Use hex key wrenches to tighten the joint connector bolts and the cap nuts.

Join the base to the top

Remove the leaf and join the top halves again. Set the assembled table base upside-down and centered on the assembled top. Use slips of poster board or similar thin cardboard as spacers to separate the slide blocks (J) about 1/32 inch from the sides of the slides (H) so that they won't bind later. Glue and screw the slide blocks to the underside of the tabletop (Photo 6), and then remove the spacer slips.

Drill pilot holes for the screws that join the slide covers (P) to the slide blocks. Cut eight 3/4 x 8-inch pieces of poster board to use as permanent shims between the slide covers and slide blocks. Screw, but don't glue, the slide covers to the slide blocks with the shims between the pieces. This ensures that no glue will seep into the joint, which would bind the movement of the tabletop.

Glue and press the glue blocks (K, L) in place, against the edging and the underside of the tabletop sections and the leaf.

Turn the assembled table over and rest it on its feet. Check to see that the top halves move freely on the slides. Sand the faces of all the side edging pieces (E, F) flush with each other at the joint for the leaf.

FINISHING THE TABLE

Unscrew the slide covers, remove the top, then disassemble the base. Finish-sand all surfaces and round over all the edges and corners. First use 100-grit sandpaper, then 120-grit paper.

Apply three coats of Danish oil finish, following the directions on the container. Make sure you finish the underside of the top too, so it won't absorb moisture and warp later.

Drill pilot holes in the bottoms of the feet for the nail-on cushion glides, and hammer them in place. Reassemble the table.

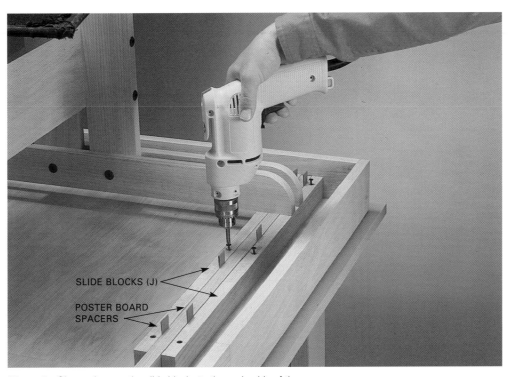

SLIDE BLOCKS (J)

POSTER BOARD
SPACERS

Photo 6. Glue and screw the slide blocks to the underside of the tabletop. Use poster board spacers between the slides and the slide blocks so the slides won't bind later.

This pantry cabinet holds an enormous amount, and it allows you

to keep everything organized and easily accessible.

Pantry Cabinet

No more boxes stacked like the Eiffel Tower or dusty cans languishing

at the back of the cupboard.

Building this cabinet is a great project for the intermediate do-it-yourselfer.

It screws together for fast, easy assembly, and incorporates

a great many very practical features.

The cabinet dimensions can be adapted to the amount of space you have available.

The easy-to-clean, plastic-coated interior does not require any laminating work.

European-style hinges permit the doors to swing fully open, out of the way.

And you can choose an exterior to match your existing

kitchen cabinets or fixtures.

Construction Plans

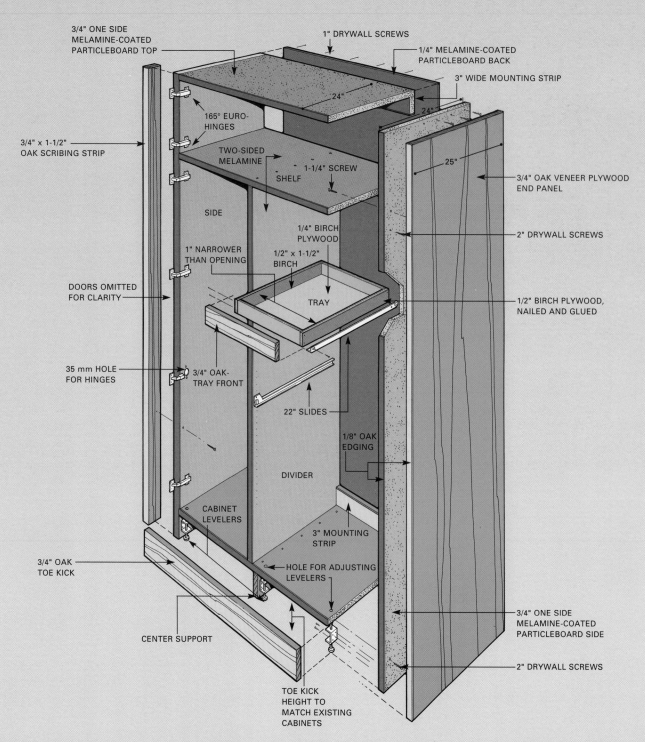

3/4" ONE SIDE
MELAMINE-COATED
PARTICLEBOARD TOP

1" DRYWALL SCREWS

1/4" MELAMINE-COATED
PARTICLEBOARD BACK

3" WIDE MOUNTING STRIP

165° EURO-HINGES

24"

24"

3/4" x 1-1/2"
OAK SCRIBING STRIP

TWO-SIDED
MELAMINE
SHELF

1-1/4" SCREW

25"

3/4" OAK VENEER PLYWOOD
END PANEL

SIDE

1/4" BIRCH
PLYWOOD

2" DRYWALL SCREWS

1" NARROWER
THAN OPENING

1/2" x 1-1/2"
BIRCH

TRAY

DOORS OMITTED
FOR CLARITY

1/2" BIRCH PLYWOOD,
NAILED AND GLUED

35 mm HOLE
FOR HINGES

3/4" OAK-
TRAY FRONT

22" SLIDES

1/8" OAK
EDGING

DIVIDER

CABINET
LEVELERS

3/4" OAK
TOE KICK

3" MOUNTING
STRIP

HOLE FOR ADJUSTING
LEVELERS

3/4" ONE SIDE
MELAMINE-COATED
PARTICLEBOARD SIDE

CENTER SUPPORT

TOE KICK
HEIGHT TO
MATCH EXISTING
CABINETS

2" DRYWALL SCREWS

Materials List

Quantity	Size and Description
2 sheets	4' x 8' x 3/4" particleboard, melamine-coated one side (frame sides, top, bottom)
1 sheet	4' x 8' x 3/4" particleboard, melamine-coated both sides (shelf, center divider)
1 sheet	4' x 8' x 1/4" particleboard, melamine-coated one side (back)
1 sheet	4 'x 8' x 3/4" oak veneer plywood (end panel or panels)
1 sheet	4' x 8' x 1/4" birch plywood (tray bottoms)
1 sheet	4' x 8' x 1/2" birch plywood (tray frames)
61 linear ft.	3/4" x 3" oak (tray fronts, toe kick, scribing strip, door frames)
1 sheet	4' x 8' x 1/4" oak veneer plywood (door panels)
14 pairs	22" drawer slides
12	Euro-style hinges, 165°
6	Cabinet levelers
As needed	Wood dowels (for door frame construction)
	1/8" oak edging
	1", 2", and 3" drywall screws
	1-1/4" wood screws
	4d finish nails

Note: The above quantities are for the 32" x 84" cabinet with one finished end panel shown in the illustrations. You will need additional quantities if your plans call for a larger cabinet.

TOP OF CABINET

1/8" GAP

UPPER DOOR HEIGHT

END PANEL

SIDE

NOTE: MEASURE DOOR WIDTH FROM CENTER OF DIVIDER EDGE TO OUTSIDE EDGE OF CABINET SIDE. DOORS DO NOT OVERLAP END PANEL OR SCRIBING STRIP.

LOWER DOOR HEIGHT

1/8" GAP

TOE KICK

FLOOR

MEASURING DOORS

NOTE: FOR FREESTANDING UNIT REPLACE SCRIBING STRIP WITH AN END PANEL.

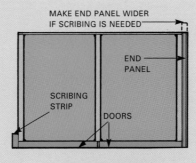

MAKE END PANEL WIDER IF SCRIBING IS NEEDED

END PANEL

SCRIBING STRIP

DOORS

CROSS SECTION— TOP VIEW

Planning the Pantry

FEATURES

How you choose to build your pantry cabinet depends on where you plan to put it and the dimensions of your kitchen. The features you choose to include will depend on your needs and preferences. The basic model shown incorporates the following features.

Roll-out trays

Roll-out trays are the best possible storage arrangement in a pantry. They use space efficiently, giving you instant access to all your groceries (Photo 1). And the weight of all those items you need to store is spread out over many separate trays, so overloading is seldom a problem.

Melamine interior

A special melamine-coated particleboard is ideal for the inside of the cabinet. Melamine is a hard plastic, much thinner than plastic laminate. It's glued to the particleboard at the factory, on one or both sides of the panel, so all you have to do is cut the panel to size. Melamine is durable and makes the cabinet bright and easy to clean (Photo 2). Because it is thin, it doesn't affect your calculations, either—3/4 inch thick is still 3/4 inch thick.

No complex joinery

This cabinet is screwed together with drywall screws. There are no rabbets or dadoes, no joints of any kind to cut, and no glue in the frame construction. If you make a mistake, the cabinet can be unscrewed and fixed. It's a forgiving way to build.

This method of assembly also means that if you cut the back square and attach it flush with the edges of the sides, the entire cabinet becomes self-squaring (Photo 3). The same is true of the roll-out trays. Cut each bottom square, and the entire tray will be square when you fasten it to its frame.

Euro-style hardware

The European or Euro-style drawer slides and door hinges are not inexpensive, but they're worth every penny. The drawer slides are easy to install and cover the exposed edges of the plywood tray bottoms. They roll smoothly and extend almost full length, making it easy to retrieve items at the back of each tray.

The hinges adjust in three dimensions, by as much as 1/8 inch, making it easy to get the doors to line up and have a uniform gap all around (Photo 4). If you've ever struggled to fit a door with butt hinges, you'll understand how great these hinges are.

LOCATION

There are any number of places to put a pantry cabinet in almost any kitchen. If there's no room to install it as a freestanding unit, you can remove a section of countertop base and upper cabinets, although that will eliminate some counter space. If you have a

Photo 1. Roll-out trays provide efficient storage. They move easily, even with a full load, and you can reach everything without difficulty.

closet that backs up to a kitchen wall, you could take up some of the depth of that closet by building the pantry through the wall, extending into that space.

DESIGN

The cabinet shown is a box of melamine-coated particleboard. The exposed edges are covered with oak trim and the exposed side is covered with a finished end panel of 3/4-inch oak veneer plywood. The doors are doweled-together solid oak frames with panels of 1/4-inch oak veneer plywood.

The interior design of the cabinet features a center panel to divide the space in half vertically. This avoids having roll-out trays so wide that they become overloaded. You can space the trays in any way you wish; they do not have to be aligned on either side of the divider. At the bottom you may prefer a roll-out basket or a tip-out bin for bulk items.

Photo 2. White melamine plastic on the inside makes the pantry bright and easy to clean. It comes attached to the particleboard, so there's no extra work.

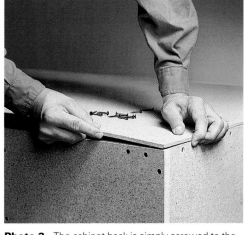

Photo 3. The cabinet back is simply screwed to the frame. The cabinet is automatically made square if you line up the edges.

Photo 4. Euro-style hinges look good and are practical because they're adjustable in every direction, which makes hanging doors a snap.

Match the finished end panel (or both panels of a freestanding unit) and the doors to the existing cabinet doors in the kitchen. Test carefully with stains and varnish to get a finish that matches your other cabinets.

Another option is to purchase doors for the pantry cabinet and then have all your other cabinet doors refaced with the same design. Many home centers and kitchen design centers offer refacing services. One potential problem with buying custom-made doors is getting the wrong size. Don't order doors for the pantry until it is completed and you know exactly what size you need. The doors cover the edges of the particleboard frame, but not the end panel or panels, and they meet over the center divider.

Draw a plan

The cabinet shown is 32 inches wide and just slightly under 7 feet high. It is an inch deeper than the adjacent countertop so the doors will clear the dishwasher and the cut edge of the countertop is concealed.

You no doubt will have to change the height, width, and depth to conform to the dimensions of your kitchen. Measure the space where the pantry will go. Determine the size of all parts and how many of them you need. Don't forget to allow for the 1/8-inch edging on the front edges of the center divider, the cabinet sides, and the end panel or panels.

There are no critical dimensions to the cabinet parts, except that the roll-out trays must be 1 inch narrower than their openings to accommodate the slides. The vertical spacing of the trays is determined by the sizes of groceries you buy—anywhere from 15 inches

for the lower trays to 6 inches in the upper trays. To save on material, keep cabinet parts 24 inches wide or less—half the width of a 4x8-foot sheet of particleboard or plywood.

Make cutting and materials lists

When the plan is complete, make a cutting list of the number of pieces and their exact measurements. Double-check all dimensions to make sure the cutting list is correct before ordering any materials.

Use the cutting list sizes to determine how much material you need. Remember what every cabinetmaker has learned: it's much cheaper to make mistakes on paper. Draw scale versions of 4x8-foot sheets of material and experiment with various layouts to get as many parts as possible from a panel with minimum waste. Then make a list of the materials and hardware you need.

Construction Procedures and Techniques

CUTTING AND DRILLING THE PIECES

Cut the sides, bottom, and top

Slowly and carefully cut the particleboard pieces to the sizes given in the cutting list (Photo 5). Don't cut the plywood end panel or panels yet, or the 1/4-inch particleboard for the back. Check that the top, bottom, and shelf are the same dimensions.

Attach the edging

Cut the solid-wood edging at least 1/16 inch wider than the particleboard edge. Glue it to the front edges of the particleboard; use clamps or masking tape to hold it in place until the glue dries (Photo 6). You can carefully plane off the excess, but it's dangerous —one cut too deep and you've cut the melamine and ruined the piece. It's easier to use a router and a flush-trimming bit instead. Stain and finish the edging now.

Drill hinge mortises and slide holes

Drill flat-bottom mortise holes for the hinges with a 35 mm Forstner bit. Use this bit in a drill guide to make holes in the cabinet sides. Use the drill guide or a drill press when you drill hinge mortises in the doors (Photo 7). Place a hinge in each mortise to mark the positions of the mounting holes. Drill pilot holes at those marks. Do not mount the hinges yet, so you have room to mark and mount the tray slides.

Tools You Need

Table saw or radial arm saw with fine-tooth carbide blade

Router with flush trimming

Drill with twist bits and 35 mm Forstner bit

Drill guide; drill press (optional)

Pipe clamps

Compass

Screwdrivers

Hammer

Stud finder

Block plane

Sander

Photo 5. Cut melamine-coated particleboard with a fine-tooth carbide blade. Make the cut slowly to avoid chipping the plastic surface.

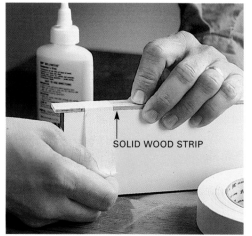

Photo 6. Glue solid wood trim to the particleboard as edging; hold it in position with masking tape. Trim the edging to width with a router.

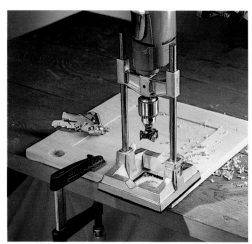

Photo 7. Drill mortise holes for the Euro-style hinges, using a drill guide. Use a 35 mm Forstner bit to make the flat-bottom holes the hinges require.

Consult your plans for the positions of the roll-out trays. Be sure that they will not interfere with the hinges. Measure and mark tray positions, then use a drawer slide at each position to mark the mounting holes for the slides. Leave a 7/8-inch space between the slide and the front of the cabinet to accommodate the tray front. Drill pilot holes at the marks and screw on the slides (Photo 8). Finally, screw the hinges to the cabinet sides.

ASSEMBLING THE CABINET

Build the frame

Use 2-inch drywall screws to fasten the 3/4-inch particleboard parts together.

Fasten the mounting strip at the rear of the top by driving screws through the top into the edge of the mounting strip.

Screw the shelf and the bottom to the center divider. Be sure the divider is exactly centered on them, and square to their front edges. Drive screws through the shelf and bottom into the edges of the divider.

Screw one side of the cabinet to the edges of the top, shelf, and bottom. Make sure the bottom will be at the proper height above the floor—high enough to put a toe kick under it that matches the existing cabinets. Use a framing square to get the bottom, shelf, and top at right angles to the side. Clamp the pieces to hold them in position while you drill pilot holes and then drive the screws (Photo 9). Countersink the screw heads. Attach the other side in the same way.

Measure the cabinet, then cut the 1/4-inch particleboard back. Check that it is square by measuring from corner to corner—the distances should be the same. Drill pilot

holes and drive 1-inch drywall screws through the back into the frame (Photo 10). Fasten the back to the rear edges of the top and one side first, then screw it to the other side, the shelf, the divider, and the bottom. If you have cut the back square, it will pull the cabinet box into square.

Install the bottom mounting strips, one on each side of the center divider. Screw into the mounting strips through the bottom and in from the sides. Then cut a center support strip to go under the middle of the cabinet bottom. Offset it to one side of the divider and drive screws down through the bottom into the support's top edge.

If your plan calls for it, cut and attach a scribing strip against the side of the cabinet that will fit against the wall (see Cross Section—Top View in the construction plans). This strip will give a snug fit against a wall.

Cutting Tip

When cutting melamine-coated particleboard, minimize chipping by placing the melamine side face-up if you use a table saw, or face-down if you use a radial arm saw. Use a fine-tooth carbide blade and feed the work slowly. If you have trouble with the two-sided melamine pieces, cut them slightly oversize, then use a straightedge and router with a straight carbide bit to clean up the edges.

Photo 8. Attach drawer slides inside the cabinet, set back to allow room for the tray fronts. Drill pilot holes before driving the screws.

Photo 9. Assemble the main cabinet parts with drywall screws. Clamp the parts in position while you are drilling the pilot holes.

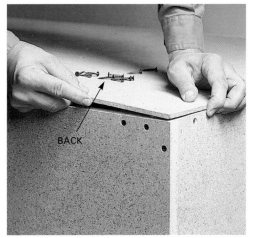

Photo 10. Line up the back and the cabinet edges carefully before screwing it on. A square-cut back will automatically square up the entire frame.

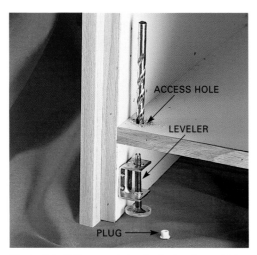

Photo 11. Drill access holes for the levelers, which adjust with a screwdriver from inside the cabinet. Put removable plugs in the holes later.

Screw on the levelers and drill the access holes for the adjustment screws (Photo 11). You may need to temporarily remove the bottom tray slides to drill the access holes.

Cut the end panel

Cut the end panel (or panels, for a freestanding unit). Make it 1/4 inch wider than the depth of the cabinet if you want to scribe it against the back wall during installation. Otherwise, cut it straight and cover any gap at the back wall with molding. Attach edging to the front edge as you did with the particleboard edges. Stain and finish the panel, but don't attach it to the side of the cabinet yet.

Make the doors

The doors consist of panels of 1/4-inch oak veneer plywood set into grooves in frames made of 3/4- x 3-inch oak (Photo 12). The frames are doweled and glued together. Stain and finish the completed doors.

Build the roll-out trays

Cut the frames for the trays from 1/2-inch birch plywood. Cut the plywood into strips 1-1/2 inches wide, then cut the strips to length for the sides, fronts, and backs of the frame. The sides are 7/8 inch shorter than the interior depth of the cabinet, to allow for a facing piece across the front. The frame fronts and backs are 2 inches smaller than the interior width between the center divider and one side. When they are fastened between the frame sides, the outside dimension must be 1 inch less than the width of the cabinet section. This clearance is necessary for the slides that support the trays to work properly. Glue and nail the frames together with 4d finish nails (Photo 13).

Measure the outside dimensions of the trays and cut the tray bottoms from 1/4-inch plywood. Cut the bottoms square and attach them to the tray frames with glue and 4d nails; they will square up the frames.

Screw the drawer slides to the tray frames (Photo 14) and test-fit the trays in the cabinet. Adjust the fit as necessary, either by sanding the tray side or shimming out the drawer slide with tape or washers.

Cut, sand, then stain and finish the solid wood facings for the trays. Fasten them in place by driving short screws through the plywood tray frames into their facings.

Position the cabinet

Place the cabinet in position in your kitchen. If it is a freestanding unit, attach the finished end panels first by driving 1-1/4 inch wood screws through the cabinet sides into the backs of the panels.

If one side of the cabinet has a scribing strip to fit against a wall, do not attach the end panel to the other side yet. Instead, put the cabinet into position with that side tight against the adjacent counter and cabinets. Adjust the levelers until the cabinet sides are plumb; check with a level.

Set a compass to 3/4 inch wide and scribe a line conforming to the shape of the wall down the scribing strip (Photo 15).

Move the cabinet out again to plane or sand the scribing strip down to the scribed line. This will ensure a snug fit with the wall.

While the cabinet is out of position, use a stud finder to locate the studs in the wall behind its location. Measure the distance of the studs from a common point—the nearest corner, for instance.

Slide the cabinet back in place and make sure that it is plumb and level. Measure and mark the stud positions on the mounting strips in the back of the cabinet. Screw through the mounting strips into the studs behind the cabinet (Photo 16). If the cabinet is not tight against the back wall, add shims behind the mounting strips before driving screws into the studs.

Slide the finished end panel into place over the exposed side of the cabinet. Fasten it in position with 1-1/4 inch wood screws driven from the inside (Photo 17).

FINAL TOUCHES

Mount the doors on the cabinet and adjust them so there is a uniform gap and a flush fit, using the screw adjustments on the hinges. Then attach the door pulls.

Cut and finish the toe kick, then nail it in place and fill the nail holes.

Photo 12. Make doors with glued-and-doweled frames and 1/4-inch plywood panels set into grooves routed or sawed in the frame edges.

FRAME

PLYWOOD

Photo 13. Assemble tray frames with glue and 4d finish nails. Clamp the pieces in position while nailing. Glue and nail the bottoms, too.

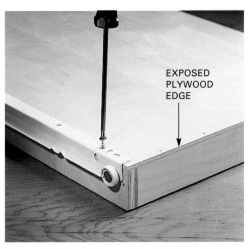

EXPOSED PLYWOOD EDGE

Photo 14. Attach drawer slides to the trays. Notice that this type of slide covers the exposed side edge of the plywood tray bottom.

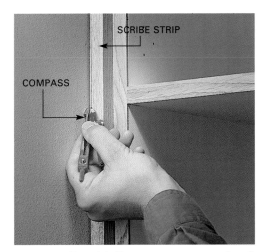

SCRIBE STRIP

COMPASS

Photo 15. For a tight fit, use a compass to mark wall irregularities on a scribing strip on the cabinet. Plane or sand the strip to the marked line.

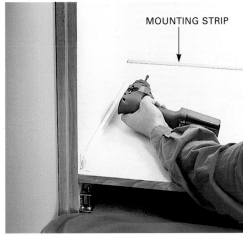

MOUNTING STRIP

Photo 16. Fasten the cabinet to the back wall. Drive 3-inch drywall screws through the top and bottom mounting strips into the wall studs.

FINISHED SIDE

Photo 17. Screw on the finished end panel from inside the cabinet. The panel is cut from 3/4-inch plywood and trimmed with solid wood edging.

Family Room

Oak Media Cabinet

This beautiful three-piece cabinet has accents of walnut and brass—and plenty of space for your audio and video gear and recordings.

Country Pine Bench

Knotty pine gives this versatile, easy-to-build bench a rustic charm. It provides both convenient seating and interior storage space.

Traditional Bookcase

It may look traditional, but it's all modern—plywood, drywall screws, and lumberyard molding. That means fast and easy building.

This media cabinet is thoroughly modern, designed to hold

all your audio and video components and provide plenty of storage

space for hundreds of tapes, CD's, and records.

Oak Media Cabinet

The construction is modern, with ball-bearing drawer slides, take-apart

fasteners, and router-based joinery. The cabinet is made of red oak plywood,

with contrasting solid walnut corners. Solid oak drawer fronts and solid

brass knobs add to the rich appearance.

The cabinet is designed in three sections: two side cases with drawers for

tapes and CD's, and a main case with shelves for media components.

You can put a TV set atop the main case or on a pullout shelf inside it.

All three cases have space below for LP's and old records,

or for tape and CD racks, depending on your needs.

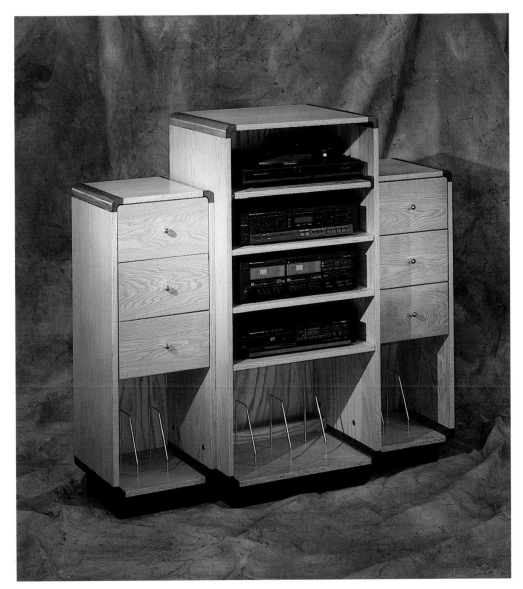

Materials List

Quantity	Size and Description
2	4' x 8' x 3/4" red oak plywood
1	4' x 8' x 1/4" red oak plywood
1	4' x 8' x 1/2" all-birch plywood
10 board ft.	8/4 walnut planed to 1-1/2"
10 board ft.	4/4 walnut planed to 3/4"
15 board ft.	4/4 red oak planed to 3/4"
6	12" drawer runners with rollers
1	16" drawer runner with rollers
12	1-1/8" joint connector bolts, antique brass
12	Cap nuts, antique brass
12	1/4" pin-style shelf supports, brass
7	Record dividers, brass (optional)
1 or more	Audio cassette holder (optional)
1 or more	Compact disk holder (optional)
6	Brass knobs
3	Walnut wire grommets
12	No. 6 x 3" flathead wood screws
2	No. 6 x 2" flathead wood screws
36	No. 6 x 3/4" flathead wood screws
12	No. 10 x 1" pan-head sheet metal screws
12	1/4" flat washers
50	1" headed nails
50	1" finish nails

Construction Plans

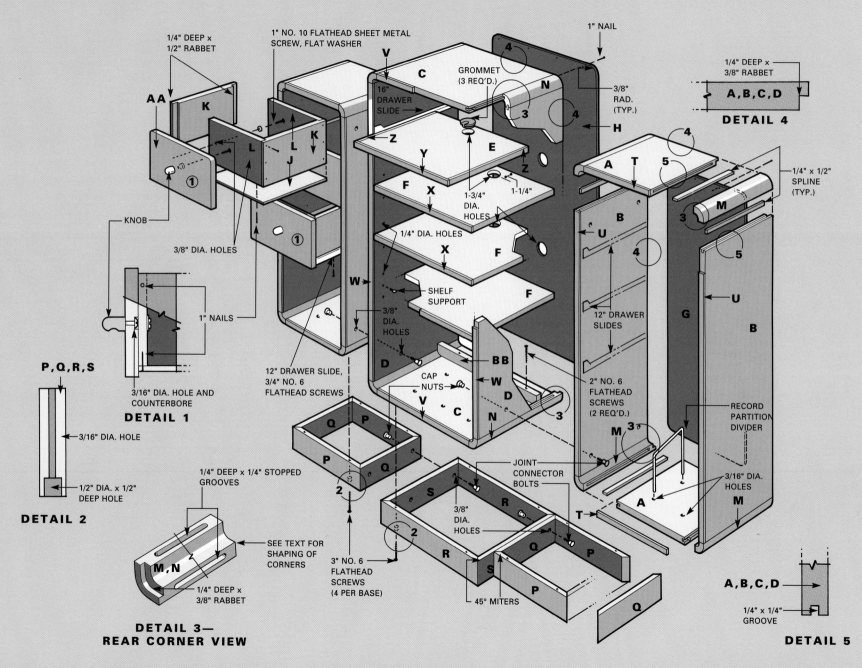

1/4" DEEP x 1/2" RABBET

1" NO. 10 FLATHEAD SHEET METAL SCREW, FLAT WASHER

1" NAIL

GROMMET (3 REQ'D.)

3/8" RAD. (TYP.)

1/4" DEEP x 3/8" RABBET

A,B,C,D

DETAIL 4

AA

K

V

C

16" DRAWER SLIDE

N

H

4

4

3

4

5

K

L

K

L

Z

Y

E

Z

A

T

5

1/4" x 1/2" SPLINE (TYP.)

J

F

X

1-3/4" DIA. HOLES

1-1/4"

M

3

KNOB

①

1/4" DIA. HOLES

B

①

X

F

U

4

5

3/8" DIA. HOLES

W

U

3/8" DIA. HOLES

SHELF SUPPORT

F

B

G

1" NAILS

3/16" DIA. HOLE AND COUNTERBORE

DETAIL 1

D

BB

W

2" NO. 6 FLATHEAD SCREWS (2 REQ'D.)

RECORD PARTITION DIVIDER

P,Q,R,S

12" DRAWER SLIDE, 3/4" NO. 6 FLATHEAD SCREWS

V

C

N

D

3

M

3

3/16" DIA. HOLE

CAP NUTS

A

3/16" DIA. HOLES

1/2" DIA. x 1/2" DEEP HOLE

Q

P

JOINT CONNECTOR BOLTS

M

DETAIL 2

1/4" DEEP x 1/4" STOPPED GROOVES

P

Q

2

S

R

3/8" DIA. HOLES

T

A,B,C,D

SEE TEXT FOR SHAPING OF CORNERS

2

R

Q

P

M,N

Z

3" NO. 6 FLATHEAD SCREWS (4 PER BASE)

S

Q

1/4" DEEP x 3/8" RABBET

45° MITERS

P

1/4" x 1/4" GROOVE

DETAIL 3— REAR CORNER VIEW

Q

DETAIL 5

Cutting List

Key	Pcs.	Size and Description
A	4	3/4" x 13-1/4" x 10-1/2" red oak plywood (side case top and bottom)
B	4	3/4" x 13-1/2" x 31-3/4" red oak plywood (side case sides)
C	2	3/4" x 16-3/4" x 18-1/2" red oak plywood (main case top and bottom)
D	2	3/4" x 16-3/4" x 39-3/4" red oak plywood (main case sides)
E	1	3/4" x 16" x 18-1/2" red oak plywood (turntable pullout)
F	3	3/4" x 16-1/2" x 20" red oak plywood (adjustable shelves)
G	2	1/4" x 12-3/4" x 34" red oak plywood (side case backs)
H	1	1/4" x 20-3/4" x 42" red oak plywood (main case backs)
J	6	1/4" x 11" x 12" red oak plywood (drawer bottoms)
K	12	1/2" x 6" x 12" all-birch plywood (drawer sides)
L	12	1/2" x 6" x 10-1/2" all-birch plywood (drawer fronts and backs)
M	8	1-1/2" x 1-1/2" x 13-1/2" walnut (side case corners)
N	4	1-1/2" x 1-1/2" x 17" walnut (main case corners)
P	4	3/4" x 3" x 13-1/2" walnut (side case base, fronts, and backs)
Q	4	3/4" x 3" x 11-1/2" walnut (side case base, sides)
R	2	3/4" x 3" x 18-1/2" walnut (main case base, front, and back)
S	2	3/4" x 3" x 15" walnut (main case base, sides)
T	4	1/4" x 3/4" x 10-1/2" red oak (side case edging)
U	4	1/4" x 3/4" x 31-3/4" red oak (side case side edging)
V	2	1/4" x 3/4" x 18-1/2" red oak (main case edging)
W	2	1/4" x 3/4" x 39-3/4" red oak (main case edging)
X	3	1/4" x 3/4" x 20" red oak (shelf edging)
Y	1	1/4" x 3/4" x 19" red oak (pullout edging)
Z	2	1/4" x 3/4" x 16" red oak (pullout edging)
AA	6	3/4" x 6-3/4" x 12" red oak (drawer faces)
BB	1	3/4" x 1-1/2" x 20" red oak (record stop)

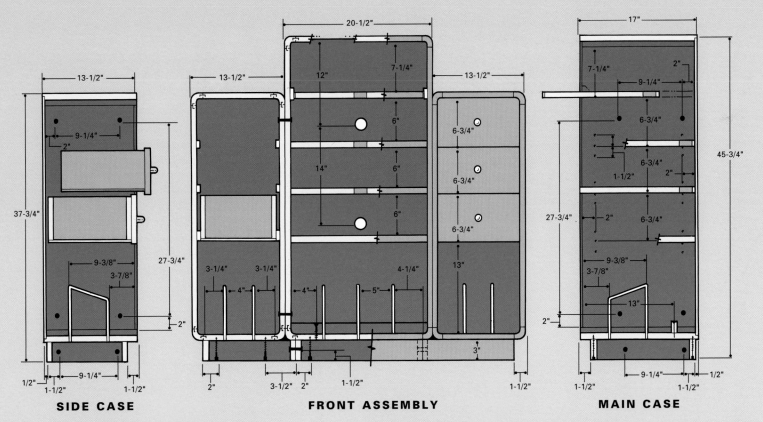

SIDE CASE   **FRONT ASSEMBLY**   **MAIN CASE**

Construction Procedures and Techniques

Tools You Need

Table saw or radial arm saw with dado blade

Saber saw

Router and router table

Planer

Drill with twist bits and self-centering Vix bit

Hole saw

Pipe clamps

Band clamps

Framing square

Sanding block

Hexagonal key wrenches

Rubber mallet

CABINET DESIGN

This handsome cabinet is composed of three cases that sit on walnut base frames. The cases are fastened to one another with joint connector bolts (Photo 1). The base frames are fastened together in the same way and are attached to the bottoms of the cases with screws. The joint connector bolts make it easy to separate the units without damage.

The shelves of the center case adjust at 1-1/2 inch increments to accommodate different sizes of equipment. The top shelf is a pullout mounted on drawer guides. In the cabinet shown it is positioned for a turntable, but it also provides enough space for a CD player or a VCR. If you prefer, mount the pullout

Photo 1. Joint connector bolts hold the three cases together and allow them to be disassembled for moving. Bolts and nuts with an antique brass finish complement the appearance of the finished cabinet.

shelf lower to make room for installing a TV inside the case. The other shelves can move down as well, with the lowest going down into the optional record storage space below.

The two side cases are identical, each with three drawers and lower storage space. To make construction simple, the six drawers are exactly the same size. You can fit the interiors of the drawers with cassette, CD, or video tape racks according to your needs. These accessories are available from woodworking specialty suppliers and audio/video stores. Or you can make dividers of hardboard or 1/4-inch plywood to whatever specifications you want.

The brass-rod record partition dividers shown in the bottom space of each case are optional. You can buy them from some woodworking specialty suppliers, or you can bend your own from 3/16-inch diameter brass rod. If you don't need them, you can install shelves or tape or CD holders in those spaces. Thus, you can customize the cabinet to your personal collection of recordings, tapes, and media components.

CUTTING THE PIECES

The 12 rounded walnut pieces (M and N) at the top and bottom corners of each case provide striking accents in contrast to the red oak sides, tops, and bottoms.

Make the walnut corner pieces

Here are detailed instructions for making the corner pieces. The finished shape and the six steps for cutting it are illustrated in the box on the opposite page.

Step 1. Cut and plane 2-inch thick walnut to pieces 1-1/2 x 1-1/2 inches square. Cut eight pieces 13-1/2 inches long for the side case corners (M), and four pieces 17 inches long for the center case corners (N).

Step 2. First mark the curved lines that show the finished shape on one end of each piece. Then use a 1/4-inch slot-cutting router bit with a pilot bearing to cut grooves in the sides located as shown. The grooves are 1/4-inch deep to accept half of the 1/4- x 1/2-inch splines used in assembling the cases. As shown in Detail 3 of the construction plans, the grooves are "stopped," meaning you cut only to within 1/4 inch of the ends of the piece. When the cabinet is assembled, there is no evidence of the spline. The rabbet at the rear of each block will be cut later.

Step 3. With a table saw set to a 45-degree bevel, cut away the corner between the grooved sides, leaving a five-sided piece of wood. You will now cut an inside curve in the angled face of the piece.

Step 4. Set up your router table with a 3/8-inch-radius core box bit and position a fingerboard to hold each workpiece tight against the fence (Photo 2). When you turn on the router to shape the work, use a push stick, not your fingers, to feed each piece into the bit. Be careful, and don't try to make a full-depth cut in one pass. The core box bit will want to push the work up and away from the fence, which could lead to kickback. Make a series of small cuts, slowly raising the router bit each time until it has cut to the desired depth.

Step 5. Now cut off the little triangular corners at the edges of the inside coved shape. Set your table saw blade 3/8 inch high and run the walnut pieces through first on one narrow edge and then the other. This makes the narrow sides of the corner pieces the same thickness as the plywood where you will make a splined joint during assembly.

Step 6. The outside corner of each walnut piece must be rounded, and a rabbet must be cut in the rear edge (plans, Detail 3). This work will be done with the corner pieces in place, after each case has been assembled. For now, finish-sand the insides of these corner pieces and put them aside until later.

Corner Tips

When making the walnut corner pieces, cut a few extra blanks for trial shaping. That will let you learn the sequence of steps and establish accurate saw and router settings before cutting the finish pieces.

Photo 2. Cut the inside curve of the corner pieces in several passes over a core box bit in a router table. Fingers are OK when lining up the piece, but use a push stick to feed the work when making the cut.

CORNER PIECES

The walnut corner pieces for all three cases of the media cabinet have the same profile, shown here at right. Make the shape in the six steps shown at the far right, using a table saw and router; specific operations are explained in the text.

1/4" x 1/4" GROOVES (STOPPED)

3/4" RAD.

3/4"

1-1/2"

3/8" RAD.

3/4"

1-1/2"

Step 1

Step 2

Step 3

Step 4

Step 5

Step 6

Cut the case pieces

Cut the plywood pieces for the sides (B, D) and the tops and bottoms (A, C). Use a sharp carbide blade with 60 to 100 teeth.

Lay out and drill the holes for the adjustable shelf pins and the joint connector bolts. Hole locations and spacing are shown in the construction plans. If you plan to include record partition dividers, drill holes for them also. It's a good idea to make tests in scrap wood for these hardware items, to be sure of boring holes that provide a snug fit.

Cut 1/4-inch grooves for splines in the plywood sides, tops, and bottoms (plans, Detail 5). Use the same slot-cutting router bit that you used on the solid walnut corners; stop each groove 1/4 inch from the edges. To ensure that the outer surfaces of the plywood and the solid corners will align properly, rest the router base on the oak face of the plywood to cut these grooves.

Cut and plane solid red oak stock to make edging 1/4 inch thick for the sides, tops, and bottoms (T, U, V, and W). Make enough stock to include the remaining edge pieces for the adjustable and pullout shelves (X, Y, and Z). The edging width is a nominal 3/4 inch, but check the exact thickness of your plywood and plane the edging to that width. Glue and clamp these solid edges to their respective plywood front edges.

Finish-sand the inner faces of all the sides, tops, and bottoms.

Clean Cuts

When cutting plywood, the saw teeth must bite into the best face as the blade rotates, to avoid chipping or tearing of that surface. To ensure this, orient the plywood with the best face upward on a table or radial arm saw, but downward if you use a portable circular saw.

Join the corners

Make splines to join the solid corners to the plywood sides, tops, and bottoms. Use any solid scrap that won't be needed for other pieces. The splines are 1/4 inch thick, 1/2 inch wide, and as long as their respective grooves. When planing or sanding the splines to final thickness, periodically check how they fit into the grooves; do not allow them to get too thin.

Glue and clamp the solid corners (M, N) to the top and bottom edges of their respective sides (B, D) with splines in their grooves (Photo 3). Go easy on the glue to avoid excessive squeeze-out onto the wood surfaces.

After the glue dries, spline, glue, and clamp the tops and bottoms (A, C) in place on the left side piece of each case. Use a framing square to make sure the tops and bottoms are square to the sides. If they aren't, adjust the position of the clamp heads to bring them into alignment.

When the glue in those joints is dry, finish assembling the cases by joining the right side piece of each case to its top and bottom with splined and glued joints. Again be sure the case is square when you clamp it.

Finish the corner pieces

Round over the square edges of the walnut corner pieces (see box on page 141, Step 6). Use a 3/4-inch radius round-over bit in a router or a rasp and wood file. If you choose this method, cut a piece of cardboard with an inside corner having a 3/4-inch radius to use as a template. Check the shape of the corner frequently by fitting the template all along the corner piece as you work, to create a uniform contour.

Photo 3. Use glue to fasten the splines that connect the corner pieces with the plywood case sides. Go easy with the glue, for minimum cleanup. Make sure the corner remains square as you clamp it.

Cut the backs

Turn each case back-side up (place cardboard on the floor to protect the front edges) and rout a 1/4-inch by 3/8-inch rabbet into the back edges. Use a self-piloting rabbeting bit. These rabbets are for the backs (G, H).

Cut the case backs (G, H) from 1/4-inch plywood. Radius the four corners on each back so that they fit snugly into the rabbets on the backs of the cases. You will not fasten the back in place until after the final finish has been applied to the cases.

Build the shelves and backs

Measure and cut the plywood for the pullout (E) and the adjustable shelves (F). Then glue the solid edging (X) to the fronts of the adjustable shelves; the side edging (Z) to the sides of the turntable pullout; and the edge piece (Y) to the front of the pullout shelf.

If you are going to store records in the bottom of the center case, measure and cut a record stop (BB), which will prevent records from being pushed too far to the rear. (The side cases do not need stops, because they are not as deep.) Radius the two bottom corners of the stop to fit into the inside bottom corners of the main case. Drill holes for the mounting screws that hold the record stop.

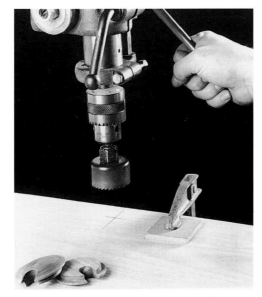

Photo 4. Drill holes for equipment cords with a hole saw. For good appearance, use walnut wire grommets to hold the cords neatly in place. Choose the hole size to match the grommets.

Using a 1-3/4 inch hole saw and a drill guide or a drill press, drill access holes for the stereo power cords in two of the adjustable shelves, the turntable pullout, and the main case back (Photo 4). You can insert walnut wire grommets (available from woodworking specialty suppliers) in these holes to help manage the equipment cords if you wish.

Assemble the drawers

The drawers are boxes constructed from 1/2-inch all-birch plywood, with solid oak finish fronts. Cut out the drawer box sides (K), and the fronts and backs (L). With a dado blade set up in a table saw or a radial arm saw, cut 1/4- x 1/2-inch deep rabbets on the front and rear edges of all the drawer sides.

Choose six of the 12 front/back pieces (L) to be the drawer fronts. Drill 3/8-inch holes in these pieces for the screws that will fasten the solid oak finish fronts to the drawers. Finish-sand the inside face of all drawer sides, fronts, and backs.

Glue and nail the drawer boxes together with 1-inch finish nails. Set the nailheads into the drawer sides and putty over the resulting nail holes. Finish-sand the outside faces of the drawer sides.

Cut the six drawer bottoms (J) from 1/4-inch plywood. Finish-sand the inside faces. Use small brads or nails to tack the drawer bottoms to the drawers. The screws used later to attach the drawer slides to the drawers will secure the drawer bottoms.

Attach the finish drawer faces

Choose solid oak stock with the best grain appearance for the finish drawer faces (AA). Measure the openings in the side cases where the fronts are to fit. Cut and sand each of the fronts to fit with 1/16-inch clearance all the way around.

In the center of each finish drawer front drill a 3/16-inch hole and countersink it from the rear for the screw that will hold the brass knob (plans, Detail 1).

Radius the upper corners of the two top drawer fronts so that they fit into the inside top corner of the cases.

Mount the drawers and pullout shelf

Study the plans, think through the procedure thoroughly, and measure carefully when mounting the drawer slides; even do a dry test of the mounting on some scrap wood. Mount the drawer slides with flathead wood screws. For accurate alignment, drill screw holes with a self-centering Vix bit, available from many woodworking and specialty hardware suppliers (Photo 5).

Fasten the sections to the drawers with No. 6 x 3/4-inch screws through the elongated holes in the slides, which allow for front-to-back adjustments. Then mount the other sections on the case sides with the flathead screws supplied with the slides.

Photo 5. Use a self-centering Vix bit to drill pilot holes for screws that hold drawer slides in place. Elongated holes in the slides allow preliminary adjustment; round holes are for final installation.

Drive the screws through the elongated holes, which allow for up–down adjustments of the case sections. The Front Assembly and Main Case details in the construction plans show basic positioning of the drawer slides; change the positions to fit your needs.

Attach the solid drawer faces to the drawers with No. 10 x 1-inch pan-head sheet metal screws and flat washers.

Now put the drawers in position and make adjustments for smooth travel and a proper fit. The elongated holes in the slides allow for overall front–back and up–down adjustments of each drawer. The 3/8-inch mounting holes in the drawer fronts allow for some minor adjustments to create an even gap between the faces and the case sides.

When all adjustments have been made, remove the drawers and drill final mounting holes in the round holes of the slides with the Vix bit. Use flathead screws to secure the drawer slides in place.

Mount the pullout shelf on drawer guides in the same way as you did the drawers.

Build the cabinet bases

Cut and plane the solid walnut pieces for the side case bases (P, Q) and the main case base (R, S). Miter the corners. Glue all the mitered corners and clamp each base together with a band clamp (also called a web or strap clamp). Make sure the base corners are square when the clamp is tight.

When the glue is dry, turn the bases upside down to countersink and drill the holes for the screws that will attach the bases to the cases (plans, Detail 2).

Drill 3/8-inch holes in the sides (S) of the center cabinet base for the joint connector bolts. Then place the bases for the side cabinets on either side of the center base, align their back edges, and mark the bolt hole locations in their center sides (Q). Drill 3/8-inch holes at the marked points.

FINISHING THE CABINET

Remove all hardware from the cases and the drawers. You'll have to take the faces off the drawers in order to remove the brass knobs. Mark the backs of the finish faces and the faces of their corresponding drawers so you can match them up again.

Finish-sand all outside surfaces and any other exposed surfaces that haven't been finish-sanded. Use a sanding block to soften all edges slightly.

Wipe all surfaces clean with a tack cloth or cloth dampened with mineral spirits. Apply three coats of Danish oil. When the final oil coat has dried sufficiently (see the product instructions for time), apply a coat of wax to create a little sheen.

Remount the slides for the drawers and the pullout shelf. Attach the brass knobs, and remount and adjust the drawer faces. Put the cabinet backs in position in their rabbets and fasten them with 1-inch headed nails. Drill tiny pilot holes for the nails.

Connect the side cases to the main case, and bases to one another, with joint connector bolts (Photo 6). Fasten the bases to the cases with No. 6 x 3-inch flathead wood screws. The backs of the bases should be set in 1/2 inch from the backs of the cases so that the mounting screws don't interfere with the rabbets for the case backs (see Side Case and Main Case details in the plans).

If you are using the lower storage space for records, mount the record stop in the center case with No. 6 x 2-inch flathead wood screws. Tap the record dividers into their holes with a rubber mallet. Put shelf pins in place and install the adjustable shelves.

Cut, fit, and install whatever racks, holders, or dividers you have chosen to use for the interiors of the drawers.

Install and connect your media components, and sit down to enjoy some well-deserved relaxation and entertainment.

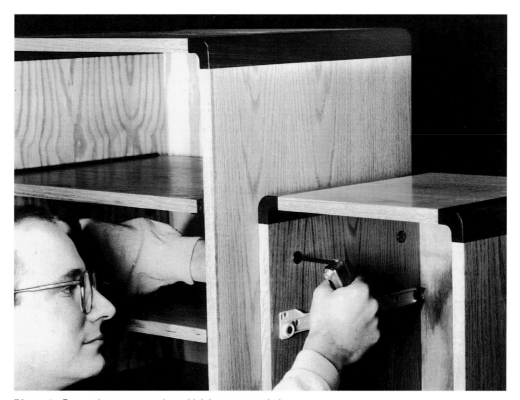

Photo 6. Fasten the cases together with joint connector bolts. Hold the bolt head with a hex key wrench and turn the cap nut with a second wrench. Join the bases in the same way.

This bench is a great project for the beginning woodworker.

It's not much more than a large hinged box made of inexpensive

lumberyard pine. The whitewash finish provides a simple, rural look

and is both easy to apply and durable.

Country Pine Bench

This is a versatile piece of furniture that can be put to good use in a child's

playroom or a bedroom, dining room, or entryway.

Beneath the hinged seat, which has a support to prop it open, is plenty of room

to store toys, bedding, linens, shoes—just about anything.

This project includes detailed instructions for cutting the curved parts of the bench.

If you've never tried transferring curved patterns to wood,

here's a project that will teach you how to do it.

Materials List

Quantity	Item
16	1x6 x 8' pine
14	No. 6 x 3" drywall screws
38	No. 6 x 1-1/4" flathead screws
1	1-1/2" x 72" brass piano hinge
1	Lid support
1 pint	White stain
1 quart	Latex urethane acrylic finish, clear, low luster

Construction Plans

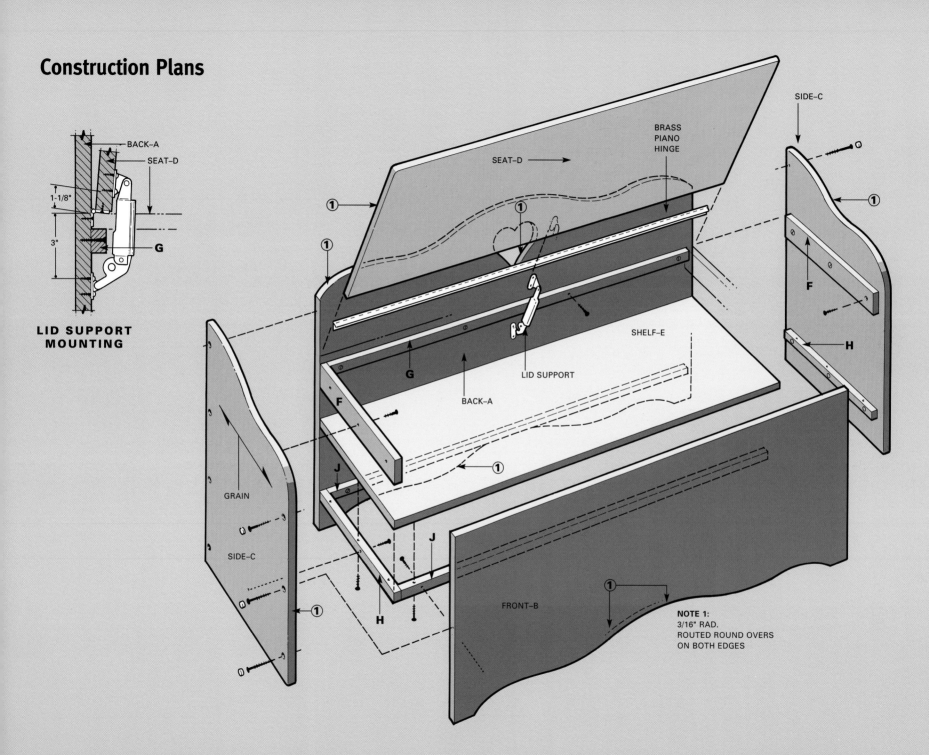

LID SUPPORT
MOUNTING

BACK–A

SEAT–D

1-1/8"

3"

G

SEAT–D →

BRASS
PIANO
HINGE

SIDE–C

F

H

SHELF–E

G

LID SUPPORT

BACK–A

F

GRAIN

SIDE–C

J

J

H

FRONT–B

NOTE 1:
3/16" RAD.
ROUTED ROUND OVERS
ON BOTH EDGES

Cutting List

Key	Pcs.	Size and Description
A	1	3/4" x 26" x 42" pine (back)
B	1	3/4" x 15-3/4" x 42" pine (front)
C	2	3/4" x 22-1/2" x 18" pine (sides)
D	1	3/4" x 17-1/2" x 41-7/8" pine (seat)
E	1	3/4" x 16" x 42" pine (shelf)
F	2	3/4" x 2" x 16" pine (seat supports)
G	1	3/4" x 1" x 40-1/2" pine (seat support)
H	2	3/4" x 3/4" x 16" pine (shelf cleats)
J	2	3/4" x 3/4" x 40-1/2" pine (shelf cleats)

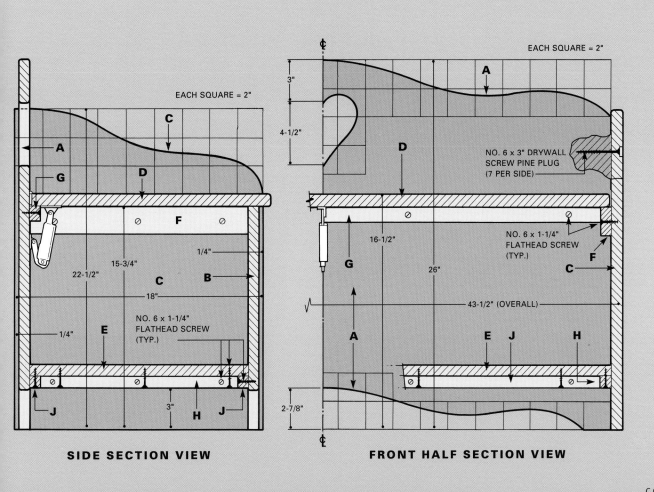

EACH SQUARE = 2"

EACH SQUARE = 2"

NO. 6 x 3" DRYWALL
SCREW PINE PLUG
(7 PER SIDE)

NO. 6 x 1-1/4"
FLATHEAD SCREW
(TYP.)

NO. 6 x 1-1/4"
FLATHEAD SCREW
(TYP.)

3"

4-1/2"

16-1/2"

26"

43-1/2" (OVERALL)

2-7/8"

22-1/2"

15-3/4"

18"

1/4"

1/4"

3"

SIDE SECTION VIEW

FRONT HALF SECTION VIEW

Construction Procedures and Techniques

Tools You Need

Circular saw

Saber saw

Pipe clamps

Tape measure

Router

Drill

Plug cutter

Sanding drum

Screwdrivers

Chisel

Hacksaw

CUTTING AND DRILLING THE PIECES

The wide components of this bench (A–E) are made by edge-gluing 1x6 boards to achieve widths that can be cut to the dimensions given in the cutting list. Choose the lumber carefully. Sight down the length of each board, along both wide faces and both narrow edges, and reject boards that are warped, crooked, or bowed. Make sure the edges of the boards do not have any splits, checks, cracks, or wanes (unsquare edges with tree bark showing).

Next, inspect the boards and mark the sections you can cut out to be glued together. Eliminate portions with large and unsound knots—that is, knots that have gaps around them or that look like they could be knocked out. You'll need eight sections 28–30 inches long for the back (A); 16 sections 25–27 inches long for the two sides (C, eight pieces each); and 24 sections 18–21 inches long for the front, seat, and shelf (B, D, E, eight pieces each). These rough lengths are a bit oversize to allow for final cutting.

Edge-glue the wide pieces

Cut out the rough lengths and assemble the pieces for each wide component. Take care to arrange the boards in each assembly so you won't have to cut through any knots on the curved edges or in the heart cutout in the back. Alternate the direction of the growth rings in the end grain of the boards when you glue them together.

Work on a flat surface. Apply the glue and align the boards so they lie perfectly flat with no raised edges. Clamp them while the glue dries (Photo 1). Alternate the clamps from one side of the assembly to the other to equalize the pressure.

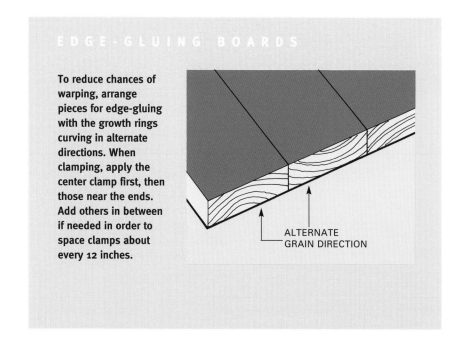

EDGE-GLUING BOARDS

To reduce chances of warping, arrange pieces for edge-gluing with the growth rings curving in alternate directions. When clamping, apply the center clamp first, then those near the ends. Add others in between if needed in order to space clamps about every 12 inches.

ALTERNATE GRAIN DIRECTION

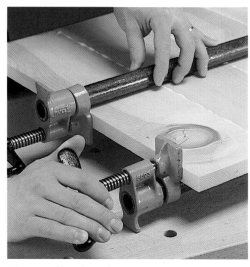

Photo 1. Use pipe or bar clamps to hold boards tightly together as the glue dries. Apply glue to both edges of each joint; alternate clamps on both sides of the glued-up assembly.

Cut the rectangular pieces

When the glue is dry, cut each large piece (A–E) to its finished dimensions.

Cut the shelf cleats and seat supports (F–J) to their finished sizes.

Draw and cut the curved shapes

Lay out and draw grids of 2-inch squares at the top and bottom of the back (A) and the top of one side (C) (Photo 2).

Transfer the curved shapes from the grids shown in the construction plans to the grids on the wood pieces as follows.

First, mark all the points with given dimensions (Photo 3)—for example, the center points of the heart cutout.

Next, transfer all the points where curved edges intersect with the grid lines (Photo 4). These points should produce a dotted outline defining the shapes.

Finally, draw in lines to connect the dots and define the curved edges. If you have trouble drawing freehand, use a French curve or a flexible drafting curve (Photo 5); both tools are available at art supply stores.

Photo 2. Draw layout grids on the bench back piece and on one side piece. Use a soft pencil and light pressure to avoid gouging the pine or leaving marks that require deep sanding to erase.

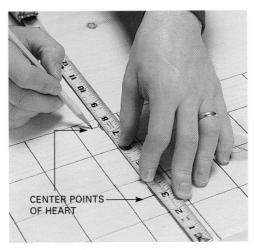

Photo 3. Transfer the shapes shown in the plan drawings to the grids on the wood. Start by marking all the points where dimensions are given, such as the center points of the heart cutout.

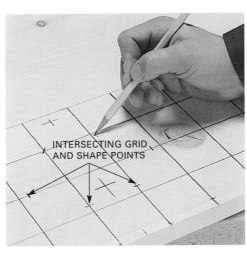

Photo 4. Mark all the points where shape curves intersect with grid lines or marked dimension points. The result will be a dotted outline pattern that delineates the curved shape.

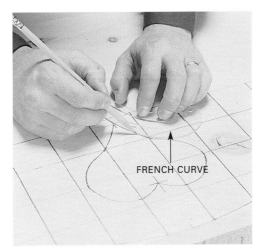

Photo 5. Connect the pattern dots to obtain a completed drawing of the shape. Drawing aids such as transparent plastic French curves or a flexible curve are helpful in making smooth lines.

Curve Layout

When laying out curved shapes, you can draw the grid and shapes directly on the wood, but that leaves you with the chore of erasing all marks. You may prefer—especially if you have never tried marking curved patterns before—to lay out the shapes on pieces of thin cardboard, cut them out, and use them as templates to trace the shapes on the wood.

Screw Holes

Even though you are working with soft pine, you need to drill pilot holes for all screws, particularly when drilling into the edge of a board. For the No. 6 screws used in this project, drill 1/16-in. diameter holes for the screw threads, and 9/64-in. diameter holes for the screw shanks.

Use a fine-tooth saw blade in a saber saw to cut out the shapes. Work slowly and cut as close as possible to the lines (Photo 6) to reduce the amount of finish sanding.

Sand the edges smooth with a sanding drum in a drill press (Photo 7) or a hand-held electric drill. Or mount a drum on the spindle of a radial arm saw motor and turn the motor so the drum is in a vertical position.

When the bottom of the back has been cut and sanded, use it as a template to mark the shape on the bottom of the front (B). Also, use the top of one side (C) as a template to mark the other sides. Cut out these shapes and sand their edges smooth.

Drill screw holes and shape edges

Lay out and drill the screw holes in the sides (C). Then drill half the depth of these holes for 3/8-inch plugs to cover the screw heads. Lay out, countersink, and drill screw holes in the shelf cleats and seat supports (F–J).

Use a 3/16-inch round-over bit in a router to shape all the edges of the sides (C); the top, bottom, and inside edges of the heart on the back (A); the bottom edges of the front (B); and the side and front edges of the seat (D).

Finish-sand all the bench pieces, eliminating any rough or sharp edges.

ASSEMBLING THE BENCH

Attach the side cleats

Align and screw the side seat supports and shelf cleats (F, H) to the sides. Center both pieces on the sides, with a 1-inch space at each end (see section views in the construction plans). Drive screws through the supports and cleats into the sides.

Construct the basic box

Butt the ends of the front (B) and back (A) against the sides (C) and flush against the ends of the seat supports and shelf cleats. Then drive screws through the sides into the edges of the front and the back (Photo 8).

Screw the two remaining shelf cleats (J) to the front and back. Place the shelf (E) inside the bench and secure it to the shelf cleats. Drill holes from underneath the cleats and drive screws up into the shelf.

Screw the back seat support (G) into position on the back. There is no seat support on the front of the chest.

CLEARANCE HOLE FOR SAW BLADE

Photo 6. A saber saw with a fine-tooth blade is best for cutting the curves. Drill a hole in the heart cutout to start the cut. Keep the blade as close to the lines as possible to save work later.

HOLE FOR SANDING DRUM

AUXILIARY TABLE

Photo 7. For easy edge sanding, use a sanding drum in a drill press. A table with a large hole lets you use the full length of the drum. You can also use a portable drill and drum, or a hand sander.

Fill the screw holes

Use a 3/8-inch plug cutter to cut 14 pine plugs to cover the screws in the sides.

Glue and lightly hammer the plugs into their holes. When the glue is dry, use a sharp chisel or a backsaw to carefully trim the protruding tops of the plugs flush with the sides. Sand the surface until it is flat.

Mount the seat

Use a hacksaw to cut the piano hinge 41-7/8 inches long. Screw it to the back edge of the seat. Set the bench on its back, then attach the piano hinge and seat to the back.

Install the lid support. It is listed in some woodworking hardware catalogs as a toy box lid support; in other catalogs it is called an internal spring counterbalance support or a back-mounted counterbalance support.

Orient and attach the support as shown in the detail in the construction plans, not according to the instructions that come with it. However, the dimensions given in the manufacturer's instructions are correct.

FINISHING THE BENCH

Unscrew the lid support, piano hinge, seat supports, shelf, and shelf cleats. Wipe all surfaces clean with a tack cloth or a cloth dampened with mineral spirits. Apply stain to all exposed surfaces. Rather than the white stain shown, you can use a darker color. If you choose to do that, first apply a stain controller (or similar product—ask your supplier) to avoid uneven, blotchy results. If you prefer the natural wood color, simply apply a clear sealer.

When the stain or sealer is dry, brush on three coats of a clear latex urethane finish. Allow each coat to dry completely before applying the next, and then sand lightly between the coats.

When you have completed the finishing, reassemble the bench.

Photo 8. All the parts are fastened with screws. Use 3-in. drywall screws to attach the sides to the front and back. Drill pilot holes for clean, split-free results.

This bookcase is quick and simple to build. The pieces are screwed

together, with lumberyard moldings covering the screwheads.

There are no dado joints, no dowels, and no fuss.

Traditional Bookcase

The bookcase shown is made from solid oak and oak plywood,

but you can substitute birch and birch plywood if you want to paint the finished

bookcase. You might consider using pine for a more countrified or colonial look.

You can adjust the height of the bookcase to include more shelves,

or increase its depth. The construction method will be the same, regardless of size.

However, don't make it wider or the shelves will sag.

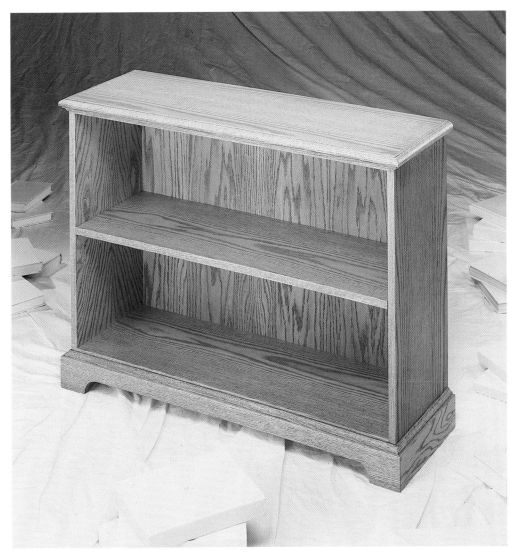

Materials List

Quantity	Item
1 sheet	4' x 8' x 3/4" oak plywood
1 piece	4' x 4' x 1/4" oak plywood
5 board ft.	4/4 oak lumber
12 ft.	1/2" x 1/2" oak cove molding
12	No. 6 x 2" drywall screws
20	No. 6 x 1-1/4" drywall screws
40	1" brads
4	1/4" brass shelf pins

Construction Plans

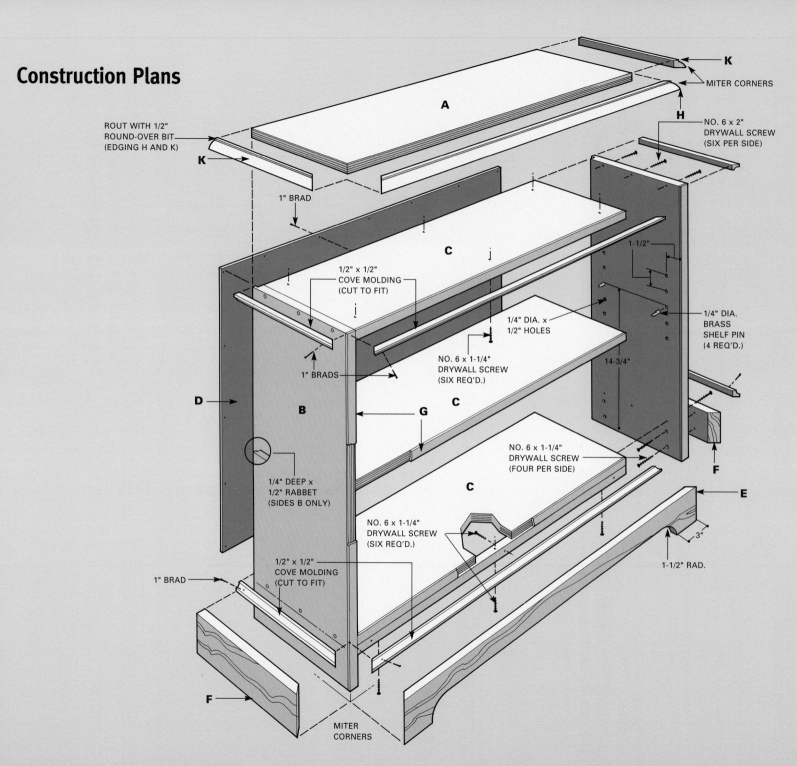

ROUT WITH 1/2"
ROUND-OVER BIT
(EDGING H AND K)

K

A

K

MITER CORNERS

H

NO. 6 x 2"
DRYWALL SCREW
(SIX PER SIDE)

1" BRAD

C

1-1/2"

1/2" x 1/2"
COVE MOLDING
(CUT TO FIT)

C

1/4" DIA. x
1/2" HOLES

1/4" DIA.
BRASS
SHELF PIN
(4 REQ'D.)

1" BRADS

NO. 6 x 1-1/4"
DRYWALL SCREW
(SIX REQ'D.)

D

B

G

C

14-3/4"

1/4" DEEP x
1/2" RABBET
(SIDES B ONLY)

NO. 6 x 1-1/4"
DRYWALL SCREW
(FOUR PER SIDE)

F

C

E

NO. 6 x 1-1/4"
DRYWALL SCREW
(SIX REQ'D.)

3"

1/2" x 1/2"
COVE MOLDING
(CUT TO FIT)

1-1/2" RAD.

1" BRAD

F

MITER
CORNERS

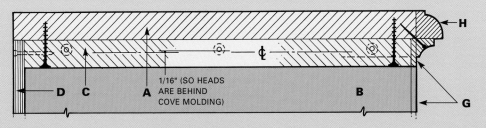

SECTION VIEW AT TOP

1/16" (SO HEADS ARE BEHIND COVE MOLDING)

D C A B G H

Cutting List

Key	Pcs.	Size and Description
A	1	3/4" x 11-1/2" x 36" oak plywood (finish top)
B	2	3/4" x 11-3/8" x 27-1/4" oak plywood (sides)
C	3	3/4" x 11-1/8" x 34-1/2" oak plywood (case top, bottom, shelf)
D	1	1/4" x 35-1/2" x 24-1/4" oak plywood (back)
E	1	3/4" x 3" x 37-1/2" oak (base front)
F	2	3/4" x 3" x 12-1/4" oak (base sides)
G	1	3/4" x 2" x 34-1/2" oak (edging strips)
H	1	3/4" x 3/4" x 37-1/2" oak (top front edging)
J	1	3/4" x 3/4" x 34-1/2" oak (base cleat)
K	2	3/4" x 3/4" x 12-1/4" oak (top side edging)

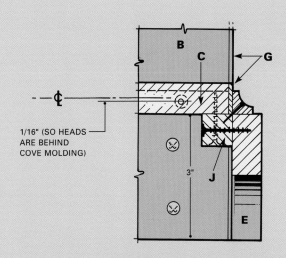

1/16" (SO HEADS ARE BEHIND COVE MOLDING)

B C G J E 3"

SECTION VIEW AT BASE

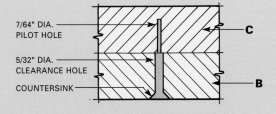

7/64" DIA. PILOT HOLE

5/32" DIA. CLEARANCE HOLE

COUNTERSINK

C B

SCREW HOLE DETAIL

Construction Procedures and Techniques

CUTTING THE PIECES

If you choose to build the bookcase from solid wood, edge-glue narrow boards to obtain wide pieces for cutting the top, side, and bottom components (see box, page 150, for edge-gluing information). Use a piece of plywood for the back as shown, because it gives the bookcase much of its strength.

Cut the sides, shelves, and supports

Begin by cutting 3/4-inch plywood pieces A, B, and C to the sizes given in the cutting list. The case top, shelves, and bottom (all C) are cut 1/4 inch narrower than the sides because the sides (B) will have a rabbet cut in the rear edges for the plywood back of the bookcase. The finish top (A) is 1/8 inch wider than the sides so it can cover the top edge of the back and the edging on the front of the case top.

Cut the pieces on a table saw or radial arm saw with the good side of the plywood facing up. If you use a portable circular saw, face the good side down. Use a carbide saw blade with 60 to 100 teeth. If you do not have such a blade, score the cutting line deeply with a sharp utility knife before sawing.

Cut the solid wood pieces E, F, G, H, J, and K a few inches longer than the cutting list dimensions, so they can be trimmed to exact size later during assembly.

Cut and glue the edging

Rip the edging (G) into 1/8-inch strips for gluing to the front edge of plywood pieces B and C. Your saw blade will be close to the fence, so use a push stick to guide the wood.

Glue the strips to the front edges of B and C (Photo 1), using carpenter's glue. After the glue is dry, cut or sand the strips flush with the surface of the plywood. Trim the ends with a small handsaw.

Tools You Need

Table saw or radial arm saw

Pipe clamps

Router with 1/2" round-over bit

Drill with countersink and brad-point bits

Hammer

Handsaw

Nail set

Miter box

Backsaw

Block plane

Sander

Photo 1. Fasten edging strips to the plywood with easy-remove masking tape for gluing. It's easier to manage than clamps, and strong enough to hold these thin strips in place.

Miter the moldings

Cut mitered ends on the 3/4-inch edging (H, K) for the top (A). Use a miter box. Cut the front piece (H) first, so the inside edges of the miters are exactly flush with the corners of the plywood, then cut the sides slightly long in back; trim them after the glue is dry. Clamp the edging on to test-fit the seams with the top and the mitered joints. Sand or plane to eliminate any gaps if necessary, then apply glue and clamp the edging in place (Photo 2). Sand the edging flush with the top when the glue is dry.

Cut the profile on the top edge with a router, using a piloted 1/2-inch round-over bit (see Section View at Top in the plans).

Photo 2. Miter the thick edging for the top at the corners. Clamp it when gluing. Do the front piece first, then the sides, which are cut long and trimmed later.

Drill screw holes

Mark the location of the screw holes in the case sides, top, and cleats. Drill the countersinks first, then the clearance holes (see Screw Hole Detail in the plans). Or use a combination countersink bit to drill both holes at the same time. You will drill the pilot holes in the pieces that the screws enter when you assemble the bookcase.

Note that these holes in the sides are off-center so the cove molding will completely cover them. The top screw holes are 1/16 inch above the center of the top thickness; the bottom holes are 1/16 inch below the center of the bottom thickness (see section views in the plans).

Drill the shelf pin holes in the inside surfaces of the sides. Be very precise in marking their positions, because all four holes at each level must be exactly aligned or a shelf placed there will wobble. Clamp the pieces side by side so they can't shift during marking. You can use a piece of perforated hardboard as a template for uniform hole spacing.

Work carefully and precisely in drilling matching holes for the shelf pins. Use an awl to prick the surface where you want the drill bit to start. Then use a brad-point drill bit, which won't wander off the mark.

Rabbet the back

Cut the rabbets on the back edges of the sides with a table saw or radial arm saw. The rabbets are 1/2 inch wide and 1/4 inch deep. Make the depth cut into the edge of the piece first (Photo 3), leaving 1/4-inch thickness to the outside. Then turn the piece flat and make the cut from the inside surface to create the rabbet for the back.

Photo 3. Cut rabbets in the sides to house the back. Cut them in two passes. Use a push stick, not your fingers, to guide the wood when making the actual cuts.

Cutting Tips

Trim the solid wood edging with a block plane or belt sander, but be careful not to cut or sand through the thin oak veneer of the plywood. If you've never done this before, experiment on some scrap plywood first.

Do not cut the curved cutout in the base front (E) until you have cut the miters on the end of the piece. This ensures that you will get the cutout centered in the piece.

ASSEMBLING THE BOOKCASE

Finish-sand all the pieces already cut. It would be difficult to sand inside corners cleanly after the bookcase is assembled.

Screw the frame together

Clamp pieces together temporarily to drill pilot holes for all screws. Be sure the pieces are square to one another before drilling. Screw the sides (B), bottom (C), and case top (C) together. Fasten the base cleat (J) and screw the finish top (A) to the case.

Cut and assemble the base

Hold the base front piece (E) against the front of the bookcase and mark the position of the end miters on its top edge. Cut miters on the top edge first (Photo 4), and then cut the miters on the base sides (F).

Test-fit the base pieces (E and F) and trim as necessary. When they fit well, cut the curved opening at the bottom of E. Give the pieces a final sanding. Attach them to the case by driving screws through the sides and base cleat and into their backs (see Section View at Base in the plans). Use carpenter's glue on the miter joints and other inside surfaces. Trim the ends of the side pieces with a handsaw.

Miter and attach the cove moldings

Mark the cove molding and cut the miter joints. Fit the pieces as you did on the finish top edging and base: front first, then sides. Drill pilot holes for the nails in both the molding and the bookcase. Glue and nail the molding in place (Photo 5). Sink the nail-heads slightly with a nail set, and when the glue is dry, trim the ends of the molding. Finally, sand the moldings.

Cut the back

Cut the back (D) to size from 1/4-inch oak plywood. Sand the face and edges, but don't fasten the back in place until you have done the finishing work.

BLADE SET AT 45°.
(BLADE GUARD REMOVED FOR CLARITY ONLY— USE YOURS)

Photo 4. Cut miters on the solid oak pieces that form the base of the bookcase by angling the saw blade. Make sure the blade guard is in place when you make your cuts.

SCREW HEAD

COVE MOLDING

Photo 5. Cove molding hides the screws that hold the bookcase together. Nail on the molding after drilling pilot holes in both the molding and the case.

FINISHING THE BOOKCASE

Lightly sand all sharp edges on the bookcase. Wipe everything clean with a tack cloth or a cloth dampened with mineral spirits. Then apply the finish of your choice.

It's a good idea to test any finish on scrap pieces of the plywood, edging, and molding to make sure they will look the same. If the plywood stains differently than the solid wood, you may want to use different stains on various parts to obtain a closer match. Experiment carefully with scrap pieces—a little bit of stain can produce a pronounced and noticeable effect.

When the finish is dry, attach the back. Drive nails into the rabbets in the sides and into the back edge of the case bottom. Finally, fill the nail holes in the cove molding with colored putty.

Assembling and Finishing Tip

Sand and finish as many pieces as you can before assembling the case. That eliminates having to sand inside corners, which are very difficult to do well. Be careful; glue won't stick to a finished surface, so all gluing must be done first, and all of the glue that oozes out carefully scraped and sanded away.

Bedroom

Futon Sofa Bed

A flick of the wrist turns a good-looking futon sofa into a comfortable bed. The special hinges that do the trick are easy to install.

164

Pine Dry Sink

Use it as a sideboard, a bar, or a hall table. This handsome piece is versatile and practical—and easy to build.

172

Cherry Wardrobe

Scaled for modern rooms, this charming wardrobe has traditional Scandinavian styling, right down to its rounded "bun" feet.

180

This futon sofa and bed is a far cry from the heavy, overstuffed piece

of furniture many people associate with the term "sofa bed."

Futon Sofa Bed

The spare design and clean lines of this versatile piece of furniture make

it both attractive and easy to use. It's also easy to make.

The key is a pair of special hinges—they eliminate the usual moving parts.

To operate the bed, you simply pull the seat forward and up, lowering the back.

Then you push down on the seat, which unlocks the hinges and allows you to lower

the seat into the open-bed position.

The whole process takes about five seconds. The futon sofa bed shown

on these pages is made from red oak and finished with a

golden oak stain, followed by Danish oil.

Materials List

Quantity	Size and Description
40 board ft.	6/4 oak
7 board ft.	4/4 oak
1 sheet	4' x 8' x 1/2" oak plywood
24	3/8" diameter x 2-1/2" dowel pins
56	3/8" diameter x 1-1/2" dowel pins
8	2-3/4" Confirmat screws
8	3" drywall screws
18	2-1/2" drywall screws
2	1-5/8" drywall screws
80	1" drywall screws
1 pair	Futon sofa bed hinges
1 quart	Stain
1 quart	Danish oil finish
1	3/8" diameter plug center
1	Futon mattress
1	24" x 60" piece of rubber antislip padding
1	Futon mattress slipcover

Note: Futon sofa bed hinges are available from The Woodworkers' Store, 21801 Industrial Blvd., Rogers, MN, 55376. Futon mattresses, antislip padding, and slipcovers are available from futon stores around the country.

Construction Plans

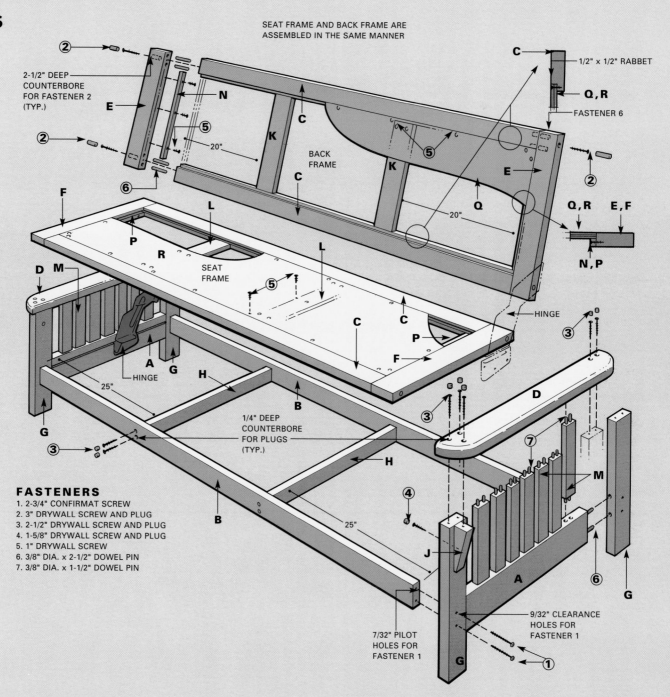

SEAT FRAME AND BACK FRAME ARE
ASSEMBLED IN THE SAME MANNER

1/2" x 1/2" RABBET

Q, R

FASTENER 6

2-1/2" DEEP
COUNTERBORE
FOR FASTENER 2
(TYP.)

E

N

C

C

K

K

E

BACK
FRAME

Q

Q, R

E, F

N, P

20"

20"

F

L

L

SEAT
FRAME

P

R

P

C

C

C

F

HINGE

D

M

HINGE

A

G

H

B

25"

G

B

1/4" DEEP
COUNTERBORE
FOR PLUGS
(TYP.)

H

D

M

J

A

G

G

25"

FASTENERS

1. 2-3/4" CONFIRMAT SCREW
2. 3" DRYWALL SCREW AND PLUG
3. 2-1/2" DRYWALL SCREW AND PLUG
4. 1-5/8" DRYWALL SCREW AND PLUG
5. 1" DRYWALL SCREW
6. 3/8" DIA. x 2-1/2" DOWEL PIN
7. 3/8" DIA. x 1-1/2" DOWEL PIN

7/32" PILOT
HOLES FOR
FASTENER 1

9/32" CLEARANCE
HOLES FOR
FASTENER 1

Cutting List

Key	Pcs.	Size and Description
A	2	1-1/4" x 5" x 25" oak (end rails)
B	2	1-1/4" x 3-1/2" x 77" oak (seat and back rails)
C	4	1-1/4" x 3-1/2" x 68" oak (seat and back frame rails)
D	2	1-1/4" x 3-1/2" x 33" oak (arms)
E	2	1-1/4" x 3-1/2" x 26" oak (back frame stiles)
F	2	1-1/4" x 3-1/2" x 23" oak (seat frame stiles)
G	4	1-1/4" x 3" x 21-3/4" oak (legs)
H	2	1-1/4" x 2-5/8" x 26-3/4" oak (seat supports)
J	2	1-1/4" x 1-5/8" x 6" oak (arm supports)
K	2	3/4" x 3-1/2" x 19" oak (back frame stiffeners)
L	2	3/4" x 3-1/2" x 16" oak (seat frame stiffeners)
M	14	4-3/4" x 2-1/8" x 11-3/8" oak (slats)
N	2	1/2" x 3/4" x 19" oak (cleats)
P	2	1/2" x 3/4" x 16" oak (cleats)
Q	1	1/2" x 20" x 68" oak plywood (back frame panel)
R	1	1/2" x 17" x 68" oak plywood (seat frame panel)

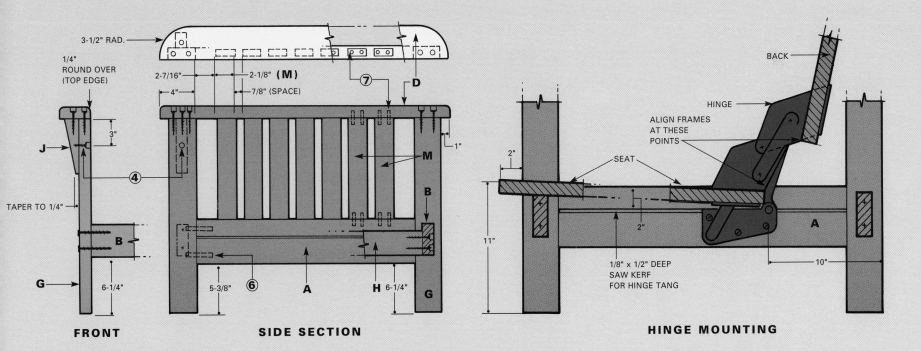

FRONT

SIDE SECTION

HINGE MOUNTING

Construction Procedures and Techniques

Tools You Need

Table saw

Drill

Drill press (optional)

Dowel jig

Router and 1/4"
round-over bit

Saber saw

Orbital sander

5/32" hex key
wrench

3/8" diameter plug
cutter

3' pipe or bar
clamps

18" bar clamps

Planer (optional)

Screwdriver

Mini-hacksaw

Mallet

CUTTING AND DRILLING THE PIECES

Before cutting any pieces to width or length, plane the oak to the thicknesses called for in the cutting list. Use 6/4 stock for parts A through J, and 4/4 stock for the other solid oak parts. If you don't own a planer, have a lumberyard do the work for you.

Shape the arm supports

The easiest way to make the wedge-shaped arm supports (J) is to lay them out in pairs on a piece of wood. Start with a piece of oak 1-1/4 inches thick, 1-5/8 inches wide, and 14 inches long. Starting at one corner, draw a diagonal line to mark a wedge that tapers from the full 1-5/8 inches to 1/4 inch at a length of 6 inches, measured along the straight sides of the piece. Continue the diagonal line to the side edge of the board. At that point, mark a cutting line across the face of the board, at right angles to the side. This lays out two pieces with their slanted faces together. Mark a second pair at the other end in the same way.

Cut out the arm supports with a saber saw. First cut along the diagonal lines, then cut across the lines that marked the wide ends in the center of the board. Finally, cut off the points so the wedges are 6 inches long.

Cut the remaining pieces

Cut the other pieces, A–H and K–R, from the appropriate solid oak or plywood stock. The dimensions of the pieces are given in the cutting list with the construction plans.

Use a table saw to cut full-length grooves 1/2-inch deep in the inside faces of the end rails (part A; Photo 1). These grooves receive the tangs of the futon sofa bed hinges (see Hinge Mounting detail in the plans).

Cut 1/2- x 1/2-inch rabbets on the inside edges of the rails (C) for the seat and back frames. The seat and back frame panels will fit into these rabbets.

Lay out the rounded corners on the arms (D) and cut them with a saber saw (see Side Section detail in the plans). You will round over the top edges later, after you have built the arm assemblies.

Consult the plans carefully to lay out the screw holes and dowel holes—there are some 44 parts to be marked. The dowel holes are 3/8 inch in diameter. Use a dowel jig to ensure that the holes are perpendicular to the surface (Photo 2), so joints will be square when you fasten two pieces together. Counterbore all screw holes; the plans show what depths the counterbores should be.

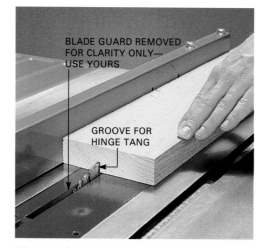

Photo 1. Cut 1/2-in. deep grooves in the end rails for the tangs of the futon sofa bed hinges. Be sure to use the table saw blade guard when making the cuts.

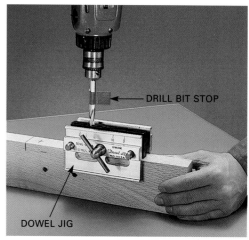

Photo 2. Drill holes for dowels with a dowel jig to guide the bit for perpendicular, centered holes. That will help ensure tight, square joints between pieces.

Sand the pieces

Sand all faces and edges of the cut wood with 120-grit sandpaper and finish off with 180-grit paper. Be careful not to round any edges that butt against another piece of wood; otherwise you will have a visible groove at the joint line. Sand the undersides as well as the top faces of the arms, and all four sides of all the slats (M). Smooth the exposed sharp edges of the slats with 180-grit sandpaper.

ASSEMBLING THE FUTON BED

The major components of this bed are assembled with glue, dowels, and screws.

However, the end assemblies are attached to the front and back rails of the frame with Confirmat screws. These screws have a unique thread design that lets you remove and insert them repeatedly without reducing their holding power or damaging the holes. This makes it easy to disassemble the bed for moving or storage. They are driven with a 5/32-inch hex key wrench.

Glue and clamp the legs

Glue, dowel, and clamp the legs (G) to the end rails (A). Make sure that joints remain square as you tighten the clamps. When the glue is dry, use an orbital sander with 120- and then 180-grit sandpaper to finish-sand the assembled legs and end rails. Then glue, dowel, and clamp the slats individually to the end rails (Photo 3).

Build the arm assemblies

Drill the pilot holes for the screws that hold the arms to the legs. Then glue and insert the dowels into the holes in the undersides of the arms. Also spread glue in the dowel holes in the tops of the slats and on the tops of the legs. Assemble the pieces by inserting the dowels into the holes in the slats. Be patient and work carefully to align the dowels in their holes. Then drive screws through the arms into the tops of the legs.

Glue and screw the arm supports (J) in place (see Front detail in the plans). Round over the top edges of the arms with a router and a 1/4-inch ball-bearing piloted round-over bit.

Assemble the back and seat frames

Glue, dowel, and screw the back and seat frame stiles (E and F) to the back and seat frame rails (C). Then glue and screw the cleats (N and P) in place.

Screw, don't glue, the back panel (Q) and seat panel (R) to their frames. Then screw, don't glue, the back and seat frame stiffeners (K and L) into place.

Assemble the base frame by fastening the seat supports (H) between the seat and back rails (B). Use both glue and screws.

Mount the hinges

The sofa bed hinges are a specialty item (see note with the Materials List, page 165). Mark the right and left hinges and identify which plates attach to the back frame and which attach to the seat frame.

Align and screw the hinges to the bottom edge of the back frame to establish the hole positions (see Hinge Mounting detail in the plans), then remove the hinges. Similarly, screw the hinges to the back edge of the seat frame and then remove them. Finally, screw the hinges to the end rails (A) and leave them in place (Photo 4).

Assembly Tip

When assembling parts with glued and doweled joints, tap the pieces together with a rubber mallet, or a wooden mallet and a smooth scrap of wood to protect the surface of the sofa bed component. When the joint fits tightly, clamp the pieces together until the glue dries. Use pads on the clamp faces to protect the workpieces.

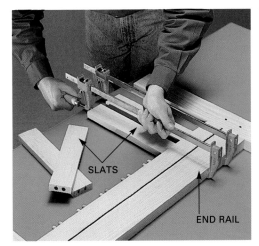

Photo 3. Fasten the slats to the end rails with glued and doweled joints. Use one clamp for each slat. When the glue has dried, glue and dowel the arms to the tops of the slats.

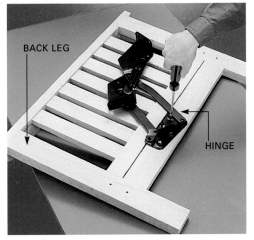

Photo 4. Fit the tangs of the futon sofa bed hinges into their grooves and screw the plates to the end rails. Use tape to label the right and left hinges, and the back and seat plates.

Locating Pilot Holes

Drill pilot holes for all screws to avoid splitting when driving screws into the narrow edges of hardwood such as oak. The easiest way to locate the pilot holes is to assemble pieces without glue, put nails in the holes already drilled in the pieces, and tap the nail heads lightly with a hammer. This will mark the precise locations of the pilot holes. Drill the pilot holes 1/16 in. smaller than the diameter of the screws you will use.

Plug the screw holes

Using a 3/8-inch plug cutter, cut out oak plugs to fill all the counterbored screw holes. Spread glue in the holes, and then tap in the plugs with a mallet.

Use a mini-hacksaw or a belt sander to trim off the tops of the screw plugs (Photo 5).

Final assembly

Drill 7/32-inch pilot holes for the Confirmat screws in the ends of the seat and back rails (B). Join the end assemblies and rails with two Confirmat screws in each rail end (Photo 6). Use a hex key wrench (Photo 7). Drive each screw up to the last 1/4 inch, then alternate among the four screws at one end for the final tightening. Tighten the screws at the other end alternately, too.

Place the seat frame in place and align the mounting holes with the screw holes made during the previous assembly. Drive screws to fasten the parts again. You'll have to work from underneath to reach most of the screws, and through the slats for the rest.

Have a helper or two hold the back frame while you clamp it to the hinge plates with the mounting holes aligned (Photo 8). Then drive the screws.

Check the operation: Pull the seat forward and up (Photo 9). The hinges are locked at this point, and the back goes down as you lift the seat. When the back is all the way down, push the seat up a bit more. This unlocks the hinges and allows you to lower the seat. Reverse the sequence to fold up the bed into a sofa. Make any necessary adjustments (see the instructions supplied with the hinges) to get everything working smoothly, then disassemble the parts.

FINISHING THE FUTON BED

Finish-sand all remaining unsanded surfaces, and smooth any exposed sharp edges with 180-grit sandpaper. Wipe everything clean with a tack cloth or a cloth dampened with mineral spirits.

Apply your choice of stain, let it dry, then apply three coats of Danish oil.

Reassemble the parts. Check that the oil finish is completely dry, then put the futon in place. For suppliers of futon mattresses and slipcovers look under "Futons" in the Yellow Pages. Cut a piece of antislip pad to fit on the seat, to keep the futon mattress from sliding forward when someone sits on it. Antislip pad is thin rubber or rubberized sheeting; it is available from carpet stores.

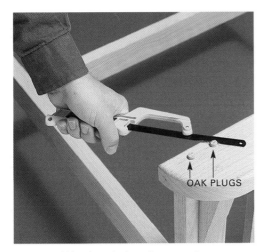

Photo 5. Trim the oak plugs that cover the screw holes in the tops of the arms with a mini-hacksaw or a belt sander. Sand them flush with the arm. Finish all other plugs the same way.

Photo 6. Use a 5/32-in. hex key wrench to drive the Confirmat screws that fasten the end assemblies to the frame rails. Rub wax, not soap, on the threads to help them go in easier.

Photo 7. Attach both arm assemblies tightly enough so the frame will stand. Then do the final tightening by alternating among the four screws at each end, to keep the joints square.

Photo 8. Clamp both ends of the back frame to the hinge plates so you can drill holes and drive screws. A helper makes it much easier to get the back in position.

Photo 9. Opening or closing the futon sofa bed takes seconds. When you check operation during final assembly, you don't need the mattress in place.

This dry sink is a modern reproduction of those used in bedrooms to hold

a washbasin and pitcher before the days of indoor plumbing.

Pine Dry Sink

Today, this piece can lend an old-fashioned feeling to any room and be immensely

practical at the same time.

There's plenty of storage behind its paneled doors, and the small shelf

and splashboard rim around the top are great for plants or for keeping the

mail from spilling onto the floor.

With an appropriate finish on the top, the sink can be a bar or a serving sideboard.

The sink is made from ordinary pine lumber and constructed with square-cut

nails to give it a more old-fashioned look.

It's a fine project for a beginning or intermediate woodworker.

Materials List

Quantity	Size and Description
4	1x4 x 10' pine
6	1x8 x 10' pine
1/4 sheet	3/4" A-B plywood (2' x 4')
1/2 sheet	1/4" plywood (4' x 4')
14 ft.	1/8" x 3/4" screen door molding
30	3/8" x 2" wood dowels
1 lb.	2" square-cut nails
15	2d (1") nails
28	5/8" wire brads
1 pint	Wood stain controller
1 pint	Stain
4	Plastic shelf supports
2 pair	Colonial "H" hinges
2	Porcelain knobs
2	Bullet catches

Construction Plans

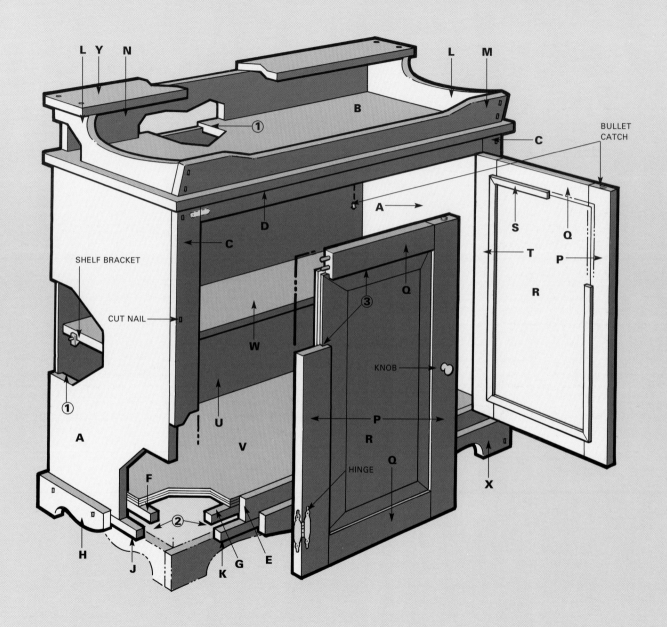

SHELF BRACKET

CUT NAIL

BULLET CATCH

KNOB

HINGE

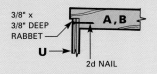

3/8" x 3/8" DEEP RABBET

A,B

U

2d NAIL

DETAIL 1

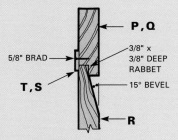

P,Q

5/8" BRAD

3/8" x 3/8" DEEP RABBET

T,S

15° BEVEL

R

DETAIL 3

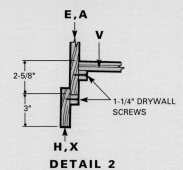

E,A

V

2-5/8"

3"

1-1/4" DRYWALL SCREWS

H,X

DETAIL 2

2"

4-1/2"

1"

15° BEVEL

DETAIL 4

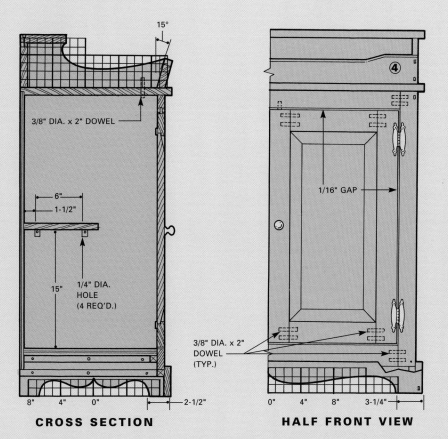

15°

3/8" DIA. x 2" DOWEL

6"

1-1/2"

15"

1/4" DIA. HOLE (4 REQ'D.)

8"   4"   0"

2-1/2"

CROSS SECTION

④

1/16" GAP

3/8" DIA. x 2" DOWEL (TYP.)

0"   4"   8"   3-1/4"

HALF FRONT VIEW

Cutting List

Key	Pcs.	Size and Description
A	2	3/4" x 16-3/4" x 33" pine (sides)
B	1	3/4" x 18-1/2" x 37-3/4" pine (top)
C	2	3/4" x 2-1/8" x 33" pine (frame stiles)
D	1	3/4" x 2-1/8" x 32" pine (top frame rail)
E	1	3/4" x 2-5/8" x 32" pine (bottom frame rail)
F	2	3/4" x 3/4" x 16-3/8" pine (side bottom shelf cleats)
G	1	3/4" x 3/4" x 33-1/4" pine (front bottom shelf cleat)
H	2	3/4" x 3-1/2" x 17-1/2" pine (base sides)
J	2	3/4" x 3/4" x 17-1/2" pine (side base cleats)
K	1	3/4" x 3/4" x 36-1/4" pine (front base cleat)
L	2	3/4" x 5-1/2" x 17-3/4" pine (splashboard sides)
M	1	3/4" x 3-1/2" x 36-1/4" pine (splashboard front)
N	1	3/4" x 5-1/2" x 34-3/4" pine (splashboard back)
P	4	3/4" x 2-5/8" x 28-1/8" pine (door stiles)
Q	4	3/4" x 2-5/8" x 10-5/8" pine (door rails)
R	2	3/4" x 11-1/2" x 23-5/8" pine (door panels)
S	4	1/8" x 3/4" x 12-1/4" screen door molding (door cleats)
T	4	1/8" x 3/4" x 24-3/8" screen door molding (door cleats)
U	1	1/4" x 33-3/8" x 35-1/2" plywood (back)
V	1	3/4" x 16-3/8" x 34-3/4" plywood (bottom shelf)
W	1	3/4" x 9" x 34-3/4" pine (half-shelf)
X	1	3/4" x 3-1/2" x 37-3/4" pine (base front)
Y	1	3/4" x 5-1/2" x 37-3/4" pine (splashboard shelf)

Construction Procedures and Techniques

Tools You Need

Table saw

Planer

Belt sander

Router with 3/8"
   rabbeting bit

Carpenter's square

Drill

Drum sander

Wood file

Dowel jig

Dowel centers

Hammer

Nail set

Chisel

Saber saw

Band saw (optional)

CUTTING THE PIECES

Lay out the lengths for the various parts that can be cut from each size of the pine boards. You will glue some pieces together to get boards of greater width. Mark out parts A, B, L, N, R, and Y on 1x8's. Mark out parts C through K, M, and Q on 1x4's. The remaining parts (S, T, U, V) will be cut from molding or plywood, as indicated in the cutting list with the construction plans.

Cut and glue the sides and top

Begin by cutting the material for the sides (A) and top (B) from 1x8 pine boards. Cut the boards an extra 1 inch long and plane or joint the edges for gluing up. Position the boards to achieve a pleasant grain pattern. Be sure to alternate the direction of the growth rings in the end grain of the boards to avoid warping. Glue them with carpenter's glue and clamp them firmly (Photo 1).

When the glue is dry, scrape off any glue and sand the panels smooth with a belt sander. Then cut the sides and top to the dimensions given in the cutting list.

Use a router and a 3/8-inch rabbeting bit to cut a 3/8-inch deep rabbet in each of the back edges of the sides (Detail 1 in the plans).

Cut the parts of the face frame

Cut the pieces of the face frame (C, D, E)— the wood frame that surrounds the doors— from 1x4 pine. Drill dowel holes for joining the horizontal and vertical pieces of the frame (Half Front View detail in the plans). Use a dowel jig to ensure that the holes are perpendicular to the edges of the frame pieces (Photo 2). Then glue and dowel the parts of the face frame together. Make sure the pieces stay flat as you clamp them to-gether, and use a framing square to see that the corners are square (Photo 3).

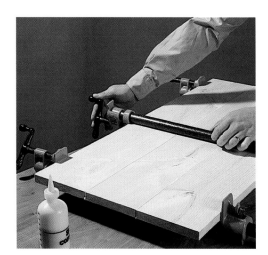

Photo 1. Edge-glue 1x8 boards together to get wide panels for the sink sides and top. Put clamps on both sides to keep the glued-up panel flat.

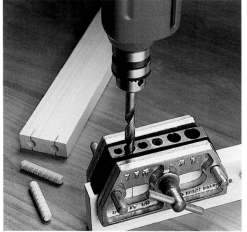

Photo 2. Use a dowel jig to bore holes for joining the face frame and door frames. Use grooved dowels to minimize glue squeeze-out.

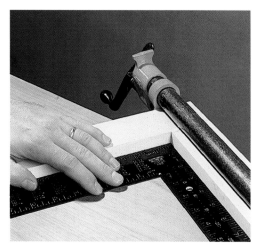

Photo 3. Glue and clamp the face frame together. Use a carpenter's square to ensure that the corner joints remain square as you tighten the clamps.

Cut the shelves and back

Glue together two pieces of 1x8 for the shelf (W), then cut it to size. Cut the bottom shelf (V) from a quarter-sheet of 3/4-inch plywood.

Cut the back (U) to the appropriate size from a half-sheet of 1/4-inch plywood.

Cut the base pieces

Cut the base sides (H) to length and width, then cut the base front (X) 1/8 inch long. This extra length gives you a bit of room to work with when constructing the base and mounting the cabinet atop it. The extra wood will be sanded off later.

Draw a 1-inch grid on the back of the pieces, and then transfer the pattern shown in the plans to the base pieces (see Cross Section and Half Front View details in the plans). Cut out the curves with either a saber saw or band saw, and sand them smooth with a drum sander (Photo 4).

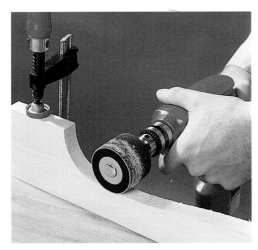

Photo 4. Sand the curved cuts in the base pieces using a sanding drum in an electric drill. Use a wood file for the tight spots in the curve centers.

Cut the splashboard pieces

Cut the splashboard parts (L, M, and Y) to the sizes given in the cutting list, using 1x8 pine boards. Cut the remaining splashboard part (M) from a 1x4 board.

The front of the splashboard rim leans outward at an angle. To achieve this, bevel the bottom edge of the front (M) at a 15-degree angle (Detail 4 in the plans). Cut the front ends of the splashboard sides (L) at a 15-degree angle to match. Then transfer the curved patterns from the plans to the splashboard front and sides and cut them out with a saber saw. Finally, sand all sawn edges.

Make the door frames

The doors are constructed of raised panels held in frames composed of vertical stiles and horizontal rails. Cut the stiles (P) to a length of 28-1/8 inches; this is the height of the face frame opening minus 1/8 inch, which allows for 1/16-inch clearance on the top and bottom of the doors.

Cut the rails (Q) of the door frames to a length of 10-5/8 inches. When combined with the width of the stiles (P), this allows for 1/16-inch clearance on the hinge sides of the doors and a 1/8 inch gap in the middle between the doors.

Drill dowel holes for the door frames (see Half Front View detail in the plans), then glue and lightly clamp the frames together. Be sure the door frame is held square and flat while the glue dries.

Cut the door panels

Glue together two pieces of 1x8 pine for each of the two door panels (R). Sand and cut them to the size given in the cutting list.

To shape the raised door panels you need to make a steep bevel cut on a table saw, one that can't be made with the blade guard in place. It's not particularly dangerous, but a firm, careful feed through the saw blade is essential. To make the operation safer and more manageable, attach an auxiliary fence to the rip fence of the table saw. Use a piece of 3/4-inch plywood that is wider and longer than the door panel.

Set the saw blade for a 15-degree bevel cut. Run each panel through on each edge to cut a bevel on all four sides (Photo 5). Note that the fence is 3/8 inch from the saw blade, so the bevel has a square edge all around. This will fit into a rabbet in the door frames.

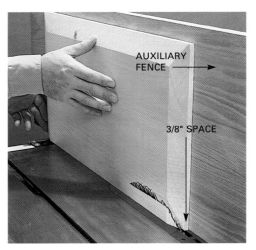

AUXILIARY FENCE

3/8" SPACE

Photo 5. Cut the raised panels for the door with a table saw. Screw an auxiliary fence to the rip fence to keep the panel steady. Note fence spacing.

ASSEMBLE THE DRY SINK

Attach the face frame

Lay the face frame on the sides and predrill holes for the nails. Because a square nail is tapered, move the drill bit gently from side to side as you drill (Photo 6) to produce a tapered hole. Check for squareness of the frame to the sides, then assemble the pieces with glue and square nails.

Attach the bottom shelf cleats (F, G) with 1-1/4 inch drywall screws (Detail 2 in the construction plans).

Photo 6. Drill pilot holes for the square-cut nails. Wiggle the bit slightly from side to side to make a tapered hole that accommodates the nails better.

Attach the top and back

Center the top on the cabinet frame, predrill the nail holes, then fasten the top to the sides and the face frame with square nails.

While you still have easy access to the inside, drill four 1/4-inch holes for the plastic shelf supports (Cross Section detail in the plans).

Rout a 3/8- x 3/8-inch rabbet in the back edge of the top to match the rabbets you cut previously in the sides (Detail 1 in the plans). Square the corners of the rabbet with a wood chisel. Place the back (U) in position in the rabbets. Make sure that the cabinet is square, then fasten the back in place with 2d wire nails or brads.

Construct the base

Join the base pieces (H, X) with glue and square nails, allowing a 1/16-inch overlap on each side. When the glue is dry, attach the cleats (J, K) to the insides with drywall screws (Detail 2 in the plans).

Put glue on the cleats and the top inside edges of the base, then set the cabinet on the base. Secure the cabinet to the base with countersunk square nails. Sand the ends of the base front (X) flush with the sides.

Assemble the doors

Rout a 3/8-inch by 3/8-inch deep rabbet around the back of the door frames (Detail 3 in the plans), then square the corners of the rabbets with a chisel (Photo 7).

Set the door panels inside the rabbets, beveled side facing down. Nail on screen door molding (S, T) with mitered corners to hold the panels in place (Photo 8). If you don't have screen door molding, you can cut thin strips of pine to nail to the back of the doors.

Attach the splashboard

Assemble the splashboard (L, M, N, Y) with glue and countersunk square nails; use a framing square to ensure squareness. Sand the ends of the splashboard front (M) so they are flush with the sides (L).

Center the splashboard assembly on top of the cabinet and trace its outline on the top. Drill dowel holes for the splashboard in the cabinet top and put dowel centers in the holes. Put the splashboard back in place, aligned with the marks on the top, and press or tap down on it (protect the top edges with scrap wood) to transfer the hole locations to the bottom edges (Photo 9). Drill dowel holes, then fasten the splashboard in place with dowels and glue, using weights to ensure that you get a tight bond.

FINISHING

Give the entire piece a final sanding. Seal both the inside and outside with a stain controller, followed by stain and varnish. The dry sink shown on these pages has three coats of stain, followed by two coats of alkyd varnish. If you plan to use the sink as a serving sideboard, be sure the finish is resistant to both water and heat.

If you are going to use it as a wet bar, check the label or ask your dealer to make sure you choose an alcohol-proof finish.

When the finish is dry, mount the hinges on the doors and then to the face frame. Use nickels as spacers to set the gaps between the face frame and the door (Photo 10).

Finally, drill holes for the bullet catches on the center stile of each door. Attach the knobs and catches. Your dry sink is done.

Photo 7. Chisel square corners in the rabbets for the back and the door panels after cutting with a router. Shown is a corner in one of the door frames.

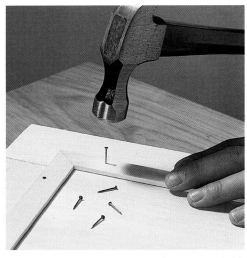

Photo 8. Nail strips to the backs of the doors to hold the raised panels in their rabbets. If you don't have screen molding, cut thin strips of pine.

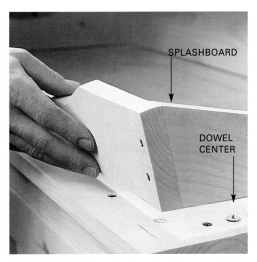

Photo 9. Attach the splashboard with dowels. Put dowel centers into the holes in the top to mark the hole positions in the splashboard.

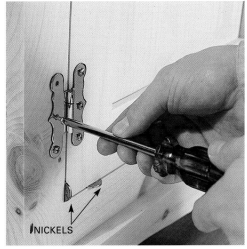

Photo 10. Screw on the hinges, leaving a 1/16-in. gap around the door. Use nickels as spacers at all four corners of each door as you work.

Many wardrobes are huge pieces of furniture that seem to dominate a normal-sized bedroom. This one doesn't.

Cherry Wardrobe

The design of this wardrobe is scaled for modern rooms, but it preserves the charm of its traditional Scandinavian styling, right down to its curved molding and rounded "bun" feet.

Although made from a simplified design, the wardrobe is a project for the advanced woodworker, particularly when it comes to crafting the molding and the feet. If you don't have access to a lathe, you can make the rounded feet with a band saw and rasp.

The wardrobe shown here is made from cherry and cherry plywood. Keep in mind that cherry's natural color can vary greatly from piece to piece, so select your lumber and plywood carefully.

Materials List

Quantity	Size and Description
2 sheets	3/4" x 48" x 96" cherry plywood
1 sheet	3/4" x 24" x 96" cherry plywood
1 sheet	1/4" x 24" x 96" cherry plywood
1 sheet	1/2" x 48" x 48" no-void birch plywood
35 board ft.	4/4 cherry
3	Solid brass hinges
1	Brass ball catch
3	1-1/4" diameter beech knobs
4	Adjustable feet
1	36" closet rod
1 set	Closet rod ends
22	3/8" x 2" spiral dowel pins
100	1" brads
70	No. 6 x 2" drywall screws
14	No. 6 x 1-1/4" drywall screws
6	No. 10 x 1" pan-head screws with 1/4" washers
1 quart	Danish oil finish

Construction Plans

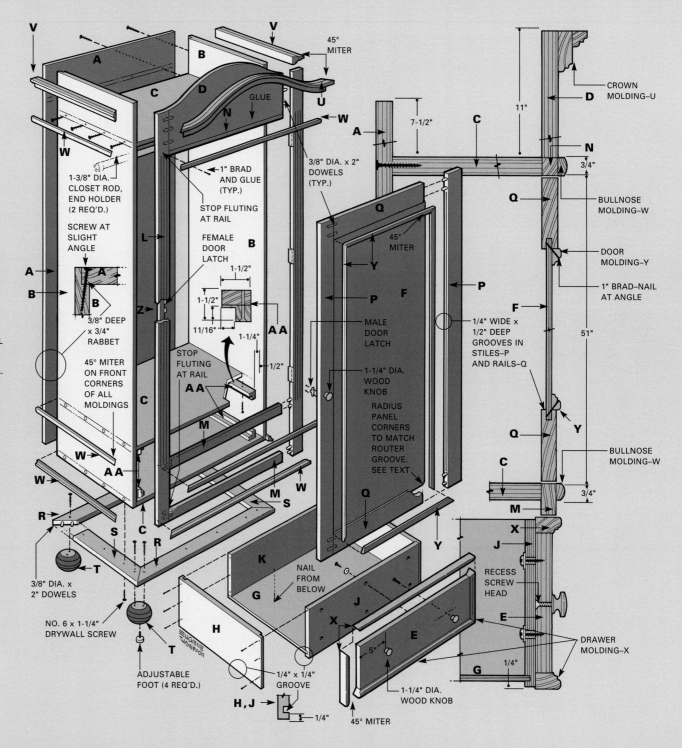

NOTES:
1. ALL SCREWS NO. 6 x 2" DRYWALL UNLESS OTHERWISE INDICATED
2. COUNTERSINK ALL SCREWS
3. SEE TEXT FOR DETAILS OF MOLD-INGS AND BUN FEET

45° MITER

B

45° MITER

CROWN MOLDING–U

D

11"

7-1/2"

C

N

3/4"

Q

BULLNOSE MOLDING–W

DOOR MOLDING–Y

1" BRAD–NAIL AT ANGLE

F

51"

Q

Y

BULLNOSE MOLDING–W

C

3/4"

M

X

J

RECESS SCREW HEAD

E

DRAWER MOLDING–X

1/4"

G

V

A

C

D

GLUE

N

U

W

A

3/8" DIA. x 2" DOWELS (TYP.)

1-3/8" DIA. CLOSET ROD, END HOLDER (2 REQ'D.)

SCREW AT SLIGHT ANGLE

1" BRAD AND GLUE (TYP.)

STOP FLUTING AT RAIL

FEMALE DOOR LATCH

1-1/2"

1-1/2"

11/16"

1-1/4"

1/2"

A

B

B

3/8" DEEP x 3/4" RABBET

45° MITER ON FRONT CORNERS OF ALL MOLDINGS

L

Z

B

STOP FLUTING AT RAIL

A A

A A

M

W

A A

W

W

R

S

C

R

3/8" DIA. x 2" DOWELS

T

NO. 6 x 1-1/4" DRYWALL SCREW

ADJUSTABLE FOOT (4 REQ'D.)

T

H

H, J

1/4"

1/4" x 1/4" GROOVE

45° MITER

Q

45° MITER

Y

P

F

MALE DOOR LATCH

1-1/4" DIA. WOOD KNOB

RADIUS PANEL CORNERS TO MATCH ROUTER GROOVE. SEE TEXT

P

1/4" WIDE x 1/2" DEEP GROOVES IN STILES–P AND RAILS–Q

Q

M

S

W

Q

Y

K

G

NAIL FROM BELOW

J

X

E

1-1/4" DIA. WOOD KNOB

5"

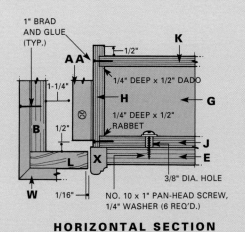

1" BRAD
AND GLUE
(TYP.)

AA

K

1/2"

1/4" DEEP x 1/2" DADO

H

G

1-1/4"

1/4" DEEP x 1/2"
RABBET

B

1/2"

J

E

L

X

W

1/16"

3/8" DIA. HOLE

NO. 10 x 1" PAN-HEAD SCREW,
1/4" WASHER (6 REQ'D.)

**HORIZONTAL SECTION
THROUGH DRAWER**

2-1/2" x 2" BRASS
HINGE (3 REQ'D.)

B

F

L

1/8"

P

Y

1/2"

1/4"

1/2"

FLUTING–STOP
11" FROM BOTTOM
AND 11-1/4" FROM TOP

**HORIZONTAL SECTION
THROUGH DOOR**

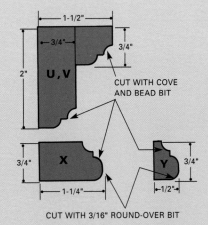

1-1/2"

3/4"

3/4"

2"

U, V

CUT WITH COVE
AND BEAD BIT

3/4"

X

Y

3/4"

1-1/4"

1/2"

CUT WITH 3/16" ROUND-OVER BIT

1/2"

3/4"

W

CUT WITH
3/8" COVE
BIT SET
3/8" DEEP

1/2"

W

3/4"

CUT WITH 1/2" ROUND-
OVER BIT SET 3/8" DEEP

3/4"

R, S

3-1/2"

MOLDING DETAILS

COVE MOLDING–W

C

3/4"

3/4"

R

T

2-3/4"

1/2"

4-1/2"

3"

1-3/4"
RAD.

3/4"

**VERTICAL SECTION
THROUGH FRONT**

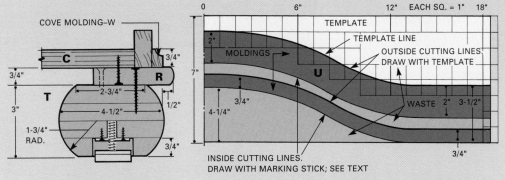

0   6"   12"   EACH SQ. = 1"   18"

TEMPLATE

2"

MOLDINGS

TEMPLATE LINE

OUTSIDE CUTTING LINES.
DRAW WITH TEMPLATE

7"

U

3/4"

WASTE   2"   3-1/2"

4-1/4"

3/4"

INSIDE CUTTING LINES.
DRAW WITH MARKING STICK; SEE TEXT

**PATTERN FOR CUTTING MOLDING
AND CROWN MOLDING TEMPLATE**

Cutting List

Key	Pcs.	Size and Description
A	1	3/4" x 32-1/4" x 70-3/4" cherry plywood (back)
B	2	3/4" x 23-1/2" x 70-3/4" cherry plywood (sides)
C	3	3/4" x 22-3/4" x 31-1/2" cherry plywood (dividers)
D	1	3/4" x 11" x 27-1/2" cherry plywood (top rail)
E	1	3/4" x 6-7/8" x 25-7/8" cherry plywood (drawer face)
F	1	1/4" x 22-7/8" x 44-7/8" cherry plywood (door panel)
G	1	1/4" x 21-3/4" x 26-3/4" cherry plywood (drawer bottom)
H	2	1/2" x 8-1/8" x 22-1/2" no-void birch plywood (drawer sides)
J	1	1/2" x 8-1/8" x 26-3/4" no-void birch plywood (drawer front)
K	1	1/2" x 7-5/8" x 26-3/4" no-void birch plywood (drawer back)
L	2	3/4" x 2-3/4" x 70-3/4" cherry (stiles)
M	2	3/4" x 1-1/2" x 27-1/2" cherry (rails)
N	1	3/4" x 3/4" x 27-1/2" cherry (top rail edge)
P	2	3/4" x 2-3/4" x 51" cherry (door stiles)
Q	2	3/4" x 3-1/2" x 22" cherry (door rails)
R	2	3/4" x 3-1/2" x 35" cherry (base frame)
S	2	3/4" x 3-1/2" x 25-1/4" cherry (base frame)
T	16	3/4" x 5" x 5" cherry (bun feet)
U	1	3/4" x 8" x 37" cherry (front crown moldings)
V	2	3/4" x 3-1/2" x 28" cherry (side crown moldings)
W	1	3/4" x 3-1/2" x 88" cherry (bullnose and cover moldings)
X	1	3/4" x 3-1/2" x 38" cherry (drawer face moldings)
Y	1	3/4" x 2-1/2" x 70" cherry (door moldings)
Z	1	3/4" x 2" x 6" cherry (door latch cleat)
AA	8	3/4" x 1-1/2" x 22" cherry (drawer runners)

Construction Procedures and Techniques

CUTTING THE PIECES

Cut all the plywood pieces A through K to the sizes given in the cutting list with the construction plans.

To cut the curved shape at the top of the top rail (D), make a template by transferring the grid and shape from the plans (see Crown Molding Curve detail in the plans) to a piece of 1/4-inch plywood or hardboard. The template has square top and side edges, and a curved bottom edge. Cut out the template and sand the sawn edges smooth.

Draw a line down the middle of the top rail D from top to bottom. Align the template to the right of this center line and trace the top curve onto the right half of D. Then flop the template over to the other side of the center line and trace the left half of the top curve. Cut out the shape.

Next cut the solid cherry pieces L through AA to size. The molding pieces U through Y are intentionally oversized so the edges can be routed first and then mitered and cut to their finished dimensions later.

Make the drawer runners

Glue two pieces (AA) face to face for each of the four drawer runners. Then cut a rabbet 11/16 x 11/16 inches in one face of each runner. The finished shape is shown in the detail inside the plan of the cabinet case.

Make the bun feet

Glue together four pieces (T) of 3/4 x 5 x 5 inch cherry for each of the four bun feet. When the glue is dry, use a combination square to make sure the blocks for the buns are square. Sand them square if necessary. You can then shape the feet with a lathe or with a band saw and rasp, as follows.

Lathe method. Mark the center point on both faces of each block, and draw a circle 4-1/2 inches in diameter on each face. Remove the waste with a band saw, cutting 1/16 inch outside the drawn circles. Then turn the feet to shape on the lathe (Photo 1).

Band saw and rasp method. The following procedure for shaping the bun feet without a lathe is illustrated in the box below left. First, mark center points on the opposite faces of the blocks. Next, draw two circles on each face—one 2-3/4 inches in diameter, the other 3-1/2 inches in diameter. Set the band saw table to a 25-degree angle and cut away the waste outside the larger circles. Finally, use a rasp to remove the rest of the waste wood to the edges of the smaller circles. Use sandpaper for final shaping.

When the feet have been shaped, drill the required holes and attach the adjustable feet (see Vertical Section Through Front detail in the construction plans). Then finish-sand the bun feet and set them aside.

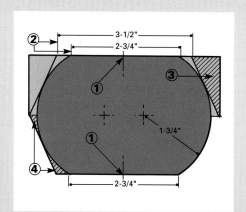

SHAPING WARDROBE BUN FEET

To shape each foot for the wardrobe with a band saw and rasp, follow these steps:

1. Mark center points top and bottom.

2. Draw circles 2-3/4 and 3-1/2 inches in diameter on both faces.

3. Cut waste around the large circle with a band saw set at 25 degrees.

4. Remove remaining waste with a rasp and sandpaper.

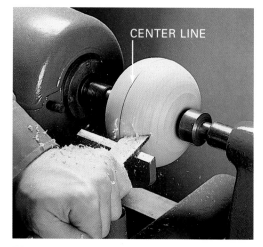

Photo 1. You can turn the bun feet on a lathe using glued-up stock. Mark a center line dividing the thickness to ensure a symmetrical shape.

ASSEMBLING THE PIECES

Construct the face frame

Align the top rail edge (N) so it is flush with the straight lower edge of the top rail (D). Glue it in place.

Drill the dowel holes in face frame pieces D, L, and M (Photo 2), using a dowel jig. Then drill matching holes in the edges of the top rail (D). Because the top rail is plywood, it will be slightly thinner than the solid wood of the rest of the face frame. To ensure that it will be flush with the solid wood on the front when the pieces are assembled, add shims of masking tape or cardboard between the back of the plywood and the inside of the dowel jig when you drill the dowel holes. Experiment with a scrap piece of plywood to determine the correct shim thickness.

Rout the flutes on the stiles (L) with a 1/4-inch core box bit (see Horizontal Section Through Door detail in the plans). Stop the fluting 11 inches from the bottom of the piece and 11-1/4 inches from the top (Photo 3).

Finish-sand the inside edges of the face frame pieces, then glue them together.

Assemble the back and sides

Rout the rabbets on the back edges of the sides (B). They will accept the back (A).

Countersink and drill the screw holes in the sides and the back. Make sure to angle the screw holes slightly at the edges of the back for the screws that go into the side rabbets (see detail of A and B in the plans).

Screw the back in place in the rabbets in the sides. This gives you a U-shaped box open at the front, top, and bottom.

Check divider fit

Each divider (C) should fit snugly inside the box—the case—but because the thickness of wood can vary slightly, check the measurement of the inside of the assembled back and sides. You might have to trim a bit of wood from the edges of each divider to get it to fit.

Finish-sand the exposed faces of the dividers and the insides of the sides and back.

Glue the dividers to the face frame

Glue the bottommost divider (C) to the bottom edge of the face frame (Vertical Section Through Front detail in the plans). If the face frame is slightly wider, align the divider so the face frame overhangs it an equal amount on both ends.

Glue a second divider (C) to the face frame so its underside is 10 inches above the bottom divider. Glue on the top divider (C) 51 inches above the middle divider.

Photo 3. Use a plunge router and edge guide to cut the flutes in the face frame stiles. Clamp a stop at both ends of the stile to control the length of cut.

STOP

1/4" FLUTES

Photo 2. Use a dowel jig to drill dowel holes. Use shims inside the jig to match hole locations in thin stock to those in thicker stock.

Tools You Need

Table saw

Drill

Dowel jig

Plunge router

Combination square

Pipe or bar clamps

Lathe (optional)

Screwdrivers

Hammer

Nail set

Band saw or saber saw

Rasp

Power miter saw

Level

Attach the face frame to the case

Glue one side to the face frame. Then screw, don't glue, the sides to the dividers.

The face frame edges will overhang the sides a bit. Cut them flush to the sides with a flush-trimming router bit. Finish-sand all outside surfaces of the case.

Add the drawer runners

The drawer runners are set 1-1/4 inches from the inside faces of their respective sides and 1/2 inch back from the front edges of the sides (see Horizontal Section Through Drawer detail in the plans). Use a block of scrap wood 1-1/4 inches wide as a spacer to set the runners the proper distance from the sides as you install them (Photo 4).

DRAWER RUNNER
(TOP AND BOTTOM)

Photo 4. Screw drawer runners to the case. Use a spacer to set the runners a consistent 1-1/4 inches from the inner faces of the case sides.

Build the base frame

Miter the ends of parts R and S, drill the dowel holes in the mitered ends, and glue the base frame together.

Drill the holes for the screws that attach the base frame to the bottom of the wardrobe case and the holes for the screws that attach the bun feet to the base frame.

Rout the rounded profile on the exposed front and side edges of the base frame (see Molding Details in the plans).

Finish-sand the base frame. Attach the bun feet with two screws into each foot. Then screw the base frame to the case.

Make the crown moldings

The crown molding is built from two pieces, a rear piece 2 inches wide, and a top face piece 3/4 inch wide (see Molding Details in the plans). The molding for the front of the case follows the curve of the top rail; it is cut from part U (see cutting list). The molding on the sides is straight and is cut from part V.

Curved molding. Make the front curved crown molding first. Use the template you made for cutting the top rail curve to draw the cutting lines for the molding. Set the template on piece U and draw one half of the outside cutting line for the 3/4-inch molding (see Crown Molding Detail in the plans). Flop the template over to draw the other side of the line. Then shift the template up on piece U to draw the outside cutting line for the 2-inch molding.

If you have a marking gauge, you can use it to draw the inside cutting lines of the crown molding. If not, make a simple marking stick: Cut a 1/4- x 3/4-inch stick 3 inches long. Measuring from one end, drill holes at distances of 3/4 inch and 2 inches to insert the point of a pencil.

Clamp the template to the outside cutting line of the 3/4-inch molding. Place the end of the marking stick against the edge of the template. Insert a pencil through the hole 3/4 inch from the end and move the stick along the template to mark the inside cutting line of the narrow molding. Flop the template to the other side and repeat.

Now clamp the template to the outside cutting line of the 2-inch molding and mark the inside cutting line, using the marking stick and the hole drilled at 2 inches (Photo 5).

Cut along the inside edge of the 3/4-inch molding with a band saw or saber saw and sand it smooth. Rout the profile on the edge with a cove-and-bead router bit (see Molding Details), then cut along the outside cutting line to separate the 3/4-inch molding from the larger piece (Photo 6). Use the same procedures for the 2-inch molding: Cut along the inside edge, rout and sand the profile there, then cut along the outside edge.

Straight molding. Make the side crown moldings (V) by routing the cove-and-bead profile on both edges of two 3-1/2 inch wide pieces of wood. Cut the 3/4-inch molding off one edge and the 2-inch molding off the other edge of each piece.

Finish-sand all the crown molding pieces and glue the 3/4-inch pieces onto the faces of their respective 2-inch pieces, keeping their top edges flush.

Miter and fit the crown moldings to the case. Cut each end of the curved molding at a 45-degree angle. Use a support block under the far end of the curved molding as you cut each miter (Photo 7). Cut the front end of each side molding at a matching angle. Glue the moldings in place.

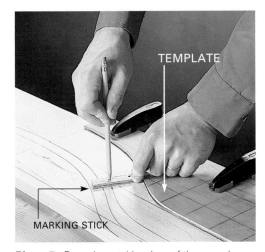

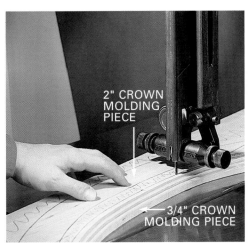

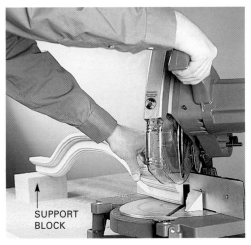

Photo 5. Draw the outside edges of the curved crown moldings with a template. Use a marking gauge or marking stick to draw the inside edges.

Photo 6. Cut out the curved crown moldings with a band saw. Cut as close as possible to the lines to reduce the amount of finish edge sanding needed.

Photo 7. Place a support block equal to the height of the miter box table under one end of the curved molding when you cut a miter in the other end.

Cut the cove and bullnose moldings

Rout a bullnose profile on both edges of piece W (Photo 8). Finish-sand the routed edges and cut off the two 1/2-inch wide lengths of molding (Photo 9).

Rout a cove profile on one edge of the remaining piece W (see Molding Details in the plans), finish-sand the routed edge, and cut off a 1/2-inch wide molding.

Miter and fit the moldings to the case. Use cove molding around the base and bullnose molding at the bottom and top of the door opening in the face frame (see Vertical Section Through Front). Drill pilot holes for 1-inch brads to avoid splitting the moldings, then glue and nail them in place.

Photo 8. Shape the edges of molding boards with a router in a router table. The door and drawer molding edges require bits for different profiles.

Photo 9. Use a table saw to cut the shaped moldings off the edges of the molding boards. Be sure to use the blade guard when making the cuts.

Assemble and mount the drawer

Cut the rabbets and dadoes in the drawer sides and front (H, J; see Horizontal Section Through Drawer detail in the plans). Drill 3/8-inch holes in the front to attach the drawer face. Finish-sand the drawer pieces G through K and assemble the drawer.

Countersink and drill the knob screw holes in the drawer face (E). Carefully finish-sand the face of the drawer.

The edge molding for the drawer is 1-1/4 inches wide. Rout both edges of piece X with a cove and bead bit (see Molding Details), then rip it down the middle to get two pieces of molding. Miter, fit, finish-sand, and glue the moldings to the edges of the drawer face.

Trim 1/4 inch off the length of the drawer knob screws with a hacksaw and attach the knobs to the drawer face. Fasten the drawer face to the drawer with pan-head screws and washers. Set the drawer in the case and then check its fit, making any necessary adjustments for travel and fit.

Assemble and mount the door

Drill the dowel holes in the door stiles and rails (P, Q). Dry-assemble the door frame with dowels and clamps, but without glue.

Rout the door panel groove in the inside edges of the assembled frame with a thin-kerf slotting cutter. Make several cuts until the width of the groove equals the 1/4-inch thickness of the door panel (F) (see Horizontal Section Through Door in the plans).

The inside corners of the door frame will have become slightly rounded as you cut the panel slots. Round the corners of the panel to match those corners.

Finish-sand the inside edges of the door frame and both faces of the panel. Unclamp and disassemble the door frame, then glue and clamp it around the panel. Do not glue the panel into the frame grooves.

Cut mortises for the hinges in the case and the door edges.

Set the case upright on a flat surface and turn the adjustable feet until the cabinet is level. Screw the hinges in place on the case. Put the door in position and adjust it for an equal gap with the case all around, then screw the hinges to it.

Attach the knob, the door latch cleat (Z), and then the door latch.

Remove the door and finish-sand any rough or unsanded surfaces.

Make the 1/2-inch wide door moldings on the edges of piece Y (see Molding Details in the plans). Miter, fit, and finish-sand the moldings. Drill angled pilot holes for 1-inch brads to avoid splitting the moldings, then glue and nail them in place.

FINISHING

Fill all nail holes with putty and finish-sand any unsanded surfaces. Smooth any sharp edges, but don't round them excessively.

Apply three coats of Danish oil. If you use paper towels or rags to apply the finish, be sure to dispose of them properly to avoid spontaneous combustion.

Reassemble the wardrobe and install a hanging rod, using end supports screwed to the sides of the case.

Index

Acknowledgments

Special thanks to Project Designer Bruce Kieffer and these members of The Family Handyman family:

Ron Chamberlain, John Emmons, Bill Faber, Roxie Filipkowski, Barb Herrmann, Shelly Jacobsen, Duane Johnson, Mike Krivit, Phil Leisenheimer, Don Mannes, Doug Oudekerk, Deborah Palmen, Don Prestley, Dave Radtke, Art Rooze, Mike Smith, Dan Stoffel, Eugene Thompson, Mark Thompson, Bob Ungar, Alice Wagner, Gregg Weigand, Gary "Mac" Wentz, Marcia Williston, Donna Wyttenbach, Bill Zuehlke.

This book was produced by Roundtable Press, Inc., for the Reader's Digest Association in cooperation with The Family Handyman magazine.

If you have any questions or comments, please feel free to write us at:

The Family Handyman
7900 International Drive
Suite 950
Minneapolis, MN 55425

More Top-Rated How-To Information From Reader's Digest® and The Family Handyman®

THE FAMILY HANDYMAN WEEKEND IMPROVEMENTS

Over 30 Do-It-Yourself Projects for the Home

Now all the how-to information homeowners need to complete short-term projects can be found in this one clear and comprehensive volume. From basic fix-ups to full-fledged facelifts, this book covers every room in the house and features great techniques for keeping the yard and the exterior of the house looking fit as well.

192 pages
10 $^{11}/_{16}$ x 8 $^3/_8$
over 500 color photographs
ISBN #0-89577-685-5

THE FAMILY HANDYMAN EASY REPAIR

Over 100 Simple Solutions to the Most Common Household Problems

Designed to help save hundreds, even thousands, of dollars in costly repairs, here is that one book that should be in every household library. It offers simple, step-by-step, quick-and-easy solutions to the most common and costly household problems faced at home, from unclogging a sink to repairing broken shingles to fixing damaged electrical plugs.

192 pages
10 $^{11}/_{16}$ x 8 $^3/_8$
725 color photographs
ISBN #0-89577-624-3

THE FAMILY HANDYMAN OUTDOOR PROJECTS

Great Ways to Make the Most of Your Outdoor Living Space

The most popular outdoor projects targeted for all skill levels are found in this easy-to-use volume. There's something for everyone in this comprehensive how-to guide—from a relatively simple garden bench and a children's sandbox to more complex structures—a spectacular gazebo and romantic garden arbor and swing.

192 pages
10 $^{11}/_{16}$ x 8 $^3/_8$
Over 500 color photographs
ISBN #0-89577-623-5

Measuring the Metric Way

Use these guides and table to convert between English and metric measuring systems.

Fahrenheit and Celsius

The two systems for measuring temperature are Fahrenheit and Celsius (formerly known as Centigrade). To change from degrees Fahrenheit to degrees Celsius, subtract 32, then multiply by $\frac{5}{9}$. For example: 68°F − 32 = 36; 36 x $\frac{5}{9}$ = 20°C. To convert degrees Celsius to degrees Fahrenheit, multiply the degrees by $\frac{9}{5}$, then add 32 to that figure. For example: 20°C x $\frac{9}{5}$ = 36; 36 + 32 = 68°F.
(See also *Some Rules of Thumb*.)

Some Rules of Thumb

Temperature:
If the Fahrenheit temperature is between 0° and 100° and you want to know the approximate degrees Celsius, subtract 30 from the number of degrees Fahrenheit, then divide by 2. For example: 70°F − 30 ÷ 2 = 20°C.

In fact, 70°F is slightly more than 21°C.

The "10 Percent and Up" Rule:
1 meter is 10% longer than 1 yard
1 liter is 10% less than 1 quart
1 kilogram is 10% more than 2 pounds
1 tonne is 10% more than 1 short ton (2,000 pounds)
1 square meter (m²) is 20% greater than 1 square yard
1 cubic meter (m³) is 30% greater than 1 cubic yard

The "30" Rule:
1 foot is slightly more than 30 centimeters
1 ounce is just under 30 grams
1 fluid ounce is almost 30 milliliters

The "About" Rule:
1 inch is about 25 millimeters or 2.5 centimeters
4 inches are about 10 centimeters
A 2-inch by 4-inch piece of lumber (a 2x4) is about 5 centimeters by 10 centimeters
3 feet are about 1 meter
10 yards are about 9 meters
100 yards are about 90 meters
1 mile is about 1.5 kilometers
5 miles are about 8 kilometers
1 pound is about 0.5 kilogram
1 imperial gallon is about 4.5 liters (1 U.S. gallon is about 4 liters)
1 quart is about 1 liter (the imperial quart is 1.136 liters; the U.S. quart is 0.946 liter)
1 pint is about 0.5 liter (the imperial pint is 0.568 liter; the U.S. pint is 0.473 liter)